# HUMAN RESOURCE MANAGEMENT BRINGS

## WHAT BENEFITS TO ORGANIZATIONS

JOHN LOK

ISBN 979-888569066-9

# Contents

# Preface

Introduction

This book explains why human resource strategy can bring organizational benefits. It will explain how reward strategy can bring what kinds of benefits to organizations. Reward management is nowadays considered as an important topic in order to achieve the goals of a company. Employees are considered as the main factor which plays an important role in the organisation. The success of each and every organisation is its dedicated employee's .Current world is filled with changes and competition. In order to survive in the current situation companies should be having employees who are loyal and expert in their own field. New technologies are developed constantly and the companies are eagerly trying to catch up those talented employees with right expertise in their own areas. So, fair award management can attract talented employees to choose the organization to work.

I write this book aims to let interviewers to know why to apply pshological methods to judge how to choose the most suitable applicant(s) more accurate to any organization in any interviews. I aim to let readers to feel that it is possible organizational behavior and training development why has relationship . This book consists three chapters.

The first chapter indicates what the common interviews are as well as explains why interviewers need to apply psychological methods to test any applicant behaviors in any interview process.

The second chapter explains how to apply psychological recruitment strategies effect/manage in the recruitment process to achieve more effective and efficient interview as well as explains how to apply occupational psychological test method to test applicant's ability.

The third chapter how selection assessment methods are applied to choose the best applicants to achieve the most effective and efficient interview result as well as how to criteria for selecting and evaluating assessment methods in interview which are the most reasonable support.

I write this book final chapter explains whether training program must be either needed to any organizations in order to raise productivities, efficiencies or improve performance etc. different aspects effect to be beneficial to any organization or waste money and time to spend training program expenditures.

Do any kinds of organizations must be beneficial, such as raise employees' efficiencies, productivities and improve performance after any training programs are arranged to be trained to trainees from their training department's trainers? Is any kind of training program useful to any organization ? How to find and design the best suitable training program to satisfy every employee individual need in any organization?

In this final chapter, I shall give my opinions to attempt to answer these above questions. In final chapter,. I shall give one organization training case study to explain how my reasons are supported my conclusion. Finally, I expect my readers can learn how to design any training courses to attribute beneficial needs to your employees and organizations.

# Prologue

Occupation psychological

test methods
How to apply psychological recruitment
strategies effect/manage in the
recruitment process?
How to apply occupational psychological
test method to test applicant's ability?
Selecting and evaluating

assessment methods
How selection assessment methods are applied
to choose the best applicants ?
How to criteria for selecting and evaluating
assessment methods in interview?
Reference
Developing a successful employee
training program steps

● What kinds of organizations need
training

● Reasons of employee training fails
and how to solve

● Prediction rewards and costs of
training program
● Can train employees raise efficiency

Training Super Talent
Human Methods

● The talent management skill
raises organizational development
and motivation of employees

● Talent in the world of work meaning
    ● Building high performance culture
talent management method
to organizations
    ● Non-training method creates
talent young people

Employee Psychological Research
    Employee satisfaction
measurement
    ● How to measure employee satisfaction ?

● How can leaders satisfy employee needs?

Raising employee efficiency
    ● How does one company raise employee
efficiency

Organizational behavior theory
● What is system approach?


Employee satisfaction methods
● How can satisfy to employees' needs?
● How to achieve work motivation strategy ?
● How can influence organizational positive behaviors ?
    Chapter 9 Human resource strategy to medical organization
    England NHS public hospital patient price
structure of marketing strategy
    ● What do you understand by the concept
of a pricing model? Critically discuss their
relevance to a public sector service p.169-171
    ● What factors should influence the level of
charges at an NHS car park?

Service-line strategies for medical organizations
● Strategies to Provide Patients With Superior
Customer Service p.172-180
● Service-line strategies for hospitals
● Changing traditional medial service to
innovative medical service front line service
method
● calculation the medical cost and charge
to patients service fee
● Learning similar medical service competitors
service attitude and medical service provision method to compare difference
● Calculation of salary level by performance measurement
● What 4 Factors Should Determine a Hospital's Service Line Strategy?

Psychosocial and medical interventions
for mental and physical health facility
management strategy

● What is the new model of healthcare facility p.181-191
management
● What is the tradition facilities management
model to hospitals
● Approach to reducing costs
● The path to a solution

# CHAPTER ONE

# Reward management strategy

What is reward management strategy?

Reward management is concerned with the formulation and implementation of strategies and policies that aim to reward people fairly, equitably and consistently in accordance with their value to the organization. Reward management consists of analysing and controlling employee remuneration, compensation and all of the other benefits for the employees. Reward management aims to create and efficiently operate a reward structure for an organisation. Reward structure usually consists of pay policy and practices, salary and payroll administration, total reward, minimum wage, executive pay and team reward.

Reward is the generic term for the totality of financial and non-financial compensation or total remuneration paid to an employee in return for work or service rendered at work. Reward, which is sometimes been refer to as compensation or remuneration, is perhaps the most important contract term in every paid-employment. Its impact on workers (or employee's) performance is in most instance greatly misinterpreted. The understanding of this term is very important; this is because the incentive scheme given to an employee will influence the behaviour and level of engagement to the organisation. However, basic pay, it is a straightforward payment scheme which may not provide incentives to individual workers because they are not based on output or performance. This pay is often in relation to a given period like an hourly rate, weekly wage or annual salary. It's also an established rate for all workers in one category. Incentive for group, Plant/enterprise-based it is refer to as grain sharing within large group or the whole organisation. This pay scheme is use in organisations where the workforce can clearly see the results of their efforts. Award can include two kinds. Intrinsic reward include- Achievement, feeling of accomplishment, recognition, job satisfaction, personal growth and status, job enlargement, job enrichment, team working, empowerment. Otherwise, extrinsic rewards also include formal-recognition; base wage or salary, incentive payments, fringe benefits, promotion, social relationship and work environment. This study will explain and define different type of pay and non-financial scheme use in today's organisations.

Reward Management is concerned with the formulation and implementation of strategies and policies that aim to reward people fairly, equitably and consistently in accordance with their value to the organization. Reward management forms the organization relationship. This if an HR manager is to succeed in successfully managing the employment relationship, he/she will have to do well in reward management, otherwise these will be an inbalance in the employment relationship, such as strikes, lockouts. Objectives of Reward Management may include: Support the organization's strategy, recruit & retain, motivate employees, internal & external equity, strengthen psychological contract, financially sustainable, comply with legislation and efficiently administered.

Basic Types of Reward include

● Extrinsic rewards

– satisfy basic needs: survival, security

– Pay, conditions, treatment

● Intrinsic rewards

– satisfy higher needs: esteem, development

Rewards by Individual, Team, Organization

● Individual: base pay, incentives, benefits

– rewards attendance, performance, competence

● Team

– team bonus, rewards group cooperation

● Organization

– profit-sharing, shares, gain-sharing

In general , a profitable reward management system should have these characteristics: Simplicity must be easily understood by everyone in the organization. People must understand why they are getting, what they are getting from the employment relationship . Fairness and equitability, every component of the system must be justifiable and consistently applied. But reward management has related problems, such as strike, staff turnover, dissatisfaction etc. An effective participatory reward management system should be negotiated and agreed better management and employees.

What is the role of Compensation and Reward in Organization? Compensation and Reward system plays vital role in a business organization. Since, among four Ms, i.e Men, Material, Machine and Money, Men has been most important factor, it is impossible to imagine a business process without Men. Land, Labor, Capital and Organization are four major factors of production.

Every factor contributes to the process of production/business. It expects return from the business process such as rent is the return expected by the Landlord. Similarly Capitalist expects interest and organizers i.e. Entrepreneur expects profits. The labor expects wages from the process. It is evident that other factors are in-human factors and as such labor plays vital role in bringing about the process of production/business in motion. The other factors being human, has expectations, emotions, ambitions and egos. Labor therefore expects to have fair share in the business/production process.

What are the advantages of Fair Compensation System?

Therefore a fair compensation system is a must for every business organization. The fair compensation system will help in the following:

● If an ideal compensation system is designed, it will have positive impact on the efficiency and results produced by workmen.

● Such system will encourage the normal worker to perform better and achieve the standards fixed.

● This system will encourage the process of job evaluation. It will also help in setting up an ideal job evaluation, which will have transparency, and the standards fixing would be more realistic and achievable.

● Such a system would be well defined and uniform. It will be apply to all the levels of the organization as a general system.

● The system would be simple and flexible so that every worker/recipient would be able to compute his own compensation receivable.

● Such system would be easy to implement, so that it would not penalize the workers for the reasons beyond their control and would not result in exploitation of workers.

● It will raise the morale, efficiency and cooperation among the workers. It, being just and fair would provide satisfaction to the workers.

● Such system would help management in complying with the various labor acts.

● Such system would also bring about amicable settlement of disputes between the workmen union and management.

● The system would embody itself the principle of equal work equal wages. Encouragement for those who perform better and opportunities for those who wish to excel.

Factors affect an organization's reward policy and strategy which include: affordability, it means what an organization can afford to pay the argument is that an organization can't borrow to reward employees, but should reward from the value created by the employees themselves. However, an organization has to afford to pay above legal minimums, legislation sets the minimum base pay ( minimum fixed pay rates), which becomes the starting point in calculating for all of an organization's policies. Workers committees/trade unions depend on the power of a union, pay levels are determined through collective bargaining. The most powerful ones will strike higher levels, external job value means the market value of the job, e.g. what is the market value or HR manager or clerical assistant? Internal job value means the value or perceived value of a job compared to other jobs which the organization will determine the reward that job, e.g. HR manager compared to finance manager. Value of the person means employees holding similar jobs can be paid differently depending on the value of the organization performance and the economy environment influence means ( labor supply/demand). A depressed economy increased the supply of labor, which reduced its price and have effect reward policy strategy.

Thus, reward system strategy means a benefit plan management procedure and it needs to implement these steps in order to achieve its fair reward as below:

Step one, deciding objective to assess what the company wants to achieve through its benefit strategy and policy, and its ability to pay for the changes;

Step two, obtaining view points and input from employees to collect employees' view points through employee surveys, focus groups and individual interviews;

Step third, analyzing competitiveness to establish or determine the company's competitive position, though conducting a customised survey or collecting available market data from external providers;

Step fourth, designing the benefit package to determine the mix and sacle of the benefit package, the allocation of benefit, the scope for flexibility and the cost of benefit provision;

Step fifth, consulting the senior management team and employees on the proposal to get input and buy in from senior management team to make amendments if necessary, collecting comments and effort the non-financial rewards as benefits; step sixth, planning the communication to inform everyone concerned what is happening, why it is happening and how it affects them,

The final step , evaluation to review the plan on a regular basis and obtain input from employees and management for evaluation purposes.

Strategy reward system pay for perform two elements: Financial reward includes base salary, pay incentives, employee benefits. Non-financial reward includes intrinsic rewards, centers in the work itself, praise, recognition , time off. Reward system is a key driver of-HR strategy, business strategy organization culture strategic reward system related to HR system. Such as skill-based pay to training, overtime pay rules to labor relations, sign-on bonus to employment, merit pay to performance management and merit pay to performance culture.

Thus one successful reward strategy system will have these characteristics. Performance and reward strategy, identify requirement and develop strategy, analyze data and performance and reward information on individuals or group and achieve collegues to aid decision making, work with managers to certain and develop reward requirements for key individuals within their area, review and analyze the organization strategy demographic profile and market activity against current reward activity to identify current reward activity to identify current and long term reward requirement to assess internal and external factors driving reward requirements agsinst plan. Explain to employees how pay and reward fits and supports overall people processes and activities, such as performance management.

In conclusion, what is award's aim ? For the organisation, reward should aim at; recruiting the quantity and quality required, encourage suitable staff to be loyal and remain in the organisation, provide rewards for good performance and incentives for further improvement in performance, maintain appropriate differentials relative to values of different levels of job, the reward adopted by organisation should be flexible enough to accommodate changes in the market rate for different skills and should be cost effective. For individual employees the reward system should be fair and equitable in valuation of the worth in comparison with others. The third which is the union of employees, the system should ensure maximum benefits for members without undue prejudices to their future security by making their reward to pace with the cost of living and the prosperity of the organisation.

What kinds of benefits of reward strategy which can bring to organizations? Good employee benefits and services can help the organization by reducing potential employee discontent, satisfying their needs and discouraging labor unrest or raisinf labor turnover. Thus, with competitive benefit programmes , an organization can be more effective in recruitment and employee retention, thus reducing labour turnover.

Employee benefits may include legally required payments, such as workers compensation, long service pay or retirement payment, sickness allowance and end of year payment, bonus as well as optional welfare plans,such as life insurance, medical/hospital /dental coverage to self and family' education allowance, housing allowance, quarters, subsidised loans, retirement, pension plan, meal allowance, travelling allowance, paid time off, pay sick leave, other specal paid leave, five day week, paid annual leave and maternity leave.

Employee service mean the organizations can choose to provide various services ranging from work related to those satisfying personal or family needs, in order to encourage employees to work happily and stay with a particular organization. The service may include social functions or recreational activities, e.g. New Year dinner, annual ball, company picnics, free transportation service, food service or canteen ,purchase of used equipment no longer required by the company, credit unions, low-interest loans, legal services, child care and elder care, conselling services, free holiday appartment, air ticket allowance etc. employees' welfares.

1.1 Why does organization need reward management system?

In compensation and benefits reward management aspect, it is not possible to imagine an offer of employment that does not indicate a salary or wage and possibly other terms of compensation as well as description of the various benefits available with the employment. So, a candidat accepts ot rejects the job offer, he/she will regard how a compensation package with a monetary of non-monetary value, such as a fair exchange for whose labor. So, the award management plan will include monetary reward and non-monetary reward both is better than monetary reward only. For example, piece rate py is good for factory workers, commissions have long been a major part of the compensation of salepeople and merit pay and bonuses are well established methods of rewarding good performance for car salepeople. So, the variable or incentive pay is a good reward implementation plan for salespeople, insurance agents.

How to evaluate the base pay level is the more accurate? Leon, M. (2002) indicated that when a company needs to determine levels of base pay, the best companies have several objectives. The most important , in a global business environment characteristized by strong demand for talented experienced employees is to be competitive. The determination of base pay level does not depend on only in one's own industry, but also in other industries competing for the same talent. In fact, a firm's closes competition for human resources often is not its closet industrial competitor. In addition, the best companies are attractive to the levels of compensation appropriate to the different regions and countries where facilites are located or where workers originate. At the same time, some are developing truly global talent managers, whose pay scales are most pay level to similar manager in other companies than they are with typical rate of pay in either the firm's headquarter country or its overseas locations.

Is one company achieves higher profits, it needs to raise higher wage to its all employees? I feel that it depends on whether situations to make decisions to raise all employees' wages , due to it has higher profit reason in the year.

Robert, P.V. (2006) summarized these rules in dealing with subordinates, their performance should be enhanced.

These rules includes using fair differential rewarding, it means that many managers try to treat all subordinates alike. When all employees receive equal rewards, superior performers begin to feel that their efforts are unappreciated, when poorer recognize that they won't be penalized for minimal effort. In response, over time, most above-average performers will drop their performance to the minimal level.

A few superior performers may persist absolutely , but most will lower their efforts to the level that they feel equals their rewards. So, when rewards are commensurate with performance, however, subordinates receive a quite different message. Superior performers get the signal that their efforts are valued, and potentially high performers are encouraged to try harder, identifying valued rewards for individual , it means that if a maneger hopes to influence an employee's behavior through the use of rewards, the rewards must have value to the employee. One of the best ways to obtain such infomation is simply to ask employees what rewards they could like to receive. Younger workers may perfer more paid vacation days, ( non-monetary value reward) or greater participation in decision making ( high position management role) . The older workers may choose better medical insurance or a longer contribution to their pension plan, instructing subordinated on how rewards are tied to performance. It means that in order for maximizing organization's effectiveness, employees must clearly understand how rewards and performance are connected. When specific information is lacking, subordinates may try to seond-guess their manager's intentions by constructing their own imagined system of rewards. Thus, much underproductivity can be avoid of a manager clearly states goals for performance and explains how rewards will be related to performance, providing information feedback on performance means that in order to meet their manager's standards of performance, employees must have instructive feedback. Their manager must evaluate their information for them, indicating how well or how poorly they are doing and suggesting specific ways to improve. In addition to providing guidance, feedback can also serve as an additional form of suggestion.

Thus, when an organization earns higher profit, it seems that it ought not raise all employees salaries to be higher, because some hard working employees will feel unfair if the lazy employees can raise the same salary level to ame to the hard working employees in the year. On the consequence, the hard working employees will be possible to underproductivity or productivity in below level efficiency or inefficiency to perform their unsatisfactory or disagreed feeling to complain whose employers. Then, the organization will encounter low productivity in possible. Hence, fair reward management plan to all employees which is needed in any organization.

1.1.1 Why do IT and bank and property managment and school organizations need reward management system?

Reward management systems have major impact on organization capability to catch, retain and motivate high potential employees and as a result getting the high level of performance. I also believe reward of employee performance can lead to differentiation between the productivity of the bank employees. In fact, bank employee performance is originally what on employee does or does not do. Performance of employees could include quantity of output, quality of output, timeliness of output, presence at work, cooperativeness.

Reward management in bank service industry, bank organization needs have effective and attractive reward management system to attract talent human resource applications. But banks are facing global saving bank competition. Reward management system is a core function of human resource discipline and is a strategic partner with company management. An good reward management can raise bank service employees performance in loan, saving mortgage etc. different departments. An effective reward management system can shorten service timeliness to raise talent employee individual bank service performance, raise the talent employee team cooperative effort in loan, mortgage, counter etc. different service departments.

However, reward management system tool includes both financial and non-financial reards which are also called as extrinsic and intrinsic rewards. In bank industry financial rewards include salary increase, bonus, commission, housing loan allowance, education loan allowance. The non-financial rewards include promotion and title, authority and responsibility, appreciation and praise, participation to decisions, vacation time, comfort of working place, social authority, customer and management positive oral and written feedback, flexible working hours, design of work recognition , social rights, etc.

Property management industry reward management practitioners include property managers, caretakers, attendants, security guards, facility maintenance workers and cleaners. It is essential for employers to formulate strategic plans and coordinate labor relations of human resource with the development. In response to the people-related challenge and opportunities to property management industry. It includes six aspects: communicating and improving staff benefits, promoting work-life balance and health and enhancing work arrangements, enhancing staff's career development and promotion prospect, improving the professional image of the industry, friendly employment practices for mature persons. Through these practices enterprises can make their job vacancie about attractive and answer misunderstandings about the property management industry.

Thus, the manpower shortage challenge will be avoid , when the people have interest to join the industry and they feel the reward is attractive to them to develop career. How to improve staff benefit? It includes new recruit entry bonus schemes, giving out little gifts and bonuses, during celebrations and festive occasions, and granting gratuities to critically ill employees or on the death of the employee's immediate family members, offers employees insurance plans, offering award schemes for employee's children by granting scholarships to outstanding students in recognition of their excellent exchange scholarships are available to subsidise their children's study abroad, promoting working-life balance to staff, such as organizing interest classes, setting up sports teams, organizing gatherings, participating in charitable activities, encouraging employees to organize social gatherings, promoting happiness at work, strengthening occupational safety and health arrangements to employees, e.g. setting up occupational safety and health committee / departments, formulating occupational safety and health policies, entertainment of work arrangement: compressed working days, five-day work week, flexible working days, flexible rostering, job sharing, part time work pattern, most rest time for frontline employee, job nature or workflow modification / re-engineering, improvement of employee's workplace environment, intra-district redeployment.

Reward is an important element in information technology industry. The IT industry had been needing a leader in changing traditional compensation strategy. Pay for performance needs to be designed effective reward system to encourage IT employee to work hardly in order to reward and contribute the most to an IT organization's technological productivity and profits.

The compensation mix depends on deliverable and the impact it has on the IT business. Consequently higher the responsibility greater the variable content in the pay package. IT industry has many IT professionals , such as programmers, software or hardware engineers, e-commerce website designer etc. different IT professionals. Hence, different IT professionals need have different skills to evaluate pay performace level fairly. However, performance related pay plans, it is a motivator the improves productivity. It helps in improving IT product productivity and performance levels when making every IT professional individual equally to encourage or motivate themm work to hardly in their IT unique professional aspects. It is a greater motivator for top performances and teams as they can get fair and reasonable reward and pay according to their contributions.

In fact, there is no standard formula for a performance -related incentive plan, it is unique for each IT professional. However, the incentive plan should need to be design to each IT professional with an organization's objectives. They include, communication and understanding of objectives, consideration of different IT professional performnce against objectives, translating evaluation into the kid of IT professional performance rating, a link between ratings and pay to the kind of IT unique professional skill.

University HR strategic reward management system( review promote monitor scheme) aims to improve systems and skills for teaching employee communication, support teaching management to play a move active role in communicatin key messages, ensure school reward policies and procedures are fair to teaching staffs and administrative non-teacing staffs in salary rank increasing level, establish improved consultation procedures at academic and teaching service level, demonstrate the values and ethics by the university through management practices and communication with teaching staffs and non-teaching staffs, improve the profile and performance of the university by recruiting and developing talent teaching employees with appropriate external recognition , certain academic disciplines present more different recruitment challenges and profile of the university as an employer could be improved in the academic labour market, recruiting sample of selection decisions through early stages of employment to assess quality of appointment and identify learning points, support and encourage recuritment messages to improve selection practive including skills and high quality appointment decisions, raise the profile of the university as an employer regionally, natinally and internationally, establish succession planning for all key roles and positions linked with clear career progression with job families, to face in a difficult economic climate the university needs to continue to attract and keep high quality staff to work in an efficient and cost effective manner. The extension of workload allocation models to all academic units is an important tool to assit in managing workload fairly and more effectively, well targeted and designed training and development is very effective in motivating and enabling staff and support productivity.

1.1.2 Why do small organizations need reward strategy?

Reward strategy can be applied to large organization, it can be also applied to small organization, e.g. family business, family business also needs compensation policies, the result encourages professional growth among family members and other employees as well as strategic business goal accomplishment. In general, compensation can be divided into the categories of base pay ( equity as a basic for fairness , benefit, e.g. health care insurance, salry , wages, incentive compensation ( e.g. bonuses, deferred compensation, stock or share options) and perks e.g. club membership, use of the company's private mountain, beach for holiday entertainment or sport activities e.g. free glof sport and company 's automobiles to provide to employees to drive in their private time.

Craig, E. A (2011) indicated that although small business has less employees , but it also needs compensatin adjustments. The reasons include: (1) performance-based increases i.e. a rise, (2) annual wage adjustments e.g. cost of living increases to remain with what comparable businesses are paying and corrective adjustments to more pay for a position into with other position in the business increases are considered to be a key component of compensation by managers and non-management employers alike. The difference between one small organization's and one large organization's performance based incresae is possible that one large organization has more a rise amount of performance -based increases in every time performance review. Otherwise, one small organization has less a rise amount of performance -based increases in every time performance review.

A good reward strategy can develop a philosophy of compensation that builds a framework for base pay and incentive tailored to the special values, goals, and needs of the particular family firm. Hence, one family or small firm's compensation -reward strategy can be explained to be needed, due to these factors : the firm can compare pay and performance levels with those of businesses with whom which compete for employees, the firm's goal is to provide total compensation between median and the percentage of comparble groups, base salary will be made more accurate decision at or high or below the median level for the comparable groups, individual salaries will be made more accurate decision within how much percent of the midpoint for the firm's comparison group's salary range, the firm can make more accurate decision on emphasizing whether performance -based incentives ought be spent at the expense of the salary, whether annual incentives ought be exceed those of comparably sized competitors, whether long-term incentives ought be based on results that add shareholder value.

However, culture can influence some business owners how to make compensation issues, culture means beliefs, values, assumption, habits and behavior patterns of the organization. The reasons staffs are paid the way, they are may be partly unconscious and may arise from the personal and family history and the deeply felt personal needs of the business leader or leaders. So, any family or small business will ought try to develop a philosophy of compensation ( reward) strategy , which may learn a great deal about itself in the process. For example, a entrepreneur has confidence in her or his ability to manage compensation on a case-by-case basis and maintain tight personal tight personal control over each individual pay, perks, incentives, dividends, and gifts in order to encourage its employees can raise more effort to increase the sale number to its different kinds of product in its shop. Otherwise, if a family member working in this kind of culture asks for a raise, the business owner will not talk to about how to raise compensation to his/her salespeople in christmas period. Hence , culture seems to influence the large organization and small organization how to make itself compensation to salepeople in christmas period.

However, a basis for fairness to base pay which can let the large organization or small organizaion's staffs to feel, it is very important , when the large or small organization needs to focus on filling a vacancy and getting new skills into key areas quickly to meet customer needs with quality and efficiency. Because if the large organization or small organization expects it sale turnover may increase or staff turnover may decrease, but hiring needed talent may become more difficult, indicating that the company's pay structure may have lost internal logic if it's basic pay is unfair to attract talent staffs choose to join to its organization to work, when they feel that the organization's base pay is not reasonable to compare its competitors ( pay for one job compared to another), and comparable jobs outide the company, the process is logical , objective and fair to be needed to judge the base pay structure to any organizations. Having a consistent, explainable rationale for how compensation or reward is critical for employee and shareholders judgements about fairness. Hence, individual employee will usually compare his/her job in the company's salary and his/her similar job in another company's salary whether whose salary is same or more or less between whose's company salary and similar company salary. Hence, a company needs to establish equitable base pay in a market value and merit system, with any adjustments , pay raises being a function of performance merit in order to make more reasonable compensation or reward to let its staffs to feel to avoid staff turnover number raises.

A rational compensation system steps can include: creating job description for all jobs, conducting a job evaluation to rank order jobs and determining which jobs that are similar in their importance to the business, obtaining extermal wage and salary survey information for representation jobs, utilizing other sources for comparable external data when needed, determining the company's reward strategy for compensation and deciding whether it wants pay to be set at the market average , whether it wants compensation at levels above or below the market average, or whther it wants to make a culture statement with pay levels, creating a wage and salary structure of starting pay levels, ( minimums ) and levels of pay for the most experienced workers ( maximums). Analyzing current pay levels against the new structure pay levels against the new structure to determine which jobs are paid appropriately and which ones are not, considerering individual, unique jobs that may have qualitative more or less important than external market comparables might suggest, making pay adjustments for those that are not of the range, accelerating regular increases for positions below the target range and decelerating or not making increased that are above the range. Finally , it needs to periodical check or review the wage and salary structure against outside benchmarket ( external similar competitors positions to maintain external equity).

The point factor job evaluation tool can help the organization to make decision whether the staff ought pay how much salary level is the most reasonable. The point method include the elements such as : The experience element means the factor appraises the length of time normally required for an individual to acquire the necessary knowledge and ability to affectively perform the duties of the job. The experience level element means that whether the worker individual working experience in the firm, e.g. up to three months, he/she can earn the lowest points, till to comprehensive over right years, he/she can earn the highest points. The direction of others element means this factor appraises the responsibility to the job , it includes for organization, selection , assignment , guidance and review of personnel and the performance of other supervisory tasks. The direction of others level can indicate the employee earns none points when whose jobs involves no responsibility or authority for the direction of others, till to the highest points when the employee can confirm to own administrative abiluty,whose job is responsible for general administrative or executive supervision of all or broad segment of company operations as well as he/she can establish general policies and procedures and formulates and applies broad plans of operations.

Compensation specialists can help the company to select representative jobs from a company and find good external comparisions. They will need to make adjustment. Some criteria for determining a jobs's market value can include position title and job description, industry, size of company, sales or revenue volume, cost of living, based on location etc. data to determine whether their company's salary level is accaptable or reasonable to a job's market value. They need to gather the data concerns the job's market value. This is helpful because the latest supply and demand factors can affect certain positions may not show up in surveys. They must need to gather similar industry's organization size, sale or revenue volume data, daily cost of living and transportation cost how to influence their employees' income and similar competitors' employees income in order to make more reasonable and accurate salary structure adjustment.

1.2 Reward management aims to bring positive influence to work performance, how to achieve high work performance?

How can reward management strategy raise job performance? In organization, work performing is affected by job characteristics and physical work environment, ability and skills and the willingness to performance to the individual employee. The major strategic rewards decisions to reward employees which include: What to pay employees, how to pay individual employees, recogntion programs? Concerning about what to pay? The employer needs to establish a pay structure balance between internal equity, ( the value of the job for the organization) and external equity , the external competitiveness of an organization's pay relative to pay in its industry.

What does reward management mean? The management discipline is concerned with the formulation and implementation of strategies and policies, the purpose of which are to reward employees fairly, equitably and consistently in accordance with their value to the organization. It deals with design, implementation and manintenace reward systems ( processes, practices, procedures) that aim to meet the needs of both the organization and its stakeholder. Thus, total reward can include non-financial as well as financial element is developed, implemented and treated. Usually , the components of total reward include two aspects: tangible rewards ( base pay, contingent pay and employee benefits ) as well as relational intangible rewards (learning and development), the work experience and achievement, growth , non-financial rewards . Then, it is the total reward. However, reward can include these tangible and intangible elements: payment, such as salary, bonus, shares etc. Praise, such as positive feedback, commendation, staff-of -the year award etc. Promotion, such as status, career development. Punishment, such as disciplinary action, criticism, withholding pay. Thus, if one employee can not achieve the satisfactory performance, he/she ought need to get disciplinary action to be punished in order to let he/she learns how to revise his/her performance to raise working efficiency.

How to implement strategic reward management? Where do we want our reward practices to be in a few years time ( vision)? How do we intend to get these ( mean)? So, a declaration of intent that defines what the organization wants to do in the longer term to develop and implement reward policies, practices and processes, that will further the achievement of its business goals, and meed the needs of the stakeholders, it can give a framework to other elements of rewards. So, the structure and content of a reward strategy may include: Environment analysis, macro-level, social, economical, demographic, industrial level, and micro-level competitors, analysis of job evaluation, financial conditions, gap analysis.

When the organization expected to apply reward strategy to raise employee individual performance successfully? It needs to know what job evaluation means. It is a systematic process for defining the relative worth/size of the jobs roles within a organization, for establishing internal relatives, for designing an equitable grade structure and grading jobs in the reward structure. For example, reward strategy can attempt to reduce wage gaps, when the wage gap can occur in the company, it can use international benchmarking in job evaluation. However, the cause is simple. The market of top managers is ususally international, they earn international wage, or they leave the firm. The market of workers with little or no qualification is locl in nearly every case. They can earn local wages. In less developed countries , this can lead to raise wage gaps between the top and bottom employee. Hence, if the firm discovered it has large distance of wage gaps between its top and bottom level positions. It ought need to find methods to adjust these positions' salaries to be reduce large distance of wage gaps fairly in order to let these large distance of wage gaps of position employees , they can feel their company is more fair to treat every employee.

Moreover, firm also need to consider that whether it ought choose which type of individual payment to excite its employee individual performance to be improved. They may include: performance -related increases basic pay or bonus -related to assessment of performance, contribution-related pay is related both to inputs and output, skilled-base pay is related to high or low skilled to the individual effort performance, service -related pay is related to whether the employee needs to spend how long service-time to satisfy customer's need in order to measure every service employee's performance, team-based pay is related to team performance, it can encourage teamwork, loyalty and cooperation and it can be demotivating on individual level.

All of these any types of reward method will improve or encourage the low performance employee individual working efficiency or raise productivity more easily as well as fair reward strategy can upgrade the high performance employee indiviual efficiency or encourage them to exceed their productive level or raise their productivity to achieve the maximum number. Hence, reward management has direct relatively to influence every employee's performance in order to bring either long term positive or negative influence to their organizations.

1.3 What factors can influence organization's reward strategy?

What is reward management strategic principle to employment relationship? employees needs to pay tangibles ( salary, wage, cars, educational , holiday allowance etc.) or/and intangible ( recognition, career development growth etc.) rewards to employees aim. Individual balance to achieve tangible output, sales and/or intangibles loyalty , service performance, commitment. Hence, reward managment forms the employment relationship, if an HR manager is to succeed in successully managing the employment relationship, he/she will have to do well in reward managment.

The reward management principle includes simplicity, it must be easily understood by everyone in the organization, fairness and equitability , every component of the system must be justifiable applied. This element is arguably the most challenging to implement and is the cause of most reward management related problems , such as strike, turnover, dissatisfaction etc. Hence, an attractive communication and training to the low skilful labour to have chance to upgrade high skilful which is needed, a participatory chance is effective one should ideally be negatiated and agreed between management and employees.

In fact, traditionally companies have always adopted the base pay strategy. It pays the legal minimum wages and salaries. However, it does not adequate in new work cultures and in terms of attracting , retaining and motivating top performers for strategic purposes, but still very commonly uded for lower level employees. The new reward strategic options include as below:

1. Knowledge and skills based strategy, because of the proven relation job performance, organizations have sought to encourage continuous skills development by trying it to rewards. A organization simply varies its pay structure according to one's level of knowledge and skill ( job evaluation systems. It can define which skills, it values and will pay for and must have a supportive training and development strategy. It is based pay with an equal base pay and a variation based on skills and knowledge. It may be costly in the short-term , but it is beneficial from a knowledge HR base through increased productivity and quality of product.

2. Performance based ( varied pay based structure strategy), employees should be rewarded only for the value they create. A company will reward employee in the same grade variably depending on each employee's performance.

3. Incentive based pay structure strategy, it measures but being different in that it focuses on group performance rather than individual performance. The starting point in strategy is to define group performance targets , such as productivity sale volumes or profitability.

What factors can influence organization's reward strategy? They include: Afforability, the argument is that an organization can't borrow to reward employees, but it should reward from the value created by the employees themselves; legislation sets the minimum base pay minumum fixed pay rate; union/workers committees' pay level are determined through collecting bargaining. For example, strike issue will bring higher salary level in possible; external job value, the market value of the job, e.g. what is the market value of an HR manager or clerical assistant; internal job value, perceived value of job compared to the other jobs which the organization will determine the reward for the jobs , e.g. HR manage compared to finance manager; value of the person, employees holding similar jobs can be paid differently depending on the value to the organization performance; the economy changing factor ( labor supply/demand) in labor market, e.g. it is a depressed economy increases the supply of labour, it will reduce the labour wage/salary market prices, due to the economy is bad , employers won't need to raise to any employees number and it has excess labour supply number to affect reward policy strategy.

1.4 What is reward system of McDonald ?

For McDonald's Corporation U.S. employees at corporate, division and region offices, McDonald benefits are organized into four Performance management includes processes that effectively communicate , company aligned goals, evaluate employee performance and reward them fairly.

Your Pay and Rewards (ref from McDonald's reward system)

Attractive program follows a "pay for appearance" beliefs: The better your results, the greater your pay opportunities.

● Base Pay

Since employees' bottom pay is the most important portion of their compensation, McDonald's maintain the competitiveness of our base pay through an annual review of both external market data and interior peer data. In our business, division and region offices, McDonald's has a broad banding compensation system. Broad banding allows for suppleness in terms of pay, movement and growth.

● Incentive Pay

Inducement pay gives our workers with the possibility to earn spirited total compensation when performance meets and exceed goals. For our corporate, parting and region office, the Target Incentive Plan (TIP) links employee presentation with the presentation of the business they hold up. TIP pays a gratuity on top of employees' base salaries base on business presentation and their person appearance.

● Long Term Incentives

Long term incentives are granted to entitled workers to both prize and retain key employees who have shown continued presentation and can crash long-term value creation at McDonald's. for the benefits of employees the long term incentives are very helpful because when the organization has a policies of incentives or long term incentives then the employees of the organization feel secured and work hardly for the organization. Similar like this any company or any Originations rewarding system always brought positive crash.

● Recognition Programs

Mc Donald's recognition programs are intended to reward and recognize physically powerful performers. For our corporate, separation and region offices, these take in the president Award (given to the top 1% of individual performers worldwide) and the Circle of fineness Award (given to top teams worldwide to be familiar with their aid for advancing our vision). Once start to hesitation your honesty, and then no one is leaving to alter their activities Appraisal system is also very helpful and makes a positive competition and encouragement in between the employees of the organization. Promotions will be appraisal based which encourage employees for hard work.

● Company Car Program

Mc Donald's company car program provides entitled employees with a company car for both business and individual / personal use. If entitled, employees can decide from. This is also very encouraging and motivating incentive for employees. It creates competition between employees and they work hard to get this incentive.

In conclusion, the assumptions the company is creation about their prospect service and its intention to support their progress. Practical processes for deploy people and delivering enlargement which are consistent with these intention. The reserve and promise for taking these types of program used. If we see in past we can get that simple ways in which the company could use the out test for the planed strategies and special and important clues for the good results.

Reference

Craig, E.A. & Stephen, L.M. & John, L.W. (2011) family business compensation: New York, US, Palgrave Macmillan, p.35

Leon, M. (2002). High performers, how the best companies find and keep them: US, Jossey - Bass, John Wiley & Sons, Inc, US pp.133-134

Robert P. V, (6 edition, 2006). organizational behavior: core concepts: US, Thomson, pp.58

# CHAPTER TWO

# Organizational development

Why do organizations need develop?

Organizational development (OD) is defined by theorists and practitioners in diffferent ways. Essentially, it is a planned, organization-wide effort to increase an organization's effectiveness and/or to enable an organization to achieve its strategic goals. Before working on organizational development activities, an essential first step is to map the organizational context in which the changes , you are hoping what will occur. It means to understand function what affect your work, which approach you may be bringing to the activities and being able to determine an organization's readiness to work with you and develop for themselves the required innovations.

Many OD projects focus on providing the more visible mateial resources, building skills, improving organizational structures and systems. Moreover, culture values have an impact on several elements of as including: the way change occurs, perception about whether change is needed, perception about leadership and ownership , perception about risk and uncertainty, perception about relationship and partnership and perception of what success looks like. It is described internal changes as relating to organizational structures, processes and human resource requirement, whereas external changes involves government legislation, competitor movements and customer demand.

In general, organizational development aims to expect to raise awareness, e.g. improved understanding, attitude, confidence or motivation , enhanced knowledge and skills, e.g. increasing ability to act through teamwork, e.g. strengthened ability to act through improved with a group a people tied by a common task. This may involve for example, among them memebers, a stronger agreement or improved, communication, coordination, contribution by the team members to the common task, enhanced networks, e.g. improved processes for stronger incentives for participation in the network ot increased traffic or communication among network members; increased implementation know -how , e.g. discovey and innovation with learning by doing formulation or implementation of policies, strategies, plans for UD aims in possible.

Why do organizations need to changed? Our business would is fasting to increase technology new methods of production and new taste of customers and new market trends as well as new strategies for best control of the organizations and motivation of employees like to accept to use new products in popular nowadays. Hence, managers need to concern how to decide about the change management in the organizations, because business activities now are globalize, and every organization needs to attract loyal customers , trained the employees, introduce and adapt new methods of production and best control the activities of the organization.

How will change organization in the good condition? The question arises in present scenario. Organizational change or change management aims to raise ability of the management benefits and support from change with reduced inefficiencies and ineffectiveness from the side of employees and encourage appreciate acceptance and support. The process of changing the activities of the organization as well as the implementation of the procedures and technologies to achieve the design objective. If the organization usually needs to change management includes different aspects, such as control change, adaptation change and effecting change.

Consequently, organizational change simply means to change the activities of the organization, it concerns change the culture of the organization, technology, business process, change of employees, rules and procedures, recruitment and selection, design of jobs, methods of appraisal , human resource , technology, physical environment of the organization, methods of training and development, job skill, and knowedge etc.

However, when the organization decides to implement change. Some employees should feel not adapt the change easily. They will quickly respond by voiling complaints, engaging in work slowdown, threateninf to go on strick etc. How to overcome change management implemenation successfully. The organizations need to implement change fairly , selection peoplw who accept change, education and communication.

However, organization development also plays an important role in the change management. It can be defined as a collectin planned change, built a humanistic values and benefits and welfare needs, that need to improve the organizational effectiveness and employees work performance and well-being.

   2.1 Why does General Motor organization need change management?

For General Motor (GM) change management case example, GM taking swift cost cutting action (2008) showed GM established in 1908s, till 1920s it was becoming the world largest motor manufacturing company, it could produce new style and design car every year. These were different brand cars which were producing by the company that time, and this every there were no other competitors to compete in the company different cars. But, the Japan automakers the company, GM felt threatened, specially Toyota Japan. Hence, GM needed to aain get his position in market by restructing and making change in the company. Now the GM company is again operating business in core brands in America, such as GMC.

GM taking swift cost cutting action ( 2008) also indicated that however, the aithoer change to GM was the high wages cost to employees as the company was paying US$74 per hour as compared to Toyota US$44 per hour, because GM was an agreement with trade union and GM run the plant with minimum 80% capacity own whether it was needed or not.

Hence, what types of changes are decided to bring or make change to GM. In fact GM decided to bring changes on some areas of the motor business. These were included, structural change, cost change, process change and cultural change. The steps which as taken to change by the GM is about cost cutting, it has reduced cost of some brands to maintain the profit level. Similarly , GM also cut pay of employees which was the major problem. The GM also changed the culture of the company. GM removed it automative producing board and automative strategy up to 8 men board. It can changed the culture to improve the efficiency of the employees and such change is to speed up the day to day decision making.

But, GM also encounters problems to change process. Such as problems in cultural change, the cultural plan was based top down approach, which ignored totally the involvement of the employees as compared to other companies, some suggested that it has not down up approach in which employees feel satisfaction. So this regard , it empowered the employees by introducing in tailoring the down top approach. Rather then telling to employees what they do, due to its employees hope have change to discuss with top management to express their opinions. Moreover, the other problem with cost cutting from the agreement of trade union, as it was an agreement with not lowering the pay of the employees and maintain the capacity level.

Driving change at GM (2005) indicated that better result of cost cutting of GM seems from its employment figure of 98 to 2009. It was reduced from 226,000 to 101,000 workers and now the GM is concentrating on sale rather than to further cut off and also GM is deciding to reduce the workerd force of the factory from 60,000 to 40,000. It certainly leads to cost saving to GM. Another better result of cultural change to GM, employees now becoming aware about the responsibility, as well as GM aso empowered the employeed to give better productivity. Hence, GM can success to solve change management problems to bring profit and win its competitors in motor sale market in global successfully.

2.1.1 Culture can influence organization development

Culture is not the way we do things around here. Culture is which we cooperate and the through we view the organization. If we view an organization as a system of interacting and interrelated part, culture defines , creates and supports that system.

● IBM computer organizational culture influences whether it's computers will be out-dated feeling to computer consumers

For IBM computer computer example, IBM had brought to change a culture means changing our findamental view of how the world works. However, IBM ran into serious financial difficulties in the late 1980 and early 1990s in large part because it was unwilling to change the ways in which it was approaching the computer market, even though the market was rapidly changing around it to break with tradition.

How is culture created to IBM? Stephen, R.B(2011) indicated IBM founder , or the influential leader, had reinforced the values of culture. When he worked for IBM many years ago, he discovered the IBM leader was one considerable person to his employees. Such as one case, how when an IBM employee was badly injured and his family killed in a car accident, the leader Tom Watson was there at the hospital when the man woke up, promising to cover the medical bills and do whatever he could. Hence, he can let IBM employees feel that IBM was seem to their home family.

Hence, what makes a successful culture to IBM ? Stephen, R.B(2011) also showed that a culture is successful if it is in harmony with its environment and unsuccessful if it it unable to function in its environment. The environment is the world in which the culture operates. So, when environment changes faster than cultures. When the environment changes, the mechanisms of the culture may no longer be valid. Such as the advent of the PC changed the business environment for IBM, and the company found it difficult indeed to adjust. Today, with the accelerating shift from desktop computers to mobile devices and the Internet, Microsoft is still. In 1992, IBM had a loss for the first time, closed down numerous divisions. However, IBM's culture contained a very strong ethic of " analyze the problem, determine the solution, and execute the solution even, if it 's unpleasant." IBM realized that it needed a fresh perspective, so it brought in Lou Gerstner, the first non-IBMer to become CEO. As Ed Schein points out, Gerstner came from a very similar marketing backgroung to IBM's founder, Tom Watson, Sr. Gerstner didn't so much change IBM's culture as revitalize an aspect of it that had become dormant. Over the year, IBM's engineering culture had become dominant, and the marketing culture had benefit to become into the background.

● IKEA organizational culture influences whether it's China furniture market in success?

Why does IKEA management cultural diversity needs to regard its staffs in China challenge? Multinational company, such as IKEA furniture company aims to increase profitability and it also needs to seek to for solutions to problems related with the saturation of existing markets, it needs to make an effort to expans operations to overseas market, such as China. However, it will face cultural difference challenge to be needed to deal if it wanted to enter China furniture sale marke successfully.

Kumar, S. (2005) indicated IKEA is the world's largest furniture retailer since the early 1990s. It offers a wide range of well- designed, functional home furniture products at low prices as many people as possible will be able to afford them. However, IKEA planned to enter China market, but it will face the cultural difference challenge between China and itself Swedish regional cultural of their staff communication and cooperational relationship.

In deed, the "IKEA" facilities its successfully international expansions , it needs to combinate vision, characteristic leadership and business principle between China and Swedish culture effectively. IKEA opened its first store in China in 1998. Although, the company has succeeded with their global strategy in the past in most of the markets, it has entered , it quickly learnt the success in the Chinese market required a different strategy in the areas of marketing and HR ( Kumar, 2005, p.2).

What are the cultural difference to influence IKEA's success to develop furniture sale in China market? The standardized strategy which is adopted by IKEA could lead to some disadvantages because Swedish managers are needed to send to other branches in other countries in other to ensure the IKEA way is implemented in the local areas. Thus, it brings the conflict between the Swedish management and local employees could occur due to the cultural differences. Especially, in the country like China where the traditional cultures and value are different to such as Swedish culture. So, Chinese employees will have their mind for long a working culture differs from the Swedish way that IKEA wants to influence to their employees, problems were unavailable.

When IKEA were keen to increase revenue in Asian markets like China, they faced the challenge to mange their staffs from the conflicts and the diversity of Chinese cultures, such as how to train people within IKEA perform in a standardized format to keep its essential value, and how to avoid the misunderstanding when improve employee performance and understanding the importance of cross cultural management between Sweden and China. So, IKEA managers definitely have responsibilities to spend time, energy and effort to understand the differences of national corporate and functional cultures before starting an arranging the strategic plans in China furniture sale market.

The another cultural difference challenge concerns China and Sweden both countries have problems on law, price competition, information, language, delivery, foreign currency, time differences and cultural differences etc. different aspects. Thus, such as this IKEA Sweden furniture international company plans to enter China furniture sale market. It will have great barriers are caused by cultural differences, such as difficulty of communicaton, higher potential transaction costs, different objectives and means of cooperation and operating methods.

These problems have led to the failure to IKEA furniture to enter China furniture sale market in possible. Therefore, IKEA needs to concern questions how to do business in China and understand China's culture and how to do business with Chinese people. It is possible that Chinese labours dissatisfy IKEA's provided cheap labour as well as the strong serious organizational bureaucracy system, high job duty demand is needed to satisfy customer's behavior in China. Hence, IKEA's culture difference challenge to China furniture sale market , it has relationship to human resource management and reward challenge.

2.2 HR development aims

Human Resource Development is the framework for helping employees develops their personal and organizational skills, knowledge, and abilities. Organizations have many opportunities for human resources or employee development, both within and outside of the workplace. By the end of this paper , I will be able to devise a human resource plan for a work area, to meet organizational objectives, identify and plan for individual development to meet organizational objectives and also initiate a personal development plan for an individual and evaluate progress. Healthy organizations believe in Human Resource Development and cover all of these bases.

The focus of all aspects of Human Resource Development is on developing the most superior workforce so that the organization and individual employees can accomplish their work goals in service to customers. We need to learn new skills and develop new abilities, to respond to these changes in our lives, our careers, and our organizations. We can deal with these constructively, using change for our competitive advantage and as opportunities for personal and organizational growth, or we can be overwhelmed by them. With all the downsizing, outsourcing and team building, responsibility and accountability are being downloaded to individuals. So everyone is now a manager. Everyone will need to acquire and/or increase their skills, knowledge and abilities to perform their jobs. By developing our knowledge and skills, our actions and standards, our motivation, incentives, attitudes and work environment we will be able to cope up with the everchanging work environment.

Reference

Driving change at general motor, 2005, online retrieved 15 Dec. 2009, www.cioleadershipnotes.com/p/gm/htm

General motor talking swift cost cutting action, 2008, online retrieved 15 Dec. 2009 from dailymarkets.com/stock/ 2008/11/24/General- motor- takingswift-cost-action-cutting

Kumar, S. (2005) "IKEA's globalization strategies and its foray in China", IBS center for management research
Stephen, R.B. Organizational development, U.S., The McGraw- Hill , 2011, pp.5-8

# CHAPTER THREE

# Human resource role in business

HR function in organization

HR role in business functions: HR ethics and code of condust includes that HR people should act legally, ethically and professionally as these aspects: Act legally, it represent the most core of obligations. HR is reponsible for keeping current with changes in employment law and keeping management informed of risk or possible library. Act ethically, HR represents all employees at all levels of the organization, regardless of sex, age , race , color, material status, religion, disability or other protected class. At the same time, HR promotes the ethical culture of an organization. They must model the highest level of ethical behavior, administer all company policies and procedures fairly in handling disciplinary.

HR must conduct thorough investigations and make recommendations or decisions based on facts. Act professionally, HR must keep employees' and companies' information in the strictest confidence and protect company information when dealing with employees or individuals outside of company. HR must follow changes in employment law, company policies and employment issues. They are also reponsible for continuing education to remain expects in the field to be a successful strategic business partner. HR staffs need own business knowlege and understand the cost of people-related activities and responsible for measurement to all HR programs and processes, subject matter expert, in this role, the HR person should passes HR knowledge in relation to the most up-to-date employment law at the best HR practices for sourcing and staffing, remuneration strategy and systems, performance management, employee relations, and people development and advice business as appropriate.

At all time, a professoional HR will keep his/her management informed of any potential risk and liability to the business , due to the change of employment law. Creating good working environment, HR needs to motivate , engage, contribute good and happy working environment to le staffs to work in the organization. HR needs to help to establish and promote the organizational culture in which people are willing to do the best performance to the jobs, and commit customer's needs and concerns.

In this role, the HR person identifies and facilitates overall talent management strategies, employee development opportunities, employee assistance programs, long term incentive and effective communication opportunities and channels between management nd employees. HR is such as one change agent. The HR person needs to know how to link changes to the strategic needs of the organization and being able to show empathy and concern employee needs to minimize employee dissatisfaction change. So, HR person needs have the ability to execute successful change strategies.

HR functions in organization include: workforce planning, sourcing staffing, organizational development, skills training , learning , talent development, reward management, compensation and benefits, employee relations, communicaton, enagement, HR policy and legal recommendation, change management, employee welfare, workplace health and safety.

Staffing source means the success plan or buy recruit from external. It is a process , a company ensures that employees are recruited and developed to fill the key roles. Through high-performing employees, develop their knowledge, skills and capabilitied and preare them for advancement or promotion into even more challenging roles in 3 to 5 years' time. So, it asks to develop the employees to special projects, team leadership roles, internal and external movement to training and development opportunities.

The success plan should identify key position, its key roles and contributions, key success factors of key positions, skill, knowledge, capabilities, reasons cause of turnover, potential success identification, development plans for potential successor to reach the required success factors.

Recruit from external or buying recruiting resource from the labour market is suitable to meet company short-term staffing needs for the junior to middle level positions. It can help new skills and new experience. Sources of supply can be from a combination of full time/part time employees, recruitment agencies' temporary workers and contract workers.

The contracting applicants arrange,ent stage means the HR needs to contract the job applicants and invite for an interview, conducts the job interview, prepares the resume in advance and highlight areas to require further during the interview, knowledgeable about the company, the role in discussion and the job application process the applicants able to answer questions they might have, enthisiastic , friendly and courteous , so the applicant will be viewed the opportunity move positively, resourceful and helpful to hire managers , such as sharing tips ar interviewer, how to manage interviewees' expectation etc.

Arranging interview stage providing the shortlisted candidates with helpful information about the interview includes: when and where the interview, who will be in the interview, how the interview will be conducted. Facilitating effective interview, the interviewer needs to ensure the interviewing environment is comfortable one free no noise, not leave the candidate waiting for too long. When closing the interview, the interviewer should advise the candidate of the possible must steps, online screening of application forms, using online to search and compare job applicant's information, job skills, years of experience, education level to identify suitable candidates for further selection processes.

Reward management is concerned with the formulation and implementation of strategies and policies that aim to reward people fairly, equitably a fact, employers nowadays can hardly rely solely on base salary to attract and motivate their employees. More emphasis has other benefits , such as retirement benefits and learning opportunites.

Performance and reward system should be market-based, equitable and cost-effective. Rewards do not only depend on skills, capabilities and experience of individuals, but also performance. In order to encourage top rate performers, employers must not only offer rewards for good work, but they must also have consequences for substandard work. Although, employers usually do not want to follow through with negative consequences, it is sometimes a necessary process. Otherwise, employees have no incentive to correct unacceptable behavior.

Employers also needs to clearly know about what is recognized by the company and how these will be measured. So that they understand the relationship of performance and reward. Total reward may include anything value resulting of employment relationship to the employee with a goal to attract, motivate and attract talent. It can include financial and non-financial rewards and that these can change over time depending on their personal circumstances. Employers need to find out what attracts, engages individuals and explore how best they can meet these needs. It is important that the company how design's the elements of the reward package to suppot.

What factors can determine rewarding for performance, qualification, experience, potential, behavior, effort, achieving goals, meeting targets. How the employees will be rewarded, the awards whether are company's work culture/characteristics are whether drived the right behavior/peformance/efforts the awards are be valued by the employees, the awards are how often to be given, how often the rewards are reviewed, the award is long or short term.

Legal framework for reward system , such as payment of wage, restriction on wages deduction, minimum wage, benefit, such as share options or housing benefits. Major benefit plans may include: retirement benefit schemes, personal security, e.g. healthcare, dental , hospitalization, accident or life insurance, financial assistance, e.g. mortage interest subsidies, rental subsidies, staff discoung, education subsidies, personal needs, e.g. holidays and leave with pay chold care, fitness and facilities, use of holiday house, employee shares purchase plan, company car etc. welfares.

3.1 What is HR's role in corporate social responsibility?

The HR function should help formulate and achieve environmental and social goals when also balancing these objectives with traditional financial performance metrics. The HR function can serve as a partner in determining what is needed or what is possible in formulating corporate values.

At the same time, HR should play a key role in ensuring that employees implement the strategy consistently. For example, encouraging employees, through training and compensation to find ways to reduce the use of environmentally damaging chemicals in the products, assisting employees in identifying ways to recycle products that can be used for play grounds for children who do not have access to healthy places to play designing a company's HRM system to reflect equity development avoid well-being , thus contributing to the long-tem health.

How HR policies shape the workplace and how HR can improve employee well-being through better working conditions and more positive workplace a cultures. Top-management can encourage particularly supervisory support, also has been identified as key to employee environment actions. In addition, adopting HRM and communicating a pro-environmental image can have a positive reputational effect. This helps to staff , the company leading to lower recuitment and training costs and a better financial bottom line. In fact, in some cases, a pro-environmental instance may be more important to potential employees. It can help a company address wider social problems that are affecting not only its external community, but also the company's financial bottom line. For example, The US postal service employees participate in more than 80 cross-functional teams across the US do drive energy reduction and resource conservation. These teams helped the postal service reduce energy, water, solid waste to landfills and petroleum fuel use as well as recycles more than 222000 tons of material. Thus, HR-related activities that can support , such as reponsible workplaces, human rights, safety practices, labor standards, peformance developments, diversity, employee compensation and more.

3.2 Human resource role in Hong Kong business environment

Andy, W.C. el.(2002) indicated that economic downturn which began in early 1998 had dramatic effects on Hong Kong's prosperity and increasing rates of Gross Domestic Product, especially during the 1990s and the early years of the 21$^{st}$ century. In late 2002s, Hong Kong's unemployment rate stood at 7 per cent and showed no immediate prospect of diminishing. This has huge implication for human resource professionals and especially for their training, as managers of the organization's most precious resource, its people. Moreover, downsizing and consequent increases in the rate of unemployment were logical consequences of this process.

However, Hong Kong's strengths in finance, trade, services and tourism provided benefits from the effects of these recessionary forces. But, Hong Kong was faced with the poor of dealing with the human resource implications and other aspect of workforce reduction. Hence, it explains why HK organizations need to consider HRM functions as part of the acquisition, development , motivation and maintenance of human resources in order to bring direct relevance of the strategic decision-making on which profits and productivity depend.

Human resource management is focused on the development and application of policies in relation to human resource planning, recruitment, selection, placement, and termination, management education , training and career development, terms of employment and methods and standards of remuneration, working conditions and employee services, formal and informal communication and consultation through employer and employee representative at all levels, negotiation and implementation of agreements on wages and working conditions , as well as procedures for the avoidance and settlement of disputes and the creation of a fairer and more equitable workforce in which discrimination in any form is viewed as unethical behaviors.

HRM responsibilities include to conduct research into local wage levels to ensure the firm's reward system is competitive with those in other companies, devising remuneration systems to excite or encourage or persuade workers into enhanced effort and efficiency, administering superannuation schemes, e.g. retirement welfare plan, and advising employees about their pensions, maintaining personnel records and statistics, preparing accurate job descriptions and other retirement documentation, implementing health and safety regulations, accident prevention and the provision of first-aid facilities, e.g. safe construction site environment, designing and evaluating management training and development schemes linked with succession planning and developing and implementation systems with facilities organizational communication.

Role of HR manager includes the control function, such as analysis of key operational data in human resource areas of labor turnover, wage cost, absenteeism, monitoring of staff performance ( staff appraisal ) and recommending appropriate remedial action to managers; the advisory function offers expect advice on human resource policies and procedures, e.g. which employees are ready for promotion, who should attend a certain training course, arrangement contracts of employment, health and safety regulations etc. related human resource related issues.

The future role of HR manager needs to concern to adopt an international insight in their work, growing concern for the application of ethical approaches to human resource management, implementation of equal opportunity , data privacy, and arranging flexible working models, such as job sharing, job rotation, permanent part –time work, increased awareness to encourage or persuade for effective employee participation in company production systems in order to achieve raising efficiencies and effectiveness, concerning the consequences for HR management of the ageing workforce discussed issues, such as prolonging / shortening working age or shortening /prolonging retirement age policy, participating legal system in human resource issues, including laws on hiring , dismissing, equal opportunities, age, country discrimination conduct of industrial relations.

HR planning can help management in making decision in the following areas: recruitment. , avoidance of redundancies ( increasing labor turnover, training, management and development, estimates of labor cost, productivity bargaining, raising effectiveness or efficiency , accommodation requirements. In order to achieve company's maximum benefits purpose, HR planning needs continuous readjustment ( annual review) , because the goals of an organization are subject to change and its internal and external environment is uncertain.

It is also complex because it involves to many independent variables, e.g. increasing skillful immigration job seeker number to compete in the country's local labor market or decreasing skillful labor, e.g. computer programmers, doctors, accountant, lawyers etc. occupation professionals sudden emigrate to other countries to seek jobs, consumer demand increases or decreases to the product. Hence , it must include feedback because if the plan can not be achieved, the objectives of the company will have to be modified so that they are feasible in human resource terms.

The human resource plan process to one company is a cycle process. The first step may include that it needs to follow issues from corporate plan's strategies and objectives. The main points to be considered such as capital equipment plans, reorganization, e.g. centralization or decentralization, how to change in product or in output, marketing plans and financial limitations.

After it gathers the company's corporate strategic plan data. Then, it will implement its second step. This step may include three aspects:

● How to achieve the reasonable present utilization of human resources in particular: numbers of employees in various categories, estimation of labor turnover for each grade of employee and the analysis of labor effects of high or low turnover rates on the organization's performance, amount of overtime worked, amount of short time, appraisal of performance and the potential of present employees and general level of payment compared with that in other comparable firms. All these HR related data is essential to be recorded in accurate attitude.

● The external environment of the company analysis, such as recruitment position, population trends, local housing and transportation plans, government policies in education and retirement.

● The potential supply of labor analysis, such as effects of local emigration and immigration, effects of recruitment or redundancy in local firms, possibility of employing categories not now employed, for example outsource employees number, part time and semi-retired workers number and changes in productivity , working hours.

The final step is that HR planning needs to be achieved. It includes recruitment/redundancy program, training and development program, industrial relations policy and accommodation plan. The issues will appear in this plan, such as jobs which will appear, disappear or change, to what extent redeployment or retraining is possible, necessary changes at supervisory and management is possible, necessary changes and supervisory and management levels, training needs, arrangements for necessary and details of arrangements for handling any human problems arising from labor deficits or surpluses , e.g. early retirement or other natural wastage procedures. Following , it needs to give feedback , what will be possible modification to company objectives to company's corporate level to review its HR plan whether it can achieve company's objectives and strategic aims.

Human resource manager can be one human resource relation consultant to give recommendation how the organization should be better equipped to cope with the HR consequences of changed circumstances, careful consideration of likely future human resource requirements could lead the firm to discover new and improved ways surpluses might be avoided, it helps the firm to create and develop employee training and management succession program, some of the problems of managing change may be foreseen or consultations with affected groups and individuals can occur at an early stage in the change process and decision can be taken and by considering all the relevant , options, rather than being taken in crisis situations, management can assess critically the strengths and weaknesses of its labor force and HR policies, wasting or excess of effort among employees can be avoided and coordination to worker's efforts is improved to raise efficiencies and productive effectivenesses.

3.3 HR role in bank industry development

What is human resource (HR) role in organization? What factors can change to influence HR? They include workforce changes, globalization, ethics, organizational growth, increased accountability. These factors can influence HR's role change in the organization. So , when you assume be one HR manager, you need to concern : How have you used you awareness of internal and external changes to guide the decision making of your stakeholders ,e.g. discussing the impact of trends in workforce skills with function leaders? Which of your knowledge , skill, abilities or other characteristics have been useful in consulting with stakeholders?

Hence, HR role needs to understand the organizational goals and the role each function plays, serves of a cross-functional bridge. Locates talent throughout the global organization, identifies and supports need for resources or training, advices core functions on how with adapts to organizational strategy. Moreover, HR leaders need own knowledge of other business functions and whose organizations' business influences specific actions by HR , e.g. understanding the type of experts needed by R&D and future trends for that need. Also, the HR leader needs to know which of whose knowledge, skills, abilities or other characteristics have been useful in repsonding to this challenge? HR also needs to consider how its organizational functions. They have disadvantges and advantages in order to achieve HR staff skill, talent to satisfy different departments' needs effectively and efficeintly. Organizational structure has three types: Firstly, functional type advantages of easy to understand, specialization develop economies of scale, communication within function, career paths, fewer people and disadvantages of weak customer or product focus , potentially weak communication among function, hierarchical structure. Secondly, product type advantages of economies of scale, product team cutlure, product expertise and disadvantages of regional or local focus, more people, weak customer focus. Finally, geographic type advantages localization, quicker response time and disadvantages of fewer economic of scale, more people potential quality control.

HR also needs to concern when it's company needs to implement outsourcing employment need rea third party contractors' successful outsourcing depends on choosing the right activities to outsource, cooperation of contractor's performance objectives with strategic requirements.

Confirmation of contractors' reliability, capacity, expertise and ethical behavior. So , when the organization feel it needs to employ outsource contractors. The HR has responsibility to lead and know how to apply whose ethical practices competency in contracting for HR services or performing , due diligence or organizational sourcing, e.g. taking steps to protect employee data. The HR leader or manager also needs to know which of his/her knowledge skills, ability or other characteristics has been useful in responding to this challenge.

Standard chartered had have good talent management strategies to train its staffs. The talent management at standard chartered bank (SCB) features include: Standard chartered bank has good performance appraisal or measurement strategy. By making it a global standard to conduct face-to-face performance appraisals every six months. SCB is reviewing its own performance management objectives to make sure that those objectives stay relevant and achievable. Being sensitive to different cultures by employing different appraisal methods, also show that SCB understands the importance of managers and staff indentifying and dealing with real, actual problems in a way that is most familiar and effective to them. Through appraisal, SCB also classifies their employees into 5 categories ranging from high potentials to critical resources, then to core contributors, followed by underachievers and fainally underperformers. By identifying areas in which they are lacking and act.

What are the relevance HR problem to bring bank crisis to SCB. SCB view of employees as human capital in the organization, it could have at least mininimsed the less to a certain extent. For one, discussions between employers and still could have been more open and problem issues coulf have been identified at an earlier stage inefficiencies in the organization would have been uncovered , influence their performance against regional offices. In a way, having a certain amount of centralized control through talent management would also enable the monitoring of its offices globally.

What are performance appraisal aims? Performance appraisal is the measurement of the effectiveness of an employee's job performance. The process is described as the collection and use of judgements, ratings, perceptions or more objectives sources of information to understand better the performance of aperson, team, unit, business, process programme in order to guide subsequent actions and decisions. The resut or performance outcomes represent the contributions tht an individual's job performance makers to an organization and its goals.

Performance appraisal focus on measuring or appraising the job performance of a individual, e.g. use of surveys or rating focus to assess and evaluate employee behavior. It brings the either positive or negative feedback to the employee in the performance view and the new goals for the next performal period may be discussed.

3.4 HR role in India automobile industry

Human resource development (HRD) is the part of human resource mangement in any organizations. It deals with training employees in the organization when the industry feels it have need to upgrade skills to its staffs. It aims to let them to learn new skills distributing resources that are beneficial for the employee's task. For automobile industry in India example, India automobile sale companies will need effective HRD in their organizations if they expect to sell automobiles to global customers attractively.

Authors ( May, June 2014) from internet essay indicated the India automobile sector is divided in four different sector which are as follow: two wheeler, which comprise of mopeds, scooters, motorcycles and electric two-wheelers passenger vehicles which include passenger cars, utility vehicles and multi-purpose vehicles, commercial vehicles that are light and material heavy vehicles and three wheelers that are passenger cerriers and product carriers.

Why do India automobile sale companies need to concern HRD? Authors ( May, June 2014) indicated the automobile industry is one of the key drivers that boost the economic growth to India. However, the year 2013-2014 has seen a decline in the industry's growth . High inflation , high interest rates, low consumer sentiment and rising fuel prices with economic slowdown and rising fuel reason for the downturn of the industry.

Except for the two wheelers, all other segments in the industry have been weakening. These is a negative impact on the automakers and dealers who offer high discounts in order to push sales. To match the decline in demand, automakers need good skillful of automakers to manufacturers attractive automobiles in order to attract foreign automobile buyers to choose to buy themselves any kinds of automobiles.

Despite the comprehensive market being under extreme burden, the luxury car market has abserved a robust double digital like during the year 2013-2014, as a result of rewarding new launches at lower price points. Hence, foreign robust luxury cars competitors influence India automobiles sale number to be reduced. Hence, India automobile manufacturers felt automobile manufacturing workers' skills need to be train or improve in order to manufacture more comfortable and good design vehicles to satisfy future global automobile consumers' driving enjoyable needs.

In fact, India automobile industry employment opportunities will trend increase in the future with the number of vehicles available on the road today, the need and requirement for people who can fix these machines is fast increasing. The automobile jobs like automobile technician, car or bike mechanics are a great option. Becoming a diesel mechanic is also a significant alternative in India, automble labor market. Diesel mechanics are responsible for repairing and servicing diesel engines. As they are also required to repaire engines of trucks and buses, other than cars. Even if communication with people instead of repairing cars in what interest to Indian, then Indian have opportunity of becoming a saleperson or sales manager in an automobile company. Career opportunities in automobile design, paint specialists, job on the assembly line and insurance of vehicles is also available.

Future India automobile industry employment trend is as the destination choice for design and manufacture of automobiles employers who need to automobile production skillful worker number will rise, because India manufacturing heavy vehicles, passenger vehicles, commercial vehicles automobile production skillful workers need number will rise.

Hence, India automobile sale employers will need have good human resource development model for the automobile companies, if they expect to raise automobile sale competitive effort in global automobile sale market. At the implementation level, India exectutives of the automobile companies need to strengthen their training, net working and more towards providing a satisfactory human resource development climate for its automobile industry vehical production, design, repair, salespeople employees and suggest suitable changes and corrections in the policy decisions for management of automobile companies and policy makers. Hence, future HRD practices in automobile industrial organizations for India automobile companies aim to identify the HRD mechanisms implemented in the selected automobile companies to achieve the training function to be effectively managed in the automobile companies in order to raise automobile sale competition effect in global automobile market.

3.5 Challenge of HR management

As a HR specialist, what are the challenges you may face and what HR intervention mechanisms would you consider using in an attempt to drive individual and organisational performance in a multinational company? Critically evaluate this question by utilising the appropriate academic literatures.

The challenges of the HR specialist when there engage in attempt of increasing the individual and organisational performances in Multinational Companies through developing a set of HRM best practices, especially relating to employee recruitment and selection, performance management and staff retention. Since the organizations are multinational number of concerns are arises such as dealing cultural issues with the organizational goals as well as individual goals. Furthermore organizational behaviors and tools such as engagement, motivation and empowerment are basically highlighted; without those it is merely a dream to achieving the business goals. Basically Multinational companies are aiming profits and there for individual and organisational performance are very vital for their existence.

HR has been organized in a different ways over the years. Some functions have emphasized delivery by location or by business structure. In these models an integrated HR team has serviced managers and employees at specific location or with in specific businesses units, with some more strategic or complex tasks reserved for the corporate centre. The degree to which these different arms of HR were centralized or co-located and the question of whether they were managed by the business unit varied. Within the HR teams, depending up on their size their might have been specialization by work area (especially for industrial relations in the 1960s and 1970s) or by employee grade or group (responsibility, say, divided between those looking after clerical staff from those covering production) The advancement of personal management starts around end of the 19$^{th}$ century, when welfare officers came in to being.

There are some organizations where HR is seen as a central, corporate function with little advancement to business units. Some other organizations position themselves in the opposite direction, with a very small corporate centre and all the activity distributed to business units. The question of best structure is how the function best organizes itself between the pulls of centralization and the pushes of decentralization.(The changing HR functions) The HR assumptions and HR practices observed in high performing firms are the key elements to the formation of the Best Practice theory. Employment security, selective hiring, self managed teams, high pay contingent on company performance, extensive training, reduction of status difference, and sharing information are the key element of the theory. However less concern about the organisational goals and culture are given as draw backs for the theory. According to the "best fit theory" a firms that follows a cost leadership strategy designs narrow jobs and provides little job security, whereas a company pursuing a differentiation strategy emphasizes training and development. In other words this argues that all SHRM activities must be consistent with each other and linked to the strategic objectives of the business. HRM uses various technologies to direct employees behavior towards objectives and tasks that deliver approved organisational performance. Many organizations try to frame these 'levers' with an overall performance management system, and attach incentives and rewards to achievements of objectives and targets within this. HR will need to reduce employment expenses to help organizations to save income. Direct costs include: Recruitment costs (advertising, admin, etc),Induction/training costs,Other admin costs associated with new hires,Overtime/ cost of temporary workers,Reduced productivity cost etc. which are related to HR expenses.

In conclusion there is evidence to suggest that including the practice out line within this organisational behaviours and tools can used to drive organisational and individual performance in Multinational companies. It is essential to have suitable recruitment and selection process, performance Appraisal System and ataff Retention plan to ensure the right people, In the right place, at the right time with right attitude. Training and development is also vital to improve HR performance. In addition HR Specialists role will be more specific when these techniques applying in to multi cultural environments where people perceptions and behavioral patterns are different from each other.

3.6 The nature of the employment relationship

John, B. & Jeff, G. ( 6 edition, 2017) indicated Human resource management defines a distinctive approach to employment management, which seeks to achieve competitive advantage through the strategic deployment of a highly committed and capable workplace using an array of cultural, structural and personnel techniques. Also, human resource management is a strategic approach to managing employment relations which emphasizes that leveraging people's capabilities and commitment is critical to achieving sustainable competitive advantage or superior public services. This is accomplished through a distinctive set of integrated employment policies, programmes and practices in an organizational and societal context. Moreover, human resource management underscores the importance of people, only the " human factor" or labor can provide talent to generate value. It should draw attention to the notion of indeterminary or uncertainty, which devices from the employment relationship: Employees have a potential capacity to provide the added value desired by the employer. It also follows from this that human knowledge and skills are a strategic resource that needs investment and skilful management. Moreover, in the environmental change factor influences to any organizations need to provide a role for HRM in improving an organization's performance in terms of overall sutainability.

What is the nature of the employment relationship ?

The nature of the social relationship between employers and the social relationship between employees and employer is an issues of central analytical importance to HRM. The employment relationship describes a relation between employees ( non-managers and managers) and ther employer. Through the employment contract, inequalities of power structure both economic exchange ( wage or salary) and the nature and quality of the work performed whether it is routine or creative. They can be short-term, primarily but not economic exchange for a relatively well-defined set of duties and low commitment or they can be complex long-term relationships defined by a range of economic inducements and relative security of employment, given in return for a set of duties and a high commitment from the employee.

Airline services: the demands of emotional labor of employment relationship between airline and airline staffs. Positive emotion at work offers an apparent win to win situaton for airline organizations and individuals as it suggests that if a job or work is correctly designed, individuals will feel better and perform better. What was once a private act of emotion management is sold now as labor in the public contract jobs? What was once a privately negotiated rule of feeling or displaying is now set by th airline company's standard practices division. However, such as airline service waiter job, a private emotional system has been subordinated to commercial logic and it has been changed by whose airline employers.

3.7 HR role in business maximizing efficiency method

John , H. ( 2013) described the work of police officers, we might dicuss the functions of preventing crome and catching criminals, the practices of patrolling, filling in report forms, breaking up disturbances, making arrests, and the qualities of commitment service. He also indicated police work is much more complicated than the brief suggestions and management work ( including the management of police work) is much more complex still. It is hard to describe the functions without detailing the practices or to make sense of the practices without involving the functions.

John, H. (2013) defined characteristics of management is responsibility for an organization or organization unit and for the work of its members. The unit might be anything from a small retail outlet with one or two shop assistants to large corporation with tens or even hundreds of thousands of employees, but most managers are directly responsible for managing the organization of a managabe number of people, typically between two and twenty and of the various processes in which they are engaged. So, we have sales managers and production managers and marketing managers and IT managers etc. organizing the work of specialists. The at the level, of the business unit or agency or regional subsidiary, we have general managers whose jobs is to organize and cooordinate the work of different specialist groups.

Maximizing efficiency method

Maximizing efficiency was a work study or time-and-motion to be exercise designed to calculate how the work could be most efficiently carried out. This involved the analysis of different possible divisions of different possible tasks of labour into specialized tasks. The optimization of the tools and machines, and the optimization of the physical movements, required to operate them, assuming workers well suited to the specified tasks concern. The optimized system would then be condified so as to become a standard requirement to be implemented with absolute regularity, so that the whole workplace operated as a machine. Workers would be selected with the skills and strengths to perform each specialised task, and trained to follow the standard procesures. They would be fairly paid for what was scientifically established to be a reasonable level of peformance ( assuming they were well pay introduced, to encourge over- performance and punish (underperformance). Both owners or employee would benefits.

It indicated conclusion was that output was determined less by working conditions or incentive systems than by the informed social pattern of the work group. Feeling mattered and wherever managers took a personal interest in the workers, made them feel important and generated mutually supportive and cooperative environment, output are enhanced management. It seems was not about mechancial optimization processes, but about leadership and team dynamics. The management characteristics were however critical and with some rearrangement they can be summarized as follows: A strong people orientation, every body is treated s part of the team and just as an replaceable resource, flexibility and teamwork value driven value system is through the company.


3.8 six situation factors can influence management's choice of HR strategy


Beer , M., et al. (1984) explained that HRM and the issue of management goals and specific HR outcomes. The Harvard framework consists of six basic components as below:

Beer, M., et al. (1984) indicated these six situation factors can influence management's choice of HR strategy. Firstly, situation factors include workforce characteristics, business strategy and conditions, management philosophy, labor market, unions , task technology , laws and societal values. Any one of situation factor can influence management's choice of HR strategy. The situation factor can bring influences to other two components. Stakeholder interests component means shareholders, management, employee groups, government, community, union as well as human resource management policy choices component, it means employee influence, human resource flow, reward system and works systems. It emphaises that management' decisions and actions in HR management can be fully appreciated only if it is recognized that they result from an interaction between constraints and choices will be influenced by situational factor component and shakeholder interests components and long-term consequences component influences.

The human resource management policy choices component will influence the human resource outcomes component, it includes commitment, competence, cost -effectiveness. It means that it needs to understand the importance of management's goals, the HR outcomes of high employee commitment and competence are linked to longer term effects on organizational effectiveness and societal well-being.

The assumptions are built into the framework are that employees have talents that are rarely fully utilized in the workplace and that they show a desire to experience growth through work. The, the human resource outcomes component will influence the long-term consequences component. It includes individual well-being, organizational effectiveness and societal well-being . The long-term consequences distinguish between three goals: individual , organizational and societal. At the level of the individual employee, the long-term HR outputs comprise the psychological rewards that workers receive in exchange for their effort. At the organizational level, increased effectiveness ensures the survival of the firm. At the societal level, as a result of fully utilizing people at work, some of society's goals ( for example, employment and growth are attained.

Finally, the sixth component is a feedback component, it is through which the outputs flow directly into the organization and to the stakeholders. However, long-term outputs can influence situational factors, stakeholder interests and HR mangement policy choices in cycle two way relationship.


3.9 Knowledge management at hotel industry

Hotels' realization led to the design and implementation of a computerized knowledge library that was accessible to every site manager in every hotel across the Australia/South pacific/ South East Asia region. The system was designed to initiate a long-term knowledge-sharing culture by making it easier to share value-added practices and processes, thus reducing wastage of time and resources through replication.

The problem- The knowledge library operated as a two way system whereby managers could both add ideas or effective innovative practices and find solutions to some of their own operational problems that demanded new ideas or innovation. To simplify its use, the system was designed to store ideas by hotel function ( that is food and beverage, housekeeping etc.) with both functional and key word search tools available , knowledge transfer was considered to have occured once an idea had been implemented at another site.

Hotel management realized that they would need to create support systems to motivate sharing between the sites and geographical regions. This opened up an opportunity to achieve the desired knowledge, sharing actions and behaviors. Throughout the performance management system, as a result, for each site manager to pass their annual performance review, they had to retrieve a minumum of two ideas from the system and implement these in their hotel, as well as add two ideas to the system for others to be able to access and use.

The idea that the hotel different site managers' knowledge and expertise can play a strategic role in achieving competitive goals to expect to achieve a strategy results in superior performance, or a competive advantage. Achieving high performance, improving employment skills, pay-for -performance, profit sharing, performance appraisal, teamworking, job evaluation, information-sharing, employment security, selective hiring, self- managed teams or teamworking, high pay contingent on company performance, extensive training, reduction in status differences, information sharing( knowledge management) benefits.

3.10 Manpower planning role in business

Manpower planning ( workforce planning) means personnel and HR managers need to ensure that necessary supply of people was forthcoming to allow targets to be met. In theory at least, a manpower plan could show how the demand for people and their skills within an organization could be balanced by supply. The idea of a balance between demand and supply reflects the influence of the language of classical labor economics, in which movement towards an " equilibrium" serves as an ideal.

The utilization, improvement and preservation of an organization's human resources. The four stages of the planning process may include: the first stage is an evaluation or appreciation of the existing manpower resources. The second stage is an estimation of the proportion of currently employed manpower resources that were likely to be within the firm by the forcast data. the third stage is an essessment or forecast of labor requirements needed if the organization's overall objectives were to be achieved by the forecast date and the fourth stage, it needs to measure to ensure that the necessary resources were available as and when required that is the manpower plan.

There were two main reasons for companies to use manpower planning. To develop their business objectives and manning levels and to reduce the " unknown" factor. Firstly organization implements strategy and targets, it brings organization practices and methods, it brings manpower review and analysis ( internal and external factors) , it brings forecast ( demand and supply), it brings adjust to balance ( recurit, retain and reduce).

Way of working includes: annualized hours, working time organized on the basis of th number of hours to be worked over a year rather than a week; it is usually used to fit in with peaks. Compresses hours, which allows individuals to work their total number of agreed hours over a shorter period. Flexi-time, employees have a choice about their actual working hours, usually outside certain agreed core times. Home working, either on a fully time basis or an a part time basis where employees divide their time between home and office. Job-sharing , which involves two people employed on a part time basis but, working together to cover a full time post. Shift-working , giving employers the scope to have their business open for longer periods than an 8 hour day. Staggered hours, employees can start and finish their day at different times. Term-time working, employees can take unpaid leave of absence during the school holidays.

Recruitment, selection and talent management stages include:

Internal factors and external factors bring to workforce planning staffing needs options: internal via external brings to recuritment attraction via sources brings to applicant pool brings to selection assessment brings to job performance measurement brings to job analysis brings to workfoce planning staffing needs opinions in cycle processing again.

Capable people who will apply for jobs within a organization. First, there is a need to attract people's interest in applying for employment. It implies that people have a choice about which organizations they wish to work for, even though during times of recession such choices might be limited. People may be capable of fulfilling a role in employment, but the extent to which this will be realized is not totally predictable. How capability is understood is increasingly determined by an organization's approach to talent management and development.

Under different labour market conditions, power in recruitment process will change between buyers and sellers of labour, the employers and employees respectively. Thus, in conditions of recession, employers are likely to reduce recruitment budgets and costs, paying more attention to developing the talent that has already been employed.

● Online recruitment

Budgetary factors will also affect how recruitment channels are used, with more use of online recruitment. For example, the ageing profile of the workforce around the world requires an adjustment of recruitment policies, the use of the internet and agencies for recruitment reflected to younger applicants, whereas older workers were more dependent on formal channels of recruitment, such as newspapers and journals. In addition, there have been many more graduates leaving university, and graduate employment is becoming very competitive. Many graduates will take longer to find employment that matches ther skills. This might affect perceptions of the value to be gained from studying for a degree compared with the price of a degree.

There is a difference, however, in what recruiters think is important to this generation and what the generation itself thinks . Although HR policies will be designed to achieve particular organizational targets and goals, those policies will also provide an opportunity for individual needs and be satisfied . This view assumes that a fit between a person and the environment can be found so that their commitment and performance will be enhanced.

This an indication that the person to environment fit includes a person to organization fit, person to group fit and person to environment fit. If there is a match between the values within each of those areas expressed by the organization at th recruitment stage. The organization and the new recruits have a clear employees and can therefore manage those expectations.

HRM could help to shape the direction of change, influence culture and help bring about the mindset that would decide which strategic issues mre considered. HR considerations, including the results of a review of the quantity and quality of people, the goals , objectives and targets whether they can achieve performance in an organization and for how work is organized into roles and jobs.

There has been a rapid growth in online recuritment , e-recruitment. As a result, organizations are advised to consider the design of websites and the terms that applicants might use to carry out job and vacancy searches.

The usability of a company's wesite affects an applicant's perception of a job, with a focus on hyperlinks and text rather than graphic images and navigation links. However, issues with e-recruitment , including the one-way communication system, the fact that it is impersonal and passive, and the fact that it creates an artificial distance between the individual and the company.

● recruitment agent

However, once a recruitment strategy has been formed, an organization might outcomes its implementation to reduce costs and take advantage recruitment expertise, especially a large number of staff are recruitment. Recruitment agents act as "labor market intermediaties" between individual recruits and recruiting organizations. Financial service organization assessment and measurement of creating customer service performance indicators include as below:

Anticipating customer needs and planning accordingly, identifying the customers who will be of value to the company, recommending change to current ways of working that will improve customer service, arranging the collection of customer satisfaction data and acting on them. The analysis and definition of competencies should allow the identification and isolation of behavior that are distinct and are associated with competent or effective performance. On this assumption, the assessment of competencies is one means selecting employees.

Recruitment channels may include walk in, employee referrals, advertising, particularly online job boards, websites, labour market intermediaries, such as social media , social professional networks, recuritment agencies, educational associations, professional associations.

● job description

Job description includes job title, department, reponsible to , relationships, purpose of job/overall objectives, specific duties and responsibilities, physical and economic conditions as well as personnel specification includes physical characteristics, general intelligene, specific attitudes, interests, impact on other people, qualification and experience, abilities, motivation. Both job description and personnel specifications have been key elements, it replies too much on the analyst's subjective judgement in identifying the key aspects of a job and the qualities that related to successful performance.

● Selection

An organization wishes to recruit new employees to define criteria against which it can measure and assess applicants. Increasingly , such criteria are set in the form of competencies composed of behavioral characteristics and attitudes. Organizations have become increasingly aware of making good selection decisions, as selection involves a number of costs include: the cost of the selection process itself, including the use of various selection instruments, the future cost of training new staff , the cost of labor turnover if the selected staff are not retained.

There are good reasons why organizations need to consider the reaction of applicants to selection methods. If the selection is viewed as the attraction of the organization may be diminished, candidates who have a negative experience can dissuade others, a negative selection experience can impact on job acceptance , selection methods are covered by legislation and regulations relating to discriminaton, mistreatment during selection will put off future applicants and may also stop applicants from buying the organization's products or using their services.

3.11 role of HR technology

What is the role of technology in Human Resource Development? Identify some key forms of e-learning and critically evaluate their advantages and disadvantages, providing appropriate examples from organisations. It will define what Human Resource Development is and why it needs technology. Also it will discuss what electronic learning (e-learning) is, and will explain some key forms of e-learning and why we need to use e-learning. It will give a brief indication as to what technology actually is, and also the progression of technology. The essay will critically evaluate the advantages and disadvantages of using e-learning in Human Resource Development. There will be appropriate examples used to show how different organisations use e-learning within their company/organisation. Finally it will offer conclusions as to why I think technology should or should not be a part of Human Resource Development.

Why does HR development need technology?

Technology is always progressing and this is very good for companies who need or even sell technology. If we look at how a few years back within companies the secretary would need to file documents manually and this could take a long time, also apart from the time issue there were more serious problems like documents going missing or being damaged. This is where technology began to progress because there was a new technology progressing and this was the database and this could hold all the documents you needed safe documents onto the computer and that way it would be a lot faster and more secure for the secretary to file the documents. This is just one example there are many more ways in which technology has helped to progress companies. The example given here is just to show that technology is progressing and it will keep progressing much further in the future years to come.

Human Resource Development is all about learning, training, developing and education the employees in the workplace. There is a difference between these four concepts but there all correlated. If for example we looked at learning; this can be learnt anywhere and you can be learning yourself the new skills, but on the other hand if you looked at education you are being taught something but in a formal way but the two are linked because from both of these you are learning new skills and then you can go on to training and developing them skills.

HRD was not always known as this, there was a shift from welfare officers to HRD. HRD was initially set up for training and development and this was to help the employers in crafts such as electricians, or engineers as an example and from this they would be learning from their masters and will be developing their skills to be able to perform in the workplace. HRD created an integration of people management and development and this could become CIPD which stands for the chartered institute of personnel and development.

HRD likes to be strategic and is more for the organisation than the employees; it is also a long term method to help to build the company. HRD does like to implement change into their methods and this is why e-learning will be very convenient to help within organisations because it is constantly changing and this change would help employees improve on their learning and training and will be able to implement new skills within the workplace.

Why does HR needs e-learning in organization? Firstly before I go into detail about how e-learning helps HRD perform you will need to know what e-learning actually is. E-learning used to be known as computer-based learning, this is basically what it still is, it is a way of learning but on a computer or even these days there is even e-learning which is through the mobile. We need e-learning in everyday life to be able to adapt the required skills in education, employment, even at home. It can be defined as any learning activity supported by information and communication technologies which is known as ICTs. There are arguments out there concerning the labels, an example of this is whether ICT-based learning is the same as e-learning, we can gather information from the world wide web channel and this would be our online materials, but we can also get materials from this internet would could be confused as being from the world wide web but instead this material is delivered through an internal network of personal computers. E-learning is in fact taken to mean any form of electronic technology which can support learning this can be opposed to the chalk and blackboard technology which used to be the main form of learning.

3.12 Why is HR strategy important to influence organizational success?
In organizational level, humans do formalize strategies as a function to direct and focus their efforts. However, in a business organizational ( a firm), such efforts will focus on creating value for profit. In fact, the environment is a market with limited resources and therefore it causes competition exists. This environment mght be more or less stable, but it is in constant change.
HR Strategy will become a systemic and rational act, a process that can be managed in order to successfully attain in the golas of the firm. HR Strategy can divide these three kinds. Firstly, a HR plan is intended to achieve a particular purpose and to develop a HR strategy for dealing with unemployment. It is overall HR strategy to gain promotion. For government ( public organization's economic HR strategy example. Seondly, it is the process of HR planning or putting a HR plan into operation in a skillful way. Finally, for war strategy, it is the skill of HR planning to be trained to the movements of armies in s battle or war. An example, of military HR training strategy, defence, strategies compare tactic.
However, nowadays, business organizations need " office of general", " command" , " generalship" skilful actions, leadership and leading warefare from one leader, such as CEO who have any effective HR strategy to manage staffs and tasks as well as leading them to serve their organizations successfully. So, an effective HR strategy can give good HR planning direction to let the organization to know whether it ought need how to do in order to achieve its HR development goals successfully.
An effective HR planning direction can achieve the organizaton's HR allocation goals more easily. For example, knowling how it can use of common resources ( e.g. available human and technological resources). A basic HR strategic advantage tool win and prevail over rivals in the market comes from the different used of such resources.
In beverage competitive industry example, Coca-Cola soft drink organization example, it was still keeping its predominance in the beverage market product " Coke", Pepsi Co was advancing fast on the base of a successfull "image" HR strategy targeting the youngest segment of the soft drinking market under the taste of the new generation. So, it can select to employ more young workers to work in its organization in order to persuade many

youngest soft drink customers to believe it is one young soft drink health drinking company. By 1983, Pepsi had begun to outsell coke in supermarkets when coke maintained its edge only through soda vending machines and fast food restaurants. Although, different marketing strategic breakthrough by far unexpected. It follows all time successful formula of coke. In 1985, the " New Coke" was introduced after an extensive study of market trended, surveys, focus group and taste tests strategies. In these survey investigation process, it must need to employ many part time or full time questionnaires staffs, they can include students, housewives, freelance workers, unemployed workers.

So, HR department needs have enough time to select the right applicants to finish the whole questionnaire investigation project efficiently and effectively. The HR arrangement need to gather information to conclude this goals, such as how to design the new formula ( or taste) was based on a different ( lower cost) source of sugar, high fructose corn syrup to replace cane sugar. All of Coca ( the plant from which comes the allealoid cocain) derivates were also removed from the old formula. So, how to design the taste is the main survey information gathering aim. Also, how HR arrangement which can have enough questionnaire staffs to carry on gathering information from the taste tests in the limited time to achieve to finish the taste test questionnaire project efficently and effectively.

What are HR strategic benefits? They include: It can assist an organization to protect its HR capital base. It is a well accepted business principle, it can also help the organization to extend this notion to the world' natural and human resources, it can help leaders to plan and measure HR employment and reward and welfare and performance management systems of business enterprises more accurately, it can help business leaders to do the best balance between narrow self-interest and actions takes for the good of unemployment or creating more opportuniy solution benefit in society as well as they can do actions in pursuit of finanaicl survival more easily.

Why can HR strategy help organizational change in success? Knowing the importance and implication of organizational change and admitting the fact that organizatonal change success and leader / leadership can play a key role in bringing and implementing these changes by deciding the desired form of an organization and taking the potential steps which are needed for the process. So, when one organization has one good HR strategy, it can assist its organization to change more people and non-people resources effectively and efficiently.

Why do organizations need to change HR strategy? Nowadays, dynamic business environments influence organizations that respond quickly and effectively to constant change. A dynamic enterprise has two important tasks. It must adapt the current business environment, e.g. people skillful shortage in the industry into a shared HR strategy and then quickly and effectively to employ talent people or potential people to do the skillful job for its organization.

Reference

Andy, W.C. and Barry, J. B. and Wai, M.M. (2002) , Managing human resource in Hong Kong, Hong Kong: Thomson, p.6

Source: The harvard model of HRM

Beer , M., specter, B., Lawrence, PR. and Mills, D. Q. (1984). managing human assets. New York: Free press.

John, B. & Jeff, G. ( 6 edition, 2017). Human resource management theory and practice, Palgrave, Macmillan publishers ltd. UK , London,pp.4-5

John, H. (2013) managment a very short introduction, Oxford university press, UK, pp.11-13

Sources

http://info.shine.com/industry/automobiles-auto-ancillaries/2.html retrieved on 14 th May 2014

https://www.kpmg.de/docs/auto-survey.pdf retrieved on 17 th June 2014

# CHAPTER FOUR

# Training and Learning

What are the technique sector to solve above aspect of problems to HR?

John, A (2018) identified the major problems relate to HR personnel management, they include that selection of personal problem aspect, he explained that even if one knows precisely what qualities are required of man to do a given job well, it is still difficult to determine whether any given candidate has these qualities. On training problem aspect , he indicated that the cost of training staff is rapidly increasing, due largely to the increasing level of skill needed to operate modern equipment in the factory and office. Poor training will bring low earnings, high proportion of scrap production, mistakes, accidnts results. Finally on salary and wage structure aspect, paid problems concern complaints of unfairness in the wage and salary differentials between levels of age, or skill, or between sections of the company.

What are the technique sector to solve above aspect of problems to HR? John, A ( 2018) explained that productivity bargaining, job evaluation, consultation and management by objectives techniques can be attempted to solve human relation problem; aptitude tests, intelligence tests, manpower planning, personality tests techniques can be attempted to solve selection of personnal problem; needs analysis, programmed learning, business games techniques can be attempted to solve training problem; productive bargaining, job evaluation, merit rating, incentive schemes, salary progression curves, time span of discretion techniques can be attempted to solve salary and wage structue problem.

John, A(2018) , he explained that how to apply the aptitude test to solve selecting personnal problem. He assumed that increasing technology needs an ever larger number of skilled and semi-skilled employees in almost every field of industry , e.g. machines and processes are more complex to operate and maintain, computers must be programmed. However , training employees to the new higher standards is expensive and it is becoming increasingly important to select any those who will be able to reach the necessary standard. One way to determine whether a candidate will satisfactorily complete his training to be test his aptitude for the proposed task before his/her training starts these kinds of aptitude tests as below:

The technique consists of analysing the physical and mental skills required to perform the task successfully and then estimating each candidate's aptitude in these by means of special tests. Typical examples of the testable skills are: mannual desterity, ability to understand complex progress for chemical plant operators, mental aptitude for system analysis. Also standard training tests are now available for estimating certain aptitudes and where exist little training is required to give a test to a candidate. The training test is often a highly specialised job. Usually it will be able of someone in the personnel department to use this training test technique, but executives should be aware of its existence. Aptitude test advantage concerns buying a standard test is low, but the cost of having are specially prepared by an expert can be high. The training required to use them and interpret the results is slight. For some of the standard tests the correlation between those failing the test and failing a achieve the necessary standard of skill after training is good, i.e. substantial savings in training costs can be made by unsuitable candidates before spending money on their training.

John, A( 2018) explained that how to apply brainstorming technique to generate new ideas. He assumes that new products have appeared on the market an ever-increasing rate, that is to say many product life-cycles are declining. So, new ideas in advertising in display in production technique to HR development is needed . Many companies are finding that their employees think creaively. They begin to the problem is that most employees not only fail to think creativity, but tend to use the old product, old market , outlets, old methods and old equipment for as long as possible habitually.

He indicated that brainstorming strategy is a way of promoting new ideas. The usual method is for six to fifteen people need to meet for half an hour and propose answer to a question from the session leader. The questions may be that how many ways, we could increase sales of product (x), how many new market , we can think for product (y), in what ways we can redesign product(z). Hence, each member needs to present and they can be drawn from all levels and from any departments in the company. The leader speaks his/her idea to let the every member to listen and no one is permitted to criticize this idea, his/her idea provokes member to think of another.

Eventually, several ideas may be developed into one that is entirely new. Only when the session has ended do they start the rational process of determining whether the ideas can be practises or not. Then, any promising ideas can be subjected to " reverse brainstorming" in which the question in how many ways might this idea fail? is asked. Hence, brainstorming technique is good training to let staffs to create new idea method.

John,A (2018) explained that intelligence test can be applied to select the right man for the job. he assumed that this problem of one of the requisites for any job is a minimum level of intelligence. How can this be measured? He explained that intelligence tests, intelligence tests consist usually of a long list of questions to be answers and problems to solved within a set time. The number of questions answered correctly within this time is an indication of IQ of the candidate. Some training is required to apply an intelligence test to a candidate and to interpret the results, even when the test used is one of the well known standard ones.

How to design a test of this sort is a highly specialised job. All personnel officers should know about this technique and in large companies it may be desirable to train one officer in their use. Its advantages include cost is low, it only takes an hour or to test one candidate or a group of them. The effor is hotly debated. Without doubt these tests accurately measure IQ is a large proportion of cases.. In particular they can indicate whether a candidate has a very high or very high or very low IQ , although some doubt exists as to their accuracy in the middle ranges. Howeve, the real debate concerns the accuracy of the results so much as their value. For IQ is said to be a measure only of a certain type of intelligence and not a guide to other types which may be more relevant to industry. Psychologists would certainly agree that an IQ test must be supported by an impression formed of the candidates ability in other ways, such as at an interview.

John , A(2018) indicated that a clear job description is needed to define what each employee is to do. In some companies , the employees have not been told exactly what their job is, with the result that sometimes two people attend to the same task neither knowing whose responsibility it is, or some task is not carried out at all, each man believing that someone else is attending to it.

In large organizations , this can lead to cause the company has intense frustration and annoyance to individual employees. The job description technique is simpe, the supervisor writes a description of each job, specifying each major activity as accurately as possible ans limitations. Very little training is requires, but obviously it is necessary for someone with a fairly detailed knowledge of the company to draw up such descriptions. This is usually done by the supervisor of the job cooperation with the present job seekers. It needs seldom take more than half an hour of two people's time to write out a fairly comprehensive description of any job. It's content may include job title , tasks , authority, superior, committees, limitations.

John, A (2018) explained that job evaluation is one effective method to select the right rate of pay for each job. He assumes that the all levels of wage or salary earners is the differential in rate of pay or between one job and another. How much more should the driver of a bus get than the conductor, how much most should a crane driver get than a fork life driver, how much more should a manager get than a foreman?

The first step in job evaluation is to carry out a job description for on can not evaluate a job unless each of several headings according to the requirements of the job. Headings according to the requirements of the job. Headings used often include such aspect as: skill needed to carry out the job, possible effects of carelessness number of months experience required to each proficiency, working conditions, including any unpleasant circumstances, such as excessive, temperatures or dustiness. Each job is evaluated in this way and then arranged in order of ascending total points into financial terms. For example, the dockside crane driver, process plant operator, canteen cleaner job's maximum points possible may include headings of skill (10), effect of carelessness (20), experience required (10) and working conditions (10) , maximum points possible.

John , A ( 2018) explained joint consultation is the effective method to improve human relations. He assumes that a large company feels junor employees who feel that nothing they can do will have any effect, and the top management is indifference to them or their happiness. The result is sometimes indiscipline and always indifference towards the company, its products, its reputation, its managers. Joint consultation is one effective employee engagemen method , which is one way of drwing junior employees into the company and making them feel part of it it to allow them or encourage them to participate in management decision making or at least to discuss with them the consequences of mangement decisions. Many of decisions that managers take are highly technical and need great skill, long experiences and the use of time very advanced management techchniques, e.g. capital expenditure appraisal is on such area. However, many decisions are more of a moral nature or affect employees more than they affect the company. Thus, joint consultation advantage can make a systematic attempt to consult with the employees to seek their opinions, ideas, reactions.

4.1 What are on-job training advantages?

On -the-job training means that having a person learn a job by actually performing it. Virtually every employee, from mailroom clerk to company president, gets some on-the job training when he/she joins a firm. It usually involves assigning new employees to experiences workers or supervisors who then do the actual training.

Coaching or understudy method means that the employee is trained by an experienced worker or the trainee's supervisor. At lower levels, traines may acquire skills for, e.g. running a machine is observed by the supervisor. Top management level, to the position of assistant is often used to train and develop the company's future top managers. Job rotation, in which an employee usually a management trainee, moves from job to job at planned schedule. Special assignments similarly, give lower-level executives firsthand, experience in working on actual problems. Its advantages include relatively inexpensive trainees learn when producing and there is no need for expensive off-job facilities like classrooms or programmed learning devices. The method also facilities learning , since trainees are learned by actually doing the job and get quick feedback about the correctness of their performances.

Stages in training needs analysis includes as below: Preparation , deciding the objectives and scope of the training needs analysis; data collection is from employees in the real world; data analysis is needed to analyze the training needs in a systematic way; recommendation to propose the training budget, training design and evaluation methods; action is needed to identify the responsible person and time frame, and implement the plan,

Training principle means the effective motivation of the trainee is needed by the design of the training programme and the methods which are used, the designing a training course is needed to consider the training requirements: attitudes, skills, knowledge. For example, a shop assistant in a convenience store, would require a certain friendly service attitude towards customers, skill in selling, displaying arrangement and knowledge of stock, sale procedures and the company's general policy.

On -the -job-training is given in the normal work situation, the trainee needs to use the actual tools, equipment, document, or materials, that he/she will use when fully trained. The trainee is regarded as a partly productive worker from the time training begins. Off-the-job training is taken away from the normal work situation, usually employing specially simplified tools and equipment. The trainee is not regarded as a productive worker from the beginning, it is exercise practice. Off-the-job training is needed to implement on the company's premises at a training centre or at an educational instituation.

On-the -job training advandages include that it is less costly because it uses noral equipment, the trainee is proficient, there is no transfer of learning problems, the trainee is in the production environment, he/she does not need to adjust to it after the less realistic conditions. Its disadvantages include the trainee may be a poor teacher and may not have enough time to give proper training, if there is a payment-by-results scheme, if may discourage the trainer from training, the training may be inplemented in an inefficient way, a large amount of spoiled work and scrap material may be produced, valuable equipment may be damaged, the production conditions, which are stressful, i.e. noisy, busy, confusing, stress of this type usually inhibits learning.

Otherwise, off-job-training advantages include the training is given by a specialist trainer and it should be of higher quality, special equipment, simplified of necessary can be used, the trainee can learn the job from easy to difficulty in planned stage, it is fee pressure of payment-by-work scheme, noise, danger, publicity, the trainee will learn correct methods from the beginning, the trainee does not damage valuable equipment or produce spoiled work or scrap, it is easier to calculate the cost of off-the -job training because it is more self contained. It's disadvantages include the higher costs of separate premises, equipment and trainers, learning difficulties to the trainee, when he/she needs to change training equipment to production equipment and a classroom environment to a production environment.

4.2 The four steps of learning requirement

Any learning requirment include four steps: identifying the problem, seeking a solution, selecting an applying training and setting objectives. In seeking solutions steps, common performance problems and solutions include: lacks of skill problem can be solved to provide suitable skill training, insufficient knowledge problem can be solved by training to broaden understanding, lack of motivtion problem can be solved by training might-re-ethuse, attitudinl problems can be solved by training of management commitment.

The important concern is that the training's topics and contents need to achieve this aim to improve employee ( trainee) individual behavior, such as improvement of efficiency is concerned primaryily with doing things right, when effectiveness is about doing the right things well. Because highly efficient training courses do not mean that the training courses and contents are effectiv relevent to the company or individuals concerned needs.

Why does training need to set objectives? Because it can let the trainer gains a better understanding of the desired behaviors when it is seeking to encourage to achieve the training efficiently and effectively, let participants to know what the course details will help to oversome any uncertainty, and assist in motivating the individual and training objectives can indicate what the needs and requirements of the company. It can reduce the waste a quantifiable return on the time and capital invested beafore it has clear objectives for the training achievement.

Why does know what the main objective for training is more important? It has difference between aims and objectives. Aims mean to provide a direction or statement of intent. So, aim is at target, but the objective could be more clear. Whether this objective is realistic one would depend on the people involved and the circurstances under which they operate. This means that when an aim might express a desired outcome, it is the objective which will seek how and when this is attained or desired more easily. So, when the trainer can predict what (are) is the more accurate objective(s) , when this objective(s) is (are) confirmed the real need to the organization's benefit. The training will be more effective or avoids ineffective training consequence ( irrelevant training courses and contents) to let trainees ( participants) to learn, it means that time and money wasting of the training course.

David, L. (2016) explained that why a lesson plan is necessary. He indicated that " the existence of lesson plan can have positive effects. It depends on whether the methodology of knowledge ( the how we do it) , but at this stage we are simply examining the knowledge itself ( what knowledge are we trying to communicate). However, there are three principle classifications of information. Firstly information that the group must know, it means that there are items of information which are essential to the understanding of the topic in question. In most cases, they will have already been identified in any training need analysis and as they are findmental to the success of any training course on the subject they must be given the highest priority. Secondly, information which trainers should know would include anything which related directly to the information in the must show category. For example, this might include other practices and procedures which interlink with those requires for safety reasons. Finally, the could know matters are those which can be described as useful to the group , but largely incident to the subject. These are items of information which , if time permits, could provide a useful background to the topic , but won't directly assist in its effective execution. This categoty would include historical details, boarder aspects, of the task, further areas of interest and general information."

The classification of information into these three categories allows each aspect of the subject to be examined and assigned to the appropriate category. In this way, it is possible to provide a degree of prioritization , enabling all the essential elements to be concerned in time available and any secondary information to be incorporated as and when circumstances permit.

However, these are number of other factors which will have an impact upon the structure topic and content of any training course . These include: level of understanding, course size, availability of equipment and material, financial constraints and timing. For example, a person's existing knowledge or cognitive inventory will influence whose level of understanding whether it is more or less easily when the trainee is learning the training course, the number of people participation will affect how much can be accomplished and what facilities and trainers are necessary for the course size arrangement, the availability of equipment and materials, e.g. what materials are needed and are available to avoid the kinds of equipment limited supply shortage, the financial constraints' aim to satisfy the course objectives at the lowest cost feasible, and achieve the highest standard of training possible at a cost tht is acceptable to the organization. If the objectives of the course can't be achieved within the limits of available budget, then it is better not to run the course at all then to run unsuccessfully. Finally, the training couse whether it has enough time to prepare all teaching arragement to avoid bad or ineffective training consequence and not to cover-estimate what can accomplished during this period.

4.3 Training and development steps

Gary, D. (2000) indicated that employee orientation provides new employees with basic background information, who need to perform their jobs satisfactorily , such as information about company rules. Orientation is actually part of the employer's new employee socialization process. Socializaton is the ongoing process of researching in all employee the attitudes, standards, values, and patterns of behavior that are expected by the organization and its departments.

Training refers to the methods used to give new or present employees the skills, they need to perform their jobs. Training might mean showing how to operate its new methods, a new supervisor how to interview and appraise employees. Training is used to focus mostly on teaching technical skills, such as teachers devises lesson plans. However, technical training likes that is no longer sufficient. Employers have had to adapt to rapid technological changes, improve product and service quality and boost productivity to stay competitive.

Improving quality ( quality improvement programs) require employee who can produce charts and graphs and analyze data. Similarly, employees need skills ( training) in team building, decision making, and communication, as wel as technological and computer skills ( such as desktop publishing, computer aided design and manufacturing) . And as competition demands better service, employees require customer service training for the tools and abilities requiries to serve customers.

Gary, D. (2000) also explaines the five step training and development process, such as below:

First step is needs analysis, which identifies specific job performance skills needed to improve performance and productivity, analysing the audience to ensure that the program will be suited to their specific levels of education , experience and skills as well as their attitudes and personal motivations, using research to develop specific measurable knowledge and performance objectives.

Second step is instructional design, which gathers instructional objectives, methods, media description of and sequence of content examples, exercises and activities. Organizing them into a curriculum that supports adult learning theory and provides a blueprint for program development. Making sure all materials, such as video scripts, leaders' guides, and participants' work tools, complement each other are written clearly into the started learning objectives, carefully and professional handle all program elements, whether reproduced on paper, film or tape to quarantee quality and effectiveness.

Third step is validation, which introduces and validates the training before a representative audience. Base final revisons on pilot results to ensure program effectiveness.

Fourth step is implementation, when applicable , boost success with a train-the-trainer workshop that focuses on presentation knowledge and skills in addition to training content.

Fifth step is evaluation and follow up, assess program success according to: reaction to document that learners' immediate reactions to the training, learning to use feedback devices or pre to measure what learners have actually learned, behavior to note supervisors' reactions to learners' performance following completion of the training. This is one way to measure the degree to which learners apply new skills and knowledge to their jobs, result to determine the level of improvement in job performance and assess needed maintenance.


4.4 How to choose learning or training method

Methods of learning, training and development plans, training sources can be internal to the company or employees are trained from an external organization. Training can range from short term to long term, from online to in-person and from low cost to high cost development programmes for senior or specialist staff could learn techniques , such as coacing and mentoring or secondment, formal or off-the-job learning or educational arrangement.

The choice of learning methods depend on several factors include: the nature and degree of priority of the learning needs, type of occupation, level of seniority and qualifications/educational background of learners, organizational culture, evaluation of the effectiveness of previous learning and training results, experience, time required to complete training, learner preference, each individual may prefer learning in different ways, some prefer classroom learning over real-life practicing , learner preference's over learning ways and styles and their individual characteristics need to be taken into account when selecting , developing and delivering learning methods. For example, in-houe courses provide an opportunity to focus on company specific issues. External courses involves interaction with people from other companies. For example, in-house, on the job training aims to deliver on a one-to-one basis at the trainee's place of work, allocated time to a specified , planned and structured activity.

Reference

David , L. ( 3 edition, 2016). The Group Trainer's Handbook, Designing And Delivering Training For groups , Kogan Page , US pp. 18-19

Gary, D. ( 8 edition, 2000), Human resource management , Prentice hall, New Jersey.pp. 248-251

John, A. (2018) Management techniques, a practical guide, London, UK and New York , US: Routledge, pp. 27, 34-37, 67, 70-71,133, 140-144.

# CHAPTER FIVE

# Performance management

Pay structure steps

Human professionals might create the pay structure for their organization, or they might work with an external compensation consultant. There are several steps to design a pay structure: job analysis, job evaluation, pay survey analysis, pay policy and development and pay structure information ( Milkovish, G., & Newman, J. 2008).

Milkovich, G. & Newman, J. (2008) explaines that the pay structure steps include as below:

Step one : Job analysis is the process of studying jobs in an organization. The outcome of this process is a job description that includes the job title, a summary of the job tasks, asjust of the essential tasks and responsibilities and a description that includes the knowledge, skills and abilities needed to perform the job.

Step two: Job evaluation is the process of judging the relative worth of jobs in an organization. The outcome of job evaluation is the development of an internal structure or hierarchial ranking of jobs. Job-based evaluation is used more often than person-based evaluation and so the former will be the focus in this case. There are three methods of job-based evaluation: The point method, ranking and classification. The job evaluation helps to ensure that pay is internally worth perceived to be fair by employees.

Step three : Pay policy identification is the process of determining whether the organization wants to lead or meet the market in compensation. The pay policy or strategy will likely influence employee attraction. Pay policies can vary across families , i.e. groups of similiar jobs, and job level of the top management feels that different areas of the organization.

Step four: Pay survey analysis is the process of analysising compensation data gathered from other employers in a survey of the relevant labor market. Gathering enternal data , e.g. base pay, bonuses , stock or share options and benefits is the essential to kep the organization's compensation externally competitive within the industry. Employee attraction can be improved by maintaining externally pay structures.

Step five: Pay structure creation is the final step, in which the internal structure ( step two of job evaluation) is combined with the external market pay rates . Step four: Pay survey analysis in a simple regression to develop a market pay line. Depending on whether the organization wants to lead or meet the market, the market pay line can be adjusted top or down. To complete the pay structure , pay grades and pay ranges are developed.

In this organization's job analysis, it can influence these positions or job titles. For example, office support department has the lower level, front line receptionist, middle level, admin. assistant and top level, assistant to the director of operatons. Operations department has the lower level, operations trainee, operations trainess, middle level , operations analyst, top level, director of regional operations, top level, director of regional operations. Human resource department has the lower level, payroll assistant, the middle level, benefits counselling service and benefits manager, the top level, HR director.

In this organization, the administrative assistants, perform similiar administrative tasks across departments and do not handle function-specific tasks , e.g. HR. Thus, this organization's administrative assiatant ought be suggested grouping the front-line administrative jobs in a separate job family called office support. However, in some organizations, administrative assistant has possible to need to handle function-specific tasks, e.g. HR. Hence, in these organizations administrative assitant can be the low level group to HR department.

In the job evaluation step, this organization chooses to apply point method to evaluate the pay worth to every job title. The evaluation points method can be weights for example the four degrees for education level are identified as below:

1=high school, 2=assocaites, 3= bacholors, 4=master/graduate points are then calculated by multiplying the degree by the weights.

The compensable factor for the evaluation for front desk receiptionist as below:

skill (50%) degree( 1,2,3,4) weight points

education level 1 25% 25

degree of

technical skills 1 25% 25

responsibility(30%)

scope of control 1 10% 10

impact of job 2 20% 40

degree of

problem solving 1 10% 10

task complexity 1 10% 10

120

The ensure that the pay structure is extremely competitive, a pay survey will be conducted. The market pay data must be from the relevant labor market. Surveys can include i.e. six organizations who recruit and hire similiar jobs in the regions. Base pay salary data from the responding organizations are reflected to ensure the summary job descriptions , sample data are appropriately similiar to those in this organization in order to compare and analyze the pay data between other similiar organizations and this organization.

Finally , it need to implement how to design the pay structure. it can be setted the pay ranges for each pay grade, pay ranges create upper and lower pay rates for each job in the pay scale. Each pay grade will have a minimum and maximum pay rate. It is important to remember that all jobs in a paygrade will have the same minimum and maximum pay rates. Percent guidelines below the midpoint the pay range will reach . For example, the maximum might be 10% percent above the midpoint and the minimum might be 10% below the midpoint. The percent guidelines can be based on imput from the organization's job evaluation committee, e.g. clerical and office positions: 10% above and below the midpoint. Entery to mid-level professional and management positions: 30 % above and below the midpoint.

5.1 What is key performance indicator (KPI) components?

Performance management strategy of performance metrics are a powerful toole of organizational change. It can measure organizational performance really. Companies define objectives , establish goals, measure progress, reward achievement, and diplay the results for all productivity. Executives can use performance metrics to define and communicate strategic objectives tailores to every individual and role in the organization. Managers can ue them to identify underforming individuals or teams and guide them and employees can use performance metrics to focus on what is important and help them achieve goald defined in their personal performance plans.

But wrong metrics can have unintended consequences: They can threaten to prolong on organizational processes, demoralize employees and undermine productivity and service levels. If the metrics do not accurately translate the company's strategy and goals into real useful actions that employees can take on a daily basis. Employees will work hard but have nothing to show for their efforts, everyone will feel tired and frustrated, also the company will be efficient but ineffective.

Performance metrics are a criticial ingredient of performance management, performance management has a four steps cycle involves strategic misson, value, goals, objectives, incentives, strategy maps. Then, it needs to plan budgets, forcasts, models, targets. Next , it needs to monitor / analyze performance report, analytical tools. Finally, it needs to adjust or make action to assess, decide and track in execution step.

A performance metrics measurement tool can fasten the business, distill an organization's strategy to serve its stakeholders,linking strategy to processes. A performance metrics can give visual information delivery system that lets users measure, monitor, and manage the effectiveness of their tactics and their progress toward achieving strategic objectives . Collecting , a performance metrics measurement tool enable users to idenitfy problems and opportunities, taken action and adjust plans and goals as needed.

What is key performance indicator (KPI) components? The only difference between a metric and KPA is that a KPI is a strategic objective and measures performance against a goal. KPI is a strategic objective , KPI measure performance against specific targets. Targets are defined in strategic planning, or budget sessions and can take different forms , e.g. achievement, reduction, absolute zero, tagets have ranges of peformance, e.g. above on, or below target. Targets are assigned time frame by which they must be accomplished. Time frame is often divided into smaller intervals, targets are measured against a baseline or benchmark. The previous year's results often serves as a benchmark.

The goals associated with KPIs are known as targets because they specify a measurble outcome rather then a conceptual destination. Ideally, executives, managers and workers collectively set targets during strategic planning or budget discussions.

In performance management view point, target can be defined five types: Achievement means performance should reach or exceed the target. Anything over the target is valuable but not required, e.g. revenue and satisfaction. Reduction means performance should reach or be lower than the targe. Anything less than the target is valubale, but not required, e.g. absolute means performance should equal the target. Anything above or below is not good, e.g. in-stock percentage and on time delivery.

Minimum/maximum means performance should be within a range of value. Anything above or below the range is not good , e.g. mean time between repairs, zero means performance should equal zero, which is the minimum value possible, e.g. employee injuries and product defects. All above these target will be key performance indicator performance tool.

For time frames example, performance targets have time frames, which affects hoe KPIs are calculated and displayed. Many organizatons establish annua targets for key processes. To keep employees on track to achieve those long -term targets, many organizations divide time frames into intervals, that are measured on a more frequent basis. For example, a group may divide the annual target to improve customer satisfaction from 60% to 68% into four quarterly intervlas with 2% target improvemet each quarter. However, in some cases, such as a retail environment is affected by seasonal shopping, groups many backweighs. The targets toward the end of the year, since most holiday season, during the Dec. holiday season.

Finally, KPI targets could be measured against a benchmark that becomes the starting point for improving performance . Typically, the benchmark is last year's output. So, for example, a sales team may need to increase sales by 20% compared to last year. Or the benchmark could be an external standard , such as the performance level of an industry leader. So, a company might want to set a goals of closing the gap in market share with its closet competitor by 50% next year.

Users can read KPIs to look at a visual display that has been properly encoded and know whether a process of project is on track. To assist users can understand KPI ( key performance indicator) performance measurement more easily. It has seven attributes for each. They include: status measures performance against the target and is usually shown with a stoplight. Trend measures performance against the prior interval or another time period and is often displayed using arrows or trend lines. The actual and target values are seld-explanatory and usually displayed with text. Variance measures the gap between actual and target and is displayed using text or a micro bar chart in performance report variance percentage divides the variance against the target. These seven attributes can combine to provide valuable insight into the state of performance.

5.2 How to Implement a Performance Management System

Depending on what kind of changes have been made we will have to prepare a communication and change management plan in order to transfer the organization smoothly from one to another PMS. While the small changes can be covered by simple communication informing about the changes in the system, major changes may even require change of mindset and old habits, which will need a more serious change management plan.

It is a system that is linked to and feeds many other HR tolls and systems meaning that the final results of those tools are highly dependent on the inputs that they get from the PMS. Having that kind of importance and influence this system, though complex in its nature, from one side has to be as simple as possible so that all managers can willingly and easily use it, while on the other side it has to offer quality results that can be used as inputs for the other HR tools and systems.

The quality of the system and the results it offers depend on the process of setting up the system itself. Doing a good job in planning, defining and introducing the system will do half of the job in securing quality results from the system. So how do we set up a Performance Management System?

Implementation of a Performance Management System is a project of its own... as every other project it needs serious approach towards all project elements and phases.

The implementation of a Performance Management System is a project of its own so it should be treated as one. So, as every other project of this character it needs serious approach towards all project elements and phases such as defining, planning, people, resource and stakeholder management, implementation, monitoring, measuring etc..

The performance management system may contain all of these components, but it is the overall system that matters, not the individual components. Many organizations have been able to develop effective performance management systems without all of the following practices.

A performance management system includes the following actions:

•Develop clear job descriptions using an employee recruitment plan that identifies the selection team.
•Recruit potential employees and select the most qualified to participate in interviews onsite.
•Conduct interviews to narrow down your pool of candidates.
•Hold multiple additional meetings, as needed, to get to know your candidates' strengths, weaknesses, and abilities to contribute what you need. Use potential employee testing and assignments where they make sense for the position that you are filling.
•Select appropriate people using a comprehensive employee selection process to identify the most qualified candidate who has the best cultural fit and job fit that you need.
•Offer your selected candidate the job and negotiate the terms and conditions of employment including salary, benefits, paid time off, and other organizational perks.
•Welcome the new employee to your organization.
•Provide effective new employee orientation, assign a mentor, and integrate your new employee into the organization and its culture.
•Negotiate requirements and accomplishment-based performance standards, outcomes, and measures between the employee and his or her new manager.

•Provide ongoing education and training as needed.
•Provide on-going coaching and feedback.
•Conduct quarterly performance development planning discussions.
•Design effective compensation and recognition systems that reward people for their ongoing contributions.
•Provide promotional/career development opportunities including lateral moves, transfers, and job shadowing for staff.
•Assist with exit interviews to understand WHY valued employees leave the organization.
•Performance Appraisals Don't Work tells you why you want to move away from the traditional appraisal system.
•Performance Management Glossary Entry provides a basic definition of performance management.
•Performance Management Is Not an Annual Appraisal provides the components of a performance management system.
•Performance Management Process Checklist gives you the components of the performance management process.
•Performance Development Planning provides the steps for preparing and implementing performance development planning.
•Performance Development Planning Form is used to write out specific goals and measurements, to be updated quarterly.
•Goal Setting: Beyond Traditional SMART Goals discusses goal setting.
•Tips to Help Managers Improve Performance Appraisals provides concrete suggestions about how those of you who have to manage in a traditional performance appraisal culture can make them better—for both you and the employee.
•Common Problems With Performance Appraisals identifies the most common reasons why appraisals are not effective.
•Phrases for Approaching Performance Reviews and Difficult Conversations shares tips about successfully holding a comfortable appraisal meeting.
Finally, performance appraisal is one part of performance management system. The process by which a manager or consultant (1) examines and evaluates an employee's work behavior by comparing it with preset standards, (2) documents the results of the comparison, and (3) uses the results to provide feedback to the employee to show where improvements are needed and why. Performance appraisals are employed to determine who needs what training, and who will be promoted, demoted, retained, or fired.

5.3 Performance managment aim
Performance management means the goal of reward programs are to attract, motivate people and it is essential for the company to clearly identify the performance and competency levels required of their employees in different roles at different levels. The company will then evaluate , differentiate and reward the employees in a fair and consistent way.
Performance management is one of the most important functions in human resource management. It is also an

important tool to link individual objectives with departmental targets. It is a part of a comprehensive human resource management strategy. It needs to let objectives into practical and realistic performance goals at each level of the company. It provides employees clear aims and forms on job expectation motivates employees to perform better, helps focus on the desired results, improves communication, helps develop employees, capabilities and helps achieve organizational objectives.

It's elements include : planning means agreement on performance goals and targets, based on job descriptions and business objectives, goals and targets have to be specific to clear, measurable, specify quantity, quality, time, money etc, achievable to solve challenges, but within each of competent and committed person, relevant to the company's objectives. So, that the individual's goals can contribute towards the company's objective, monitoring and coaching means on ongoing nd continious process, monitor performance against agreed goals and targets, provide direction/ support and feedback on how well people are doing, recognize and reinforce desirable behaviours, coach and help solve diffculties in achieving desirable performance, identify problem at early stge, take corrective action in a timely manner.

Then, performance review or appraisal meeting means that it is a formal review on the individual's performance, it is usually done once or twice a year to review, monitor and employees for promotion, help identify the training and development needs of employees, achieve a better two way communication between the line manager and the employee with regards to performance.

Next, preparation for the appraisal meeting, it is necessary to keep a record of the individual's performance and achievement with gives support to rating, allow sufficient time for preparation on, what performance problems are to be mentioned, views on the possible reasons for success or failure, any suggestions to solve the problem, give sufficient notice to employee regarding the meeting and respect employee to have a self-appraisal before the meeting they they can identify their own achievements and problems. Finally preparation of the appraisal form, it should be as simple and brief as possible and allow sufficient time for comments, terms should be easily understood, with some notes for guidance, information to collect on the form includes: Key result areas, agreed objectives/targets , assessment of performance against the key result aras details of the development plan to improve performance.

What are the development activities participated for current appraisal period mean? Review the development activities are participated by the employee for the past appraisal period and to agree on a development plan for the coming appraisal period. Management coaching for performance means that managers and supervisors have an important role to play in performance management, which is to provide feedback and coaching on employee's performance when necessary, coaching is a process that helps the employee gain how to win overcome barriers to improve job performance on a as need basis, when training uses a structured design to provide the employees with the knowledge and skills to perform a task.

The other difference betwen coaching and training is that the former is normally done in real time. That is , it is performed on the job, at the workplace. The coach uses real-life tasks and problems to help the learners increase their performance. Otherwise, training and learning is taught to a group students to learn in a coaching is effective when it is specific to the individual and it is positive and it is positive and occurs as soon as performance problems are identifies.

Coaching for individual benefit performance includes to identify performance problem by pointing out the facts/describing the behaviours observed in a professional manner, support with evidence if possible, clarify the expectations/standards of the job, explain the consequence of inappropriate actions/behaviours, ask for the employee's view point and how they assess their own actions/behaviours , discuss the causes of the problem/analyze reasons for sub-standard performance, develop and agree on solutions, decide on specific action(s) to be taken.

Why is reward communication important? for this case, a company could be wasting the money spent on salaries and benefits by leaving employees when they listn the true value of the total package. Without employee understanding, reward programs won't motivate employee effort reward achieving business objectives. So, effective reward communication can let candidates existing staff appreciate or understand the value of the retirement scheme or other benefits, such as subsidised meals, life insurance and critical illness insurance. However, if rewards are used to motivate employees, or to encourage higher performance aims, it is essential to have an effective communicating information about pay scales, the provision of benefits and allowances, grading systems, job evaluation , performance-related pay schemes and how pay decisions and made for different individuals or groups of employees.

In conclusion, performance management is not an annual appraisal meeting. It is not preparing for that appraisal meeting nor is it a self-evaluation. It's not a form nor is it a measuring tool although many organizations may use tools and forms to track goals and improvements, they are not the process of performance management.

Note: Performance management is the process of creating a work environment or setting in which people are enabled to perform to the best of their abilities.

Performance management is a whole work system that begins when a job is defined as needed. It ends when an employee leaves your organization. Performance management defines your interaction with an employee at every step of the way in between these major life cycle occurrences. Performance management makes every interaction opportunity with an employee into a learning occasion.

Performance management aims at building a high performance culture for both the individuals and the teams so that they jointly take the responsibility of improving the business processes on a continuous basis and at the same time raise the competence bar by upgrading their own skills within a leadership framework. Its focus is on enabling goal clarity for making people do the right things in the right time. It may be said that the main objective of a performance management system is to achieve the capacity of the employees to the full potential in favor of both the employee and the organization, by defining the expectations in terms of roles, responsibilities and accountabilities, required competencies and the expected behaviors.

The main goal of performance management is to ensure that the organization as a system and its subsystems work together in an integrated fashion for accomplishing optimum results or outcomes.

The major objectives of performance management are discussed below:

?To enable the employees towards achievement of superior standards of work performance.

?To help the employees in identifying the knowledge and skills required for performing the job efficiently as this would drive their focus towards performing the right task in the right way.

?Boosting the performance of the employees by encouraging employee empowerment, motivation and implementation of an effective reward mechanism.

?Promoting a two way system of communication between the supervisors and the employees for clarifying expectations about the roles and accountabilities, communicating the functional and organizational goals, providing a regular and a transparent feedback for improving employee performance and continuous coaching.

?Identifying the barriers to effective performance and resolving those barriers through constant monitoring, coaching and development interventions.

?Creating a basis for several administrative decisions strategic planning, succession planning, promotions and performance based payment.

?Promoting personal growth and advancement in the career of the employees by helping them in acquiring the desired knowledge and skills.

Some of the key concerns of a performance management system in an organization are:

?Concerned with the output (the results achieved), outcomes, processes required for reaching the results and also the inputs (knowledge, skills and attitudes).

?Concerned with measurement of results and review of progress in the achievement of set targets.

?Concerned with defining business plans in advance for shaping a successful future.

?Striving for continuous improvement and continuous development by creating a learning culture and an open system.

?Concerned with establishing a culture of trust and mutual understanding that fosters free flow of communication at all levels in matters such as clarification of expectations and sharing of information on the core values of an organization which binds the team together.

?Concerned with the provision of procedural fairness and transparency in the process of decision making.

The performance management approach has become an indispensable tool in the hands of the corporates as it ensures that the people uphold the corporate values and tread in the path of accomplishment of the ultimate corporate vision and mission. It is a forward looking process as it involves both the supervisor and also the employee in a process of joint planning and goal setting in the beginning of the year.

5.4 What is the difference between performance management and performance appraisal?

Performance appraisals are one of the crucial aspects of professionally managed organizations across the world. Each organization has set an appraisal system in place in order to raise its employees' performance over a period of time. They are based on a review of the performance of an employee on the tasks assigned to it. They are used for many aspects such as salary revision, bonus provisions, promotions etc. These reviews are mostly conducted annually, but may be considered quarterly or half-yearly as well depending upon the HR policies of the organizations. Mostly, Human Resource department takes the lead in conducting formal performance appraisals.

Otherwise, performance management systems are set in place to guide the employees to achieve a desired level of performance. It is basically a definition of what organization expects from employee over the next appraisal period. Specific objectives are set for short term (say next quarter), and employee is prepared to achieve the desired outcomes by meeting these short term targets.

These targets are defined by the job description along with the desired outcome of the jobs. This helps employees to determine the gaps in their performance and thus helps them to improve before the final performance appraisal happens after a year or six months. However, performance management aims at overall personal development of the employees. It is a form of constructive feedback which encourages continuous improvement. It is helpful to both employee as well as appraiser. There is frequent communication between them which helps in setting right goals for the employee and possible guidelines from appraiser to achieve those goals in an effective manner. It therefore saves employees from the bitter feeling that comes at year end when they feel that they have wasted one whole year without any substantial value addition.

5.5 What are performance management system

The common goals of performance management system consider our daily work routine about our purpose in an organization. It is important to let organizational members understand what their organizations' visions and goals are, how their work fits into the organization, and how they contribute to their mission accomplishment. Hence one effective performance management system can encourage and improve the organization's members to raise their effort to contribute to their organizations. So, it brings this question: How to design one effective performance management system?

A clear understanding of job expectations is needed. When employees and supervisors have a clear understanding of their specific job duties in the workforce are eliminated. Each employee will be expect to contribute their own duties and responsibilities efficiently. All effective performance management system can empower employees to think about and clarify every employee's role in the organization. Organizations need to set clear goals and expectations to help with them. Employee performance plans must provide for balanced, credible measuring expected results, the performance plans include results, the performance plans include appropriate resources, such as quality, quantity, timeliness, and/or cost-effectiveness. Moreover, performance expectations must be based on job anaysis and understandable, reasonable and attainable and clear specific.

Regular feedback facilitates better communication in the workplace factor is important. Performance strengths and weaknesses. How can employee individual performance can get improvement? In fact, performance management can be a motivational tool, when this tool can let employes to feel more satisfactory. Then, the supervisors can have a performance feedback process that facilitates between the supervisors and their employees. Hence, performance feedback ought need to be regular feedback facilitated better communication in the workplace. It can reduce from normal pressures of work.

How to design effective performance management system ? AN effective management system can measure organizational and employee performance. Performance management involves multiple levels of analysis, and is clearly linked to the topics studied in strategy HRM as well as performance appraisal. The objectives of performance management system often include motivating performance, helping individuals, developing their skills, building a performance culture, determining who should be promoted, eliminating individuals who are poor performers, and helping implement strategies.

Hence, the main purposes of a performance include: The work is performed the best by employees, employees have a clear understanding of the quality of work expected from them, employees effectively these are performing relative to expectation, awards and salary increases based on employee performance are distributed, opportunity for employee development and finding reasons and solutions why the employee performance that does not need expectation. These issues will be performance management usually main purposes.

However, performance management system usually have these phases: Phase 1 ( developing and planning performance) , It includes outline development plans, setting objectives and getting commitment for the organization. Phase 2 ( managing and review performance), it includes assess against objectives, feedback, coaching , document reviews, . Phase 3 ( reward performance) , it includes personal development, link to pay , results performance.

What is the performance management aim? On setting objectives stage, the management needs to know how to achieve and help to enourage commitment and understanding by linking. The employees' work with the organization's goals and objectives. It needs to let employees to know how to achieve its missions clearly. So, targets need to be setted for each performance and goals setting is the fundamental aspect for an organization. They further indicated that productivity gains will be supported for and employees' participation in the process of setting objectives. It is a motivational process which also gives the individual the feeling of being involved and creates a sense of ownership for employees.

In management and review stage, this involves maintaining a positive approach to work, updating and revising initial objectives, performance standard and job competency areas as conditions change, requesting feedback from a supervisor, providing feedback to supervisors, suggesting career development experiences, employees and supervisors working together, managing the performance management process.

Hence, performance needs to be compared. It is between desired performance and actual performance. When they are measured , then they will give feedback and development. Then, feedback will five opinions to desired performance in order to make performance revision again, even again. Finally, when the desired performance can be achieved the best actual performance measurement result and it will bring actual performance development to achieve actual vision, mission, strategy, value drivers consequently.

IN the rewarding performance, it has three activities: personnel development, linking to pay and identifying the results or performance. In fact, all personnel development is basically self-development. Opportunity for development is valuable only if the individual capitalizes on himself/herself. Development should be designed to improve performance on the current job and then prepare the employee for promotion. In fact, it is only the employees who get promoted , who are currently doing outstanding work and this have been able to demonstrate their capacity to assume greater responsibilities. Furthermore, training activities should ideally to based on performance gaps that are identified during the performance review phase.

So, regular performance feedbacks are important factors to influence skills development. In addition organizations need a growing interest in pay-for -performance plans focused on small groups or teams. Small group pays pkan provide monetary rewards based on the measured performance of the group or team. However, high performing, effective organizations have a culture that encourages employee involvement. Therefore, employees are more willing to get involved in decision-making, goal setting or problem solving activities, which subsequently result in higher employee performance.

Thus, one effective performance management system needs to follow these steps to implement, such as developing and planning performance step: it includes to set what the main objectives , the organization needs. Then it is managing and review performance step, the organizations need to review whether what differences are between its desired performance and actural performance to prepare review their performance difference. Next, it is reward management implementation, the organization needs to give better reard to the talent employees in order to encourage they develop their skills in the maximum effort as well as it also needs to punish the poor performance employees in order to expect they can review their error. In consequence, all these steps must be followed step by step to implement the performacen management system effectively.

Reference
Milkovich, G., & Newman, J. (2008). Compensation, MC Graw-Hill Irwin. 0*NET. Available at http:// online.onetcenter.org

# CHAPTER SIX

# Sourcing and staffing

How to build talent staffing source

Marion, D. & Michel, S. (2014) explained talent is the sum of a person's abilities, his or her intrinsic grifts, skills, knowledge, experience, intelligenc, judgement, attitude, character and drive. It also includes his or her ability to learn. At the international level, talent shortages are more severe. During the past decade, an internationally mobile group of employees, who can pick and choose where they work. As firms in employing markets also begin competing in the global economy, these people are in ever-greater demand. For example, Sinapore has had on an intensive recruitment programme for skilled foreigh workers, with more liberal criteria for eligibility to work in the country. Some 90,000 now work in the city-state, the majority from the US, UK, France, Australia, Japan and South Korea.

Marion, D. & Michel, S. (2014) indicated several factors need to be taken into account to understand the market for skilled labour. Hays and Oxford Economics pooled their data to identify seven components that together give a better picture of skill shortages as below:

Labour-market participation means the degree to which a country's talent pool is fully utilised, for example, whether women and older workers have access to jobs; labour -market flexibility means the legal and regulatory environment is faced by business, especially how easily immigrants can fill talent gaps; wage pressure overall means whether real wages are keeping pace with inflation; wage pressure in high-skill industries means which wages in high-skill industries outpace those in low-skill industries; wage pressure in high-skill occupations means rises in wages for highly skilled workers are a short -term indicaton of skills shortages, talent mismatches means the mismatch between the skills are needed by businesses and those available, are indicated by the number of long-term unemployed and job vacancies; educational flexibility means whether the educational system can adapt to meet the future needs of organizations for talent, especially in the fields of mathematics and science.

Firms operating in knowledge-intensive industries depend on their most capable staff to help create value through intangible assets, such as patents, licences and technical know-how. In fact, globalisation and technological competition brings to much complexity of many jobs and occupations. Firms are now looking for individuals with an range of abilities that might include specialized skills, broader functional skills, industry expertise and knowledge of specific geographical markets. The skills include: digital skill means the fast growing digital economy is increasing the demand for highly skilled technical workers. Companies are looking for staff with social-media based skills, especially in " digital expression". Agile thinking means the regulatory and environment uncertainty, such as life sciences and energy and mining industry's talent knowledge, ability skill is needed for employee's personal effort and characteristic needs; interpersonal and communication skill, H R managers predict that co-creativity and brainstorming skills be greatly in demand, it will bring relationship building and teamwork skills; global operating skill means that ability to manage diverse employee is seen as the most important global operating skill,, glocalisation ( where home-market products and services are tailored to the taste of overseas customers and innovation ( where staffs lead innovation and then the company applies these new ideas to mature markets).

Talent is a relative concept, it includes these components, such as technical specialists, especially in areas key to the organization's core capabilities, individuals with hard-to-recruit skills, bright individuals from underrepresented groups whom the positions , the best-performing graduates or school leavers and managers with the potential to move into senior management positions at the local, national or internatonal level. However, judgement effort is the main factor to influence organizations to select individuals whose behavior and values fit with those of the organization. How performance and potential are measured is for senior managers to decide.

In many cases, the definition of exceptional performance is explained in competency frameworks and appraisal systems. Defining high potential can be more difficult and might include a range of assessment tools, such as development centres, psychometric testing and the personal judgement of those whose insights into talent are widely repected.

Talent plan has three components: talent gaps mean HR works with business management levels. Once a year to identify which leadership , management and functional skills are needed, how those roles and responsibilities and whether the talent processes are producing people who will be able to solve these skill gaps; talent supply means most of the focus is on management trainees and a smaller porportion of people who are recurited mid-career; talent development means recruiting high-potential individuals at the start of their careers and taking them through a structured development programme.

Talent strategy means how senior leaders can identify the capabilities that help achieve the company's strategy strategic objectives and provide a competitive effort. These capabilities are not just tactical or operational skills, which although important, do have as much of an impact on business performance and profit. Operational management or senior levels and the talent management team then break down each capabilities into parts, such as specific skills, knowledge and expertise. They look at how these skills sets enable each business unit to deliver their part of the strategic plan.

This analysis should indicate the roles where knowledge and expertise are needed for maximum business value. There are not automatically senior leadership or management values. They also extend to technical and specialist roles or to previously overlooked roles, e.g. positions within the organization that help sure that expertise from one part of the business. Part of review many necessitate a fresh look at knowledge management processes across the business. The HR team should also review its own ways of working and thinking to make sure that its processes for recruitment, selection, learning and development, appraisal , reward and recognition and concentrates on the skills, cultural values and behaviors most critical to business performance.

Talent review aims to assess how well employees are performing currently in the critical roles, identified by the strategic review, and their potential to move into more demanding roles. Some of the required data will be held centrally by HR, but almost certainly, the team carrying out the review will need to speak directly to operational and line managers to get feedback about the performance and potential of key individuals.

At part of the review, gap analysis will help identify gaps in skills necessary to carry out the business's strategy and plans and whether any critical roles are unfilled. Succession planning is a important factor here as it may well be that insufficient numbers of potential successors have been identified for certain critical roles. A talent based gap analysis main aim is to focus on hiring and/or training needs as part of a talent strategy, it is the company's strategic planning process. It draws on wide source of data, both internally and externally. It looks at strategic needs both current and future, and makes judgements about operational needs.

This analysis determines whether the right talented people are in the right position at the right time. These three factors will influence whether talent planning needs to be improved. For example, right people, but wrong time, it means that people who might not be being used currently because of ao downturn in markets, but who the organization does not want to lose as it takes too much time and money to replace them when demand increases. The organization must therefore determine its strategy for retaining and motivating them; wrong people means that people are not employed to perform the work .

This suggests that a mistake is between HR processes and the business strategy, learning and development processes may not be kept good with changing business needs. There may be needed to appraise and promote to make right decisions that are leading to a mismatch between roles and people, right people, but wrong location. It means that people who can do the work , but are in the wrong location as a result of a reorganization and constraints on mobility, make more creative use of temporary assignments and virtual working, or relocate work to where it can be done by the most skilful employees.

Finally, once the talent review has identified any shortages of talent, an organization has three options: either buying talent through external recuritment or building talent through tailored learning and development programmes that involve work experiences that will help talent employment development or borrowing talent by resorting to temporary workers or outsourcing.

Buying talent is an obvious choice when a company needs particular skills or expertise that it does not have time or ability ro develop in existing staff is to buy in that talent. The task is then to source this expertise, and offer the right set of inducements to recruit and retain individuals with the desired skills. However, buying talent can be costly as the going rate for sought-after specialists is high and they are often in a strong negotiating position. For example, swift recruitment processes and flexible remuneration package can attract talent employees' applications through external recruitment seeking recritment method.

Borrowing talent is a temporary need for specialist skills it makes sense to borrow or " rent" what is required by contracting with, for example, freelancers, independent consultants, staff on seondment or firms that will supply staff. This form of flexible labour means uncertain times such flexibility becomes more attractive because it enables firms to assemble new combinatins of skills in swift reponse to sudden shifts in their environment. It provides firms with access to wider pool of talent, especially in the case of work that can be performed in any location.

This, building talent means that a larger firm will seek to build its own talent by creating a reliable high potential and high performing employees. The aim is to rise and train talent skilful employees' qualities and efforts and to invest in their careers in the expectation that they will progress to senior positions in the business. So, these individuals are placed in a talent pool where their progress is monitored and where they are given extra opportunities for training and development. To keep talented people to develop, there is an emphasis on performance management, so any weaknesses or developments are needed to find.

6.1 sourcing staff methods

Internal sources advantages of filling a vacancy internally, they include better motivation because employee capabilities are more ensured to promote or transfe, improved moral, performance and loyalty to the employee, lower staff turnover rate, better utilisation of employees because he/she owns more abilities in a different job or capacity , less training required, greater reliability than external recruitment because a present employee is the terms of personality, attitudes, values, work habits etc. known more, being quicker and cheaper than external recruitment. External source advantages when the company need to expand and growth contribute to the need for recruitment. Other factors include resignation, dismissal, retirement and relocation. Althougm internal recruitment has many advantages,many positions are filled by external applicants. When an internal candidate is transferred or promoted, it means that his/her position then because a vacancy, presuming that there is no reduction in staff numbers and no organizational restructing. Hence, external recruitment can be time consuming , expensive and uncertain. However, organizations still need to conduct the external sources selecting method on a regular basis. The external recruitment source channels may include internal online or newspaper advertising, private employment agencies, professional bodies appointment services, local employment services office of government labor deparment, direct links with universities, colleges and schools, unsolicited applications, recommendations by present employees or by othe employers' referrals.

Talent management steps in validating a test. Test aims to ensure whether the testee's listening and speaking competence, he/she owns the skilful effort is enough to do the vacancy or position in the organization. The steps in validating a test is as below:

The organization needs to analyze the job. It is necessary to conduct a careful job analysis to produce a good job description and an appropriate job specification. These requirements can then become the objectives of the selection tests. Then, it needs to choose the test from among the various testing means, choose the one that is the most valid and reliable. Next, it needs to administer the test. One can either tesst current employees and find out of there is any significant differences between the scores and the employees' performances , it means concurrent validation or test potential candidates before they are hired and compare their scores with their performances after they have been in their jobs, it means predictive validation.

However, predictive validation may have disadvantages, e.g. job performance may be difficult to assess objectively, the process of validation may be lengthy, the results of the test are compared with the performance of a selected group only, it is not completely validated. Concurrent validation is quick, but its disadvantages may include standardisation is difficult, the test is validated against a non-typical group only, i.e. present employers rather than candidates for employment, the present employe may not behave normally when they do the test.

Reference

Marion, D. & Michel, S. (2014) the economist, Managing talent, Profile books ltd, London, UK, pp.1-2, 6.

# CHAPTER SEVEN

# Employee engagement

employee engagement aim

What is employee engagement? The term employee engagement needs to be clearly understood by every organization. Some organizations perceive it as job satisfaction others say it's the emotional attachment towards the organization. Employee Engagement is a fundamental concept in the effort to understand and describe, both qualitatively and quantitatively, the nature of the relationship between an organization and its employees. An "engaged employee" is defined as one who is fully absorbed by and enthusiastic about their work and takes positive action to further the organization's reputation and interests. An engaged employee has a positive attitude towards the organization and its values.

An organization with "high" employee engagement might therefore be expected to outperform those with "low" employee engagement. Employee engagement improves the productivity of an organization as the practice helps the employees in teamwork, co-ordination and inter-personal skills. It means that such as morale and job satisfaction. Despite academic critiques, employee-engagement practices are well established in the management of human resources and of internal communications. Employee engagement today has become synonymous with terms like 'employee experience' and 'employee satisfaction'. The relevance is much more due to the vast majority of new generation professionals in the workforce who have a higher propensity to be 'distracted' and 'disengaged' at work.

The workplace environment impacts employee morale, productivity and engagement - both positively and negatively. The work place environment in a majority of industry is unsafe and unhealthy. These includes poorly designed workstations, unsuitable furniture, lack of ventilation, inappropriate lighting, excessive noise, insufficient safety measures in fire emergencies and lack of personal protective equipment. People working in such environment are prone to occupational disease and it impacts on employee's performance. Thus productivity is decreased due to the workplace environment. It is the quality of the employee's workplace environment that most impacts on their level of motivation and subsequent performance. How well they engage with the organization, especially with their immediate environment, influences to a great extent their error rate, level of innovation and collaboration with other employees, absenteeism and ultimately, how long they stay in the job.

Creating a work environment in which employees are productive is essential to increased profits for your organization, corporation or small business. The relationship between work, the workplace and the tools of work, workplace becomes an integral part of work itself. The management that dictate how, exactly, to maximize employee productivity

center around two major areas of focus: personal motivation and the infrastructure of the work environment.

In today's competitive business environment, organizations can no longer afford to waste the potential of their workforce. There are key factors in the employee's workplace environment that impact greatly on

their level of motivation and performance. The workplace environment that is set in place impacts employee morale, productivity and engagement - both positively and negatively. It is not just coincidence that new programs addressing lifestyle changes, work/life balance, health and fitness - previously not

considered key benefits - are now primary considerations of potential employees, and common practices among the most admired companies.

In an effort to motivate workers, firms have implemented a number of practices such as performance based pay, employment security agreements, practices to help balance work and family, as well as various forms of information sharing. In addition to motivation, workers need the skills and ability to do

their job effectively. And for many firms, training the worker has become a necessary input into the production process.

THE PROBLEM STATEMENT

The work place environment in a majority of industry is unsafe and unhealthy. These includes poorly designed workstations, unsuitable furniture, lack of ventilation, inappropriate lighting, excessive noise,

insufficient safety measures in fire emergencies and lack of personal protective equipment. People working in such environment are prone to occupational disease and it impacts on employee's performance. Thus productivity is decreased due to the workplace environment. It is a wide industrial

area where the employees are facing a serious problem in their work place like environmental and physical factors. So it is difficult to provide facilities to increase their performance level. Thus, effective employee engagement strategy can assist the organization's employees feel they are the organization's important members to serve their organizations to work more hardly in order to raise productivities easily.

7.1 What is employee welfare mean?

Employee welfare includes everything, such as facilities, benefits and services, that an employer provides or does to ensure comfort of the employees. Good welfare helps to motivate employees and ensure increased productivity. Providing good welfare to employees may be a costly decision, but the long-term benefits are immense. It is one way of complying with the law, thus ensuring that an employer avoids legal issues. It allows accompany to retain its good and skilled employees for long periods of time. Employees work well in workplaces where they are treated well and respected. Good welfare also helps to create a good company image for a particular employer.

Employee welfare facilities in the organization affects on the behavior of the employees as well as on the productivity of the
organization. While getting work done through employees the management must provide required good facilities to all employees.
The management should provide required good facilities to all employees in such way that employees become satisfied and they work harder and more efficiently and more effectively.

Welfare is a broad concept referring to a state of living of an individual or a group, in a desirable relationship with the total
environment – ecological economic and social. It aims at social development by such means as social legislation, social reform
social service, social work, social action. The object of economics welfare is to promote economic production and productivity and through development by increasing equitable distribution. Labour welfare is an area of social welfare conceptually and operationally.
It covers a broad field and connotes a state of well being, happiness, satisfaction, conservation and development of human resources

Employee welfare is an area of social welfare conceptually and operationally. It covers a broad field and connotes a state of well being, happiness, satisfaction, conservation and development of
human resources and also helps to motivation of employee. The basic propose of employee welfare is to enrich the life of
employees and to keep them happy and conducted. Welfare measures may be both Statutory and Non statutory laws require the employer to extend certain benefits to employees in addition to wages or salaries.

Labour Welfare Measures

Labor welfare includes various facilities, services and amenities provided to workers for improving their health, efficiency,
economic betterment and social status.
Welfare measures are in addition to regular wages and other economic benefits available to workers due to legal provisions
and collective bargaining. The purpose of labor welfare is to bring about the development
of the whole personality of the workers to make a better workforce. The very logic behind providing welfare schemes is to create efficient, healthy, loyal and satisfied labor force for the organization. The purpose of providing such facilities is to make their work life better and also to raise their standard of living.

7.2 Measurement the level of employee engagement factor
There are a number of external and internal factors that help measure the level of employee engagement. External factors include organization environment; its culture and values, manager-subordinate relationship, relationships

with co-workers, monetary benefits and appraisals. Whereas internal factors include the personal values of employee, personality type and commitment to work. Gallup's research on employee engagement shows that there is a strong relationship between well being of an employee and the level of their engagement. An engaged employee is efficient an effective for the organizational outcomes.

Employee engagement has direct effect on productivity and growth. If employees are engaged they will try level best to fulfill their job responsibilities which will consequently lead to not only increase in organization productivity but will also enhance the self performance of employee. In the world of globalization only those organizations which have highly engaged workers can survive and grow. But an organization can engage its employees only if the employees have the desired attitude. Therefore an organization should train its employees to change their attitudes if they want to properly manage workforce engagement.


7.3 employee engagement survey reasons

Nowadays, increasing diverse and geographically workforces bring global competition to live nd retain qualified employees aim. Organizations need to attract, motivately and engage employees though not only the core HR functions of compensation, benefits, performance management and talent development, but engagement programs, such as work life effectiveness, recognition and reward systems.

In fact, one strategic employee engagement if designed correctly, is cost-effective program and valuable tools that can measured and increase employee involvement and ethusiasm in their work and contributions to their employer's goals or values. Industry research analysts indicated that companies in the top employee engagement designed program, which can brough 16% higher profits and 18% higher productivity in general. They also evaluated the relationship between employee engagement and employee turnover.

Companies with light effective recognition engagement programs have 31 % lower ineffective turnover than organizations with ineffective recognition programs. However, to be most impactful engagement solutions require innovative features to enble full service, effective management of strategic engagement programs. Social communicative elements along with rich analytics and mobile capabilities that interoperate with existing HR solutions are necessary to keep more efficient and effective changing HR needs and organizational goals.

As the economy slowly makes its way back in recovery mode and more employees are concerned with issues beyond job security. So organizations need to concern how to a focus on employee engagement and the criticial factor ithin organizations that drives performance. HR conulting forms point out a relationship between high levels of engagement and high levels of financial performance. Achieving overall employee engagement is overview to have need. For years, companies around the globle have conducted employee engagement surveys in an effort to determine why their organizations function the way they do, and how they can pull organizations to improve performance. The results of there employee engagement surveys sometimes reflect, better and accurate key business decisions and impacting the day-for-day lives of employees, shareholders and customers.

But is that really all these is to real reflection? Should company focus on employee engagement as the key indicator of success or failure within their organization? Is high employee engagement brings some sort of better management skills? It is absolute no answer. When employee engagement should be measured as an important organizations human resource and social system, truly understanding how to optimize performance in your organization requires understanding your organization requires understanding your culture. For example, we know that with some people, we can increase their engagement and satisfaction by simply, making their work easy-opertating in a go along to get along manner and more generally encouraging passive behaviors.

Employee engagement becomes a popular topic of the workplace instead of job satisfaction and organizational commitment which is approved to effect the organizational outcome. In HR department behaviors that affect th structured interviews were conducted in corporate HR to explore the employee engagement and techniques for improving employee engagement were recommended based on the interview.

The quantitative research results show that job autonomy , performance feedback, challenging work, worker person fit, development support and the connection with co-workers have a strong relationship with employee engagement. And the recommended solutions like building on action team, have more team activities and develop a formal both for big team ( corporate HR ) and smaller team will improve their engagement over time.

Organizations need to increase their performance by both efficiency and productivity. Managers would hardly deny that employees make a criticial difference in innovation, organization performance, competitiveness and lead to the business success. Hence, HR plays an important role in the employee engagement program with the responsibilities of the survey, providing feedback on results, prommoting communication in different groups of people, encouraging people to take action and providing educational opportunities.

Employees growth, teamwork mangement support and basic needs are needed to measure by relevant questions in viewpoint survey by using five point scale. Personal growth is measured by talking about the progress and having job opportunity grow. The options count, mission and purpose fellow employees who committed to quality work and having a best friend at work and identified as the questions for measuring team work . Management support is measured by opportunity to do the best , recognition or praise care and encourage the development.

Employee survey can reflect employees engagement , e.g. one viewpoint survey for the past three years and every time survey has chance to let employees fill the survey in, then HR managers can get the results to give scores. Managers should take get move real feedback from different department staff's positive or negative emotion or feeling aboug whose job tasks, whether they worry about any job difficulties. Hence, surveys can let organizations try to figure out of their employees are engaged and how to make them engaged by using different surveys and tools to stay competitive and improve performance.

In survey contents, there are four main topics in the engagement survey: growth, teamwork, managment support and basic needs. The result can show the most items in engagement support were scored relatively low or high as mean of development support from manager. Hence, many organizations were focusing on designing a successful reward system to keep employees engaged and productive line or the low level managers who can serve their employees are typically the ones who work or fail the engagement tools because line managers need often communicate and contact workers when they are working. They can know what their feeling to their job tasks whether it is positive or negative emotion in order to find solutions how to raise their performance.

Essentials of organizational behavioral learning

The importance of management skills is essential, if any organizations hope to raise efficiency or improve performance. Organizations need to learn how to balance hard and soft skill, how to manage social and human skills whch reflect the ability to get along with other people are increasingly important attributes at all levels of management.

Managers ought need to spend most time operating between the " hard skills" , such as conducting disciplinary matters or how to allocate of budgets, and " soft skills" , such as counselling, or giving support and advice to a member of staff. Managers also needed to be trained to raise technical competence, related to specific tasks, how to supervise and train subordinate staffs, and with day-to-day subordinate staff, and with day-to-day operations concerned in the actual production of goods and services; social and human skills relates to interpesonal relationship in working with and through other people, and how to judge to achieve effective teamwork and direction, and leadership of staff to achieve co-ordinated effort to particular situation and flexibilty in adopting the most appropriate style of management, raising conceptual ability in order to view he complexities of the operations of the organization as a whole, including environmental influences.

Mc Donald soft skill organizational behavior

It also involves decision-making skills, relates to the overall making of the organization and to its stragegic planning in long time, such as McDonald restaurant has good strategic management to manage its global branches of franchise restaurants in organizational behavioral view successfully. So, it can attract many investors buy its franchises to learn how to do McDonald fast food restsurants . It's investors number is increasing, due to it has good significant organizational behavior as well as its managers know how to apply " soft skills" and " hard skills" to manage them effectively.

So, organizational behavior and organizational performance seems have close relationship. If the organization can build the most effective and efficient organizational behavior, managers know how to manage employee individual behavior, then the performance ought will be improved , even customers won't complaint or feel unsatisfactory easily, they will feel satisfactory to their staffs service performance, such as McDonald fast food restaurant case, global McDonald fast food franchise restaurants eating customers complain bumber is low in general, because instead of their front line service staffs performance and attitude can let them to feel satisfactory,

The most influential soft skill to bring its fast food eating customers feel satisfactory or they are persuaded to choose its sale service to replace other similar fast food restaurants sale service. The reason is because that , when they buy its fast food, or soft drink, they must be arranged to give one number ticket. So, they do not need to spend long time to queue in any McDonald fast food restaurants, they can leave McDonald restaurant to go to other places and they wont' worry that McDonald staffs forget to make their fast food or soft drink when they leave. Because they can give the number ticket to indicate their number to the staff to take their fast food or soft drink any time. For example, if the eating customer's ticket number is 30, and the screen indicates next number future cooking is 10, then he will feel that he can leave McDonald to spend about 15 minutes to come back. Even, if his coming back time is exceed 15 minutes, and the screen indicates number is 40. Although, he is late, but he may ask the staff to take his fast food or soft drink immediately. So, he does not need to worry about that he can take his fast food or soft drink even he is late to come back. So they avoid to queue long time in McDonald, they can come back after half hour, even after one hour. When they come back, they only need to give their number ticket to confirm that the had paid money to buy fast food or soft drink. When the front line staff see that number from their ticket. They will go to kitchen to take their prepared fast food or soft drink to give them immediately. it is one effective time management " soft skill" to avoid eating customers feel angry or bad emotion when they need to queue in long time in any one Mc Donald restaurant. They can choose to leave Mcdonald restaurants any long time. It is one efficient and effective 2 soft skill customer service management skill in any one nowadays McDonald front line . So , it's success depends on its front line staff " don't need eating people to queue long time" in any one McDonald restaurant.

Convenient framework of analysis of organizational behavior

Any organizations ought need have a convenient framework of analysis if they hope to manage their organizational behavior efficiently. I shall explain what a convenient framework of organizational behavior analysis means as below: The top level is what nature and purpose of the organization, then next middle level concerns learning how to manage " behavior of people", " process of management", " organizational context" , next is middle level learning how to adapt any environment influences. The final process to any organizations. They hope to achieve improving organizational performance in success as well as organizational processes as well as how to execution of work to the most success.

It is one important service soft skill method to let global McDonald restaurants can continue to attract many eating people to choose to but their fast food or soft drink , instead of reduced price or coupon sale method in global fast food restaurant market. So, its success depends on how to mix of the practical and the soft skill service performance strategy to eating customer long time queue bad emotion theoretical psychological strategy, it must be linked to a single aim, such as Mc Donald has its single aim to front line staffs, is that how to avoid eating people need to stay in McDonald restaurant to queue long time to let them to feel angry and unsatisfactory to its global any McDonald franchise restaurants. So it comfirms that , many its global eating people don't like to queue and to stay in McDonald long time, when the Ms Donald has many people are staying in McDonald in busy time.

Thus, in organizational behavioral view, they will be persuaded to choose to buy MsDonald fast food in perference, because its unique service feature, when other fast food restaurants can not implement this front lines do not need queue method in their fast food restaurants. It implies that effective front line service skill may be one important factor to influence any clients' choices in preference.

How to apply hard skill and soft skill to solve inefficient problem?

The theme of inefficiency will experience to any organizations, if they lack effective organizational behavioral management strategy. It assumed that workers who were not good at one particualr task, would be best at some other tasks in any teams. There is however, no certainty of this in practice. It concerns workers from an engineering view point and as machines , but the one best way of performing a task is not always the best method for every worker. So, the reduction of physical movement to find the one best way is or always beneficial and some " wasteful" movements are essential to the overall rhythm of work.

So, if the organization hopes to achieve effective organizational behavior, the organization needs to concern these soft skill and hard skill issues they may include:

1. High wages from increased output.

2. The removal of physical strain from doing works the wrong way.

3. Development of the workers and the opportunity for them to undertake tasks , they were capable of doing and

4. Elimination of the " boss" and the duty of management to help workers.

For example on factory raising efficient organizational behavior aspect, the factory may implement these soft skill and hard skill both strategies, such as: To assist the stores in better customer service by having the merchandise ready to go on the floor, saving space in the stockroom, and creating customer goodwill, to increase the units per hour produced, to performance the job duties as efficiency and effectively as possible, avoiding bureaucracies organization, it emphasised the importance of administration based on experise ( rules of experts) and administration based on discipline ( rules of officials). Because one when burea staffs are working in one serious or strict bureaucracies organization, they will feel not happy and unsatisfactory to their manager behavior. So, managers' soft management skill ought often need to revise when need to be changed to be better or improve their performance, such as:

The tasks of the organization are allocated as official duties among the various positions, there is an implied clear -out division of labor and a high level of specialisation, a hierarchical authority applies to the organization of offices and positions, uniformity of decisions and actions is achieved through formally established systems, of rules and regulations. Together work a structure of authority , this enables the coordination of various activities within the organization, an imperaonal orietnation is expected from officials in their dealings with clients and other officials. This is designed to result in rational judgments by officials in the performance of their duties as well as employment by the organization is based on technical qualifications and constitues a lifelong career for the officials, e.g. how to apply specialisation more to the job than to the person undertaking the job.

This makes for continuity because the job usually continues of the present job holder leaves, hierarchy of authority it makes for a sharp distination between administrators and the administered or between management and workers, within the management ranks these are clearly defined levels of authority, system of rules aims to provide for an officials and impersonal operaton, sules are generally stable although some rules may be changed as modified with impersonality means that how allocation and exercise authority should not be complex.

# CHAPTER EIGHT

# Interview psychology methods

What are common psychology methods of recruitment choice?

Can any psychology methods are used to choose who will be the best recruitment applicant(s) in any recruitment stage more accurate? Can the interviewer observe the applicant's psychological phenomenon to judge whether the applicant can be the best or the most suitable applicant in the recruitment stage more accurate? To answer above these questions. We need to know why a systematic scientific procedure is an essential component to achieve any psychological method(s) to test candidate individual ability to judge whether who is the best or the most suitable applicant to do any position in any organization.

A psychologist can follow a systematic scientific procedure which has theoretical base in order to explain and interpret the psychological phenomenon of the applicant to decide whether who is the best or the most suitable applicant to do the position in the organization.

On the one hand, in order to obtain the applicant's psychological response from individual applicant, there are a number of psychological tools or instruments are used during the interview process. The responses are taken on these tools constitute the basic data which are analyzed to study the applicant experiences, e.g. working experiences, life experiences, mental processes and behaviors. On the other hand, in order to understand every applicant's behavior during the interview process. The different psychological methods can be applied for solving different applicant's individual behavior ( individual mental problems) to judge who will be the best or the most suitable applicant to the position in any organization. Because different situations will cause the applicant to choose how to do or perform different behaviors to persuade the interviewer believes who is the best or the most suitable applicant to do the position in the organization. Thus, whose performances will be shaped by many factors both intrinsic and extrinsic to him or her in any interview process.

The common psychological methods of interview process include such as: For observation psychological method example, when shopping in the market , the researcher must have noticed various activities of the consumers . When he/she observes the consumers their activities, the researcher also think about as to why who are doing those activities and probably the researcher reaches a conclusion about the causes of such activities. So, observation is as a psychological method of enquiry is often understand as a systematic registering of events without any deliberate attempt to interface with variables operating in the event which is being studies.

Thus, observation psychological method seems to be applied to judge who is the best or the most suitable applicant to do any position in any organization in any interview process. Such as in any interview process, the interviewer ( observer) can use this method to judge or observe every applicant's face and behavioral performance to feel whether who is the best or the most suitable applicant who own ability or confidence or qualification or experience to already to do the job to achieve the recruitment result is more accurate. For example, the interviewer ( observer) can attempt to give one simple or difficult task to test whether whom the applicant has the more effort of the induced stress on task performance in the short time observation test in the on part stage of the interview process.

However, observation is also divided into either participant or non-participant both types, depending on the role of observer ( interviewer). In the case of interview participant observation, the interviewer mixes up with the job ( task) performance event test under study and conducts concerns the interview test, e.g. group discussion interview test, the applicants and the interviewer will discuss one or more than one topic(s) which concern(s) on relating the position requirement issue. So, the interviewer can analyze whom applicant(s) can talk the most reasonable evidences to support whose opinions to argue the topic against the other applicants together among of them in the short time group discussion, e.g. between 15 minutes to 30 minutes. It aims to let the interviewer can have enough time to record whose opinions to analyze whose opinions are the most reasonable argument to support whose main points to win this position among these interview competitors in the short time group discussion.

Thus, the interviewer needs to participate the group discussion to ask every applicant any questions and let them to attempt to solve any challenges in the whole group discussion. After the group discussion, then the interviewer can have more effort or confidence to judge whom applicant (s) is/are the most suitable or the best applicant (s) to do the job for his/her organization more accurate.

Otherwise, as in the case of interview non-participant observation, the interviewer maintains an optimum distance and has little impact on the interview event. Such as the interview group discussion test. The interviewer won't ask any questions to let the applicants to attempt to answer. Otherwise, he/she will let the applicants have chance to ask any questions or answer the questions among of their discussion related to the topic. So the interviewer's role is a listener, who only needs to listen every applicant how who can ask and can answer any questions to decide who can talk the most correct or the right or the most reasonable answers to answer their questions in the short time group discussion. Then, the interviewer can record all applicants' questions and answers to make the judgement to decide who will be the right or the most suitable applicant to do the position in her/him organization more accurate.

Why does need to test the applicant's psychological behavior in the interview process?

To answer this question, we need to know why any large or middle size organizations which need have human resource department. To challenge of today's HR managers is to create a pool of good employees in the organization.

It starts from selection process of the employees. So, interview has been used as an important selection method by HR managers for long time. The cost of rehiring the importance of hiring the right person for right position first. It requires a reliable and valid interview process. Although, any interview won't guarantee 100 percent success in hiring the best employees into any organization, but the proper application is at least, will improve the chances of hiring the best applicant for the job the organization. The importance is given to the selection of right employees for the right positions. Firms are now realizing the value of the good employees because who can make a difference through their job performance. So, various selection methods are now being used to identify the right candidate.

" Interview" has emerged as a very useful tool in this regard. It is a very common selection method and has a high predictive validity for job performance ( Robertson, & Smith , 2001). The main purpose of the interview is to select the right candidate for the right job. The importance of conducting an effective interview is also rising. So consensus was found among the HR experts regarding the effective interview techniques. There are a number of existing literatures regarding the techniques of an effective interview, but every few literatures exist regarding a systematic approach of conducting exist regarding a systematic approach of conducting an effective interview.

This is a very few literatures exist regarding a complete interview process that shows a clear path to the employers for selecting right employees. A lot of interview technique are available, but the problem arises regarding the use of these techniques in a concrete manner. A systematic approach of interview will facilitate the tasks of HR managers in selecting the right applicant for the right position.

( Stevens, 1997) author indicated the whole process of the interview has been described in terms of "3D"- Development, discussion and decision. This study is particularly important for three reasons. First , it will help the HR mangers to think about the employee selection interview in a concrete manner. Second, it will help them to use a number of interview techniques in an effective way that will ultimately increase the chance of hiring the right person for the right position. Third, it will enrich the existing literature of selection interview.

( Stevens, 1997) author also explained that the growing importance of good employees will cause a challenge to the HR managers. The selection process of today's HR manager is becoming complex and challenging. Undoubtedly, the overall aim, of the selection process is to identify the candidates who are suitable for the vacancy or wider requirement of the HR plan. " Interview" has been used as a ' critical selection method ' by HR managers. The interview is the most valid method in determining an applicant's organizational fit, level of motivation and inter-personal selects.

Whetton & Cameron (2002) cited steps of process of conducting an interview, what they named as People-oriented selection interview process. Here is explains the interview process: P=prepare, E=establish rapport, O=obtain information, P=provide information, C= lead top close and E= evaluate.

So, it seems that the candidates' behavior individual performance in the interview process can be predicted whether who is(are) the most suitable or the best to do the position in the organization from the interviewer's observation. So, it also means the candidate's attitude in the interview process can perform to let the interviewer to feel whether who is suitable or the best to do the position in the organization . Thus, observation of the applicant individual performance, it is an interviewer's best interest to find good prospects, hire them and have them stay in the organization.

Therefore, the interviewees are needed to be provided sufficient information about the job and organization to have enough time to prepare before who will go to interview fairly. It aims to let every candidate has enough confidence to prepare to answer any questions in further interview process fairly. So, the development stage is a good preparation for the interview facilitates the effective interview process. To aim to let the candidate have enough preparation to interview , it should begin long before the first question is ever asked fairly.

In conclude, HR department seems an essential department to any middle or large organizations nowadays. It does not attribute only recruitment function to any organization, it also attribute the chance to give one psychological test function to evaluate whom applicant has the more experience and qualification and effort to do any position in any organization. If the interviewer has not prepared any psychological method to test any applicants to judge whether who has the more effort to do the position. Then, I believe the interview result will be more failure and more inaccurate to employ the most suitable applicant , due to who lacks the enough effort and qualification and experience to perform to finish any tasks or duties of the position . So, it is important why any organization needs have good psychological method to test and observe the applicant's psychological behavior in the interview process?

Occupation psychological
test methods
How to apply psychological recruitment
strategies effect/manage in the
recruitment process?

HR ( human resource) managers understand accept that poor recruitment decisions continue to affect organizational performance and limit goal achievement. In this case, many jurisdictions to identify and implement new effective hiring strategies will be serious issue to any HR departments to concern.

Acquiring and retaining high-quality talent is critical to any organization's success. So, recruiters need to be more elective in their choice. Since poor recruiting decisions can produce long term negative effects, among their high training and development costs to minimise the incidence of poor performance and high turnover to impact staff morale, the production of high quality goods and services. Thus, HR managers must seek all possible methods for improve their output and provide the satisfaction to their clients require and deserve. The provision of high quality goods and services begins with the recruitment process.

( Schuler, Randalls, 1989) explained recruitment is as " the set of activities and processes used to legally obtain a sufficient number of qualified applicants at the right place and time. So that the applicants and the organization can select each other in their own best short and long term interests.

Thus, it seems that successful recruitment begins with proper employment planning and forecasting. So any one organization needs analyze what kinds of positions of future needs talent available within and outside of the organization and the current and anticipated resources that can be expected to attract and retain such talent. Thus,

HR manager needs have one successful strategy to be prepared to employ in order to identify and select the best candidates for its developing pool of human resources.

In common, one successful recuruitment strategy involves these several processes of :

Step one : Development of a policy on recruitment and giving life to the policy.

Step two: Needing assessment to determine the current and future human resource requirement of the organization.

Step three: If the activity is to be effective , the HR requirements for each job category and functional division /unit of the organization must be assessed, identification within and outside the organization of the potential human resources pool.

Step four: Job analysis and job evaluation to identify the individual aspects of each jobs and calculate its relative worth, assessment of qualifications profiles, job descriptions that identify responsibilities and requirement skills, abilities , knowledge and experience, determination to pay salaries and benefits within a defined period.

Step five: identification and documentation of the actual process of recruitment and selection to ensure equity and laws.

Thus, the psychological recruitment strategy for the interviewer includes how to ask interview questions, how to give interview scores and panellists' comments, results of tests ( where administered). Because and length of interview time for the interview. There are any interview main contents to any interviewer needs to concern how to arrange interview process.

For example, nowadays, it is popular internet recruiting. Although, interviewer can reduce time to arrange and spend time to interview any applicants, due to the interviewer can interview any applicants from whose organization website . Specially, there are many similar potential interview competitors to apply to the position at the same time. Otherwise, internet recruiting is not all positive. Such as some applicants skill place great value in face-to-face interactons in the hiring process. Such applicant;s are likely to ignre jobs posted, impersonally on time.

I shall indicate these sample recruitment strategy to explain how to influence every applicant's choice to apply the job or not apply the job as below:

The first is online recruiting. This online recuritment strategy has a large percentage of employees are hired by human service agencies for every level jobs are seeking their first career job. The newspaper want ads are not an effective recruitment source for most of today's applicants. Placing vacancy announcements online is more effective and economical than using most traditional forms of advertising. However, online recruitment is designed to close this gap: Not reaching majority of applicants, especially young graduates.

The second is campus recruiting and job fairs. This campus recruiting strategy attracts both professional and paraprofessional applicants, who can be effectively recruited at job fairs sponsored by state workforce development agencies. However, college recruiting can be a very effective method for attracting applicants for professional jobs. The possible psychological advantages to applicants that includes any employers will send team of HR representatives to any colleges to provide an opportunity for job seekers to ask both job specific and hiring process/benefits questions; sending an ambassador to classrooms to quest lecture; schedule experienced employees or supervisors to ask on a hot topic in the human or service field at a local college or university. However, this campus recruiting strategy has a large percentage of employees hired, but need to improve overall applicant.

The third is university partner developing a variety of recruitment strategy. University partnership benefits include to collaborate with university deans and professors to help student interest in the field as well as to develop program partially covering college tuition and other expenses of college students who agree to work for the human service agency for specified periods of time. Its recruitment strategy aims to develop a variety of recruitment strategies with area universities, community colleges and schools of social work to encourage students to pursue careers in the human services. It's weakness lacks enough applicants with specialized social work degrees.

The fourth recruitment strategy is target recruitment. Employers may used a more diverse workforce that better reflects the client population who serve. For example, employers may need to recruit employees with specific lannguage skills or with specialized degrees , e.g. criminal juice. It' weakness lacks of diversity in targeted jobs.

The fifth recruitment strategy is internships. Interns sometimes are paid stipend, but in most instances interns are fulfilling an academic requirement of the college or university. Although supervisors and/or cause work staff must spend time supervising and training interns, the potential payoff is having a known applicant who is familiar with agency operations. Its weakness is needed to improve overall applicant pool.

The sixth recruitment strategy is maintain a pre-screened applicant pool. It has a pool of pre-screened, interviewed applicants always available to be called for a second interview with the hiring supervisor. When, using this approach, it's important to minimize the amount of time between the initial interview and the second interview to prevent top quality applicants from being hired human resources will need to do continuous recruiting and screening , even when there are no current vacancies. It's weaknesses include that some
human services organizations delay hiring until staff vacancies reach crisis proportions. They than initiate a recruitment process that is designed to bring new employees on board as soon as possible . The unfortunate result is hiring employees who meet the minimum requirements, but nothing more. It also has too many applicants get hired with only the minimum credentials.

The seventh recruitment strategy is realistic job previews. Realistic job previews are designed to prevent applicants from taking jobs that who have life knowledge of or are not suited to perform. It is a recruiting tool is designed to reduce early turnover by communicating both the desirable and the undesirable aspects of a jobs before applicants accept a job offer. It can be in the form of videos, oral presentations, job shadowing opportunities. It's weakness includes unwanted turnover among new workers who did not understand their job when who were hired.

The final recruitment strategy is improved hiring flexibilities in highly centralized systems. It means many public-seator human service agencies are regulated by merit systems that make it different to attract and maintain the interest of top-qualify applicants. Top applicants in today's economy are searching the interest for jobs that are available now. They aren't interested in taking a civil service exam and sitting on eligibility lists for months. In some systems requirements and lengthy inflexible scoring processes wash out well qualified applicants. It's weaknesses include hiring process takes too long, high qualify applicants are looking elsewhere for jobs.

How to apply occupational psychological
test method to test applicant's ability?

Occupational psychological interview method is the application of the science of psychology to test applicant individual work ability. For example, any interviews can apply occupational psychologists' test method to attempt to test applicant individual performance, motivation and wellbing of the organization in the workplace. If any interviewers can attempt to apply occupational psychologist test method to test any applicant individual working abilities in interview. It brings this question: How can the interviewer develop, apply and evaluate a range of tools and interventions to test the applicant individual working abilities across many different areas of the workplace?

The occupational psychological test method can include these psychological skills to test every applicant individual ability in interview. Such as : Psychological assessment means selecting and assessing the applicant individual ability using interview enquiring method, e.g. in interview, enquiring applicant concerns on how to solve crisis deal issues when challenges cause in any workplace, assessments of what the applicant's main ability centres are. Situational judgement tests, e.g. how to solve challenges in different situations and personality questionnaires and cognitive ability tests. Profiling jobs are matching requirements to the applicant's future performance. Developing and choosing is valid, reliable, fair and suitable selectin procedures.

Thus, the psychological enquiring questions can concern on work motivation, performance, appraisal and management, leadership power influence and negotiation, employee engagement and commitment, citizenship and positive behaviors or counterproductive in workplace, psychology of group teams and teamwork different aspects, which have similar points , such as concern organizational behavior questions. It aims to test the applicant how to deal any immediate crisis in the organization if the interviewer decides to employ him/her.

The key focus of how to achieve one effective psychological test to the applicant in the interiew. It focuses on key areas , such as the applicant personal goal attainment, interview performance, the applicnt's mind on innovation and creativity aspects, and well being in the workplace how the applicant explains who will perform supposes who did the job in the workplace.

In the interview, the interviewer needs the applicant to explain to let him/her to understand how the applicant's relation and motivation in the organization. The interviewer also needs to know how the applicant can solve any challenges in workplace in the suitation test interview. Because conflict resolution is a challenging environment to work in. However, any downsides are offset by the rewards of being able to help protect both the organization and its employees from the psychological , physiological and economic costs of conflict. Because conflict will occur in possible in any workplaces. Thus, the interviewer ought to ask the question to let him/her to know the applicant will solve if who did this position.

Human factors is a discipline concerned with how the successful interview applicant ( future employee) works effectively and safely. It considers a employee's environmental , organizational, job and individual characteristics. These factors will affect the organizational successful interview applicant ( future employee) behavior and it is past of the interviewer's job to analyze these and to give recommendations for change to improve human performance to the organization if who selected to employ these applicants in every time interview. Thus it seems occupational psychological test method can give benefits to the interviewer to understand more to the applicants to judge whether who will be the most suitable applicant(s)to do any positions in whose organization more accurate decision in any interviews.

Selecting and evaluating
assessment methods

How selection assessment methods are applied to choose the best applicants ?

Organizations compete in the war for talent. So, one effective selection assessment method can help any organizations to choose the best applicant(s). Using scientifically proven assessments to make selection decisions, even though such assessments have been shown to result in significant productivity increases, cost savings, decrease other critical organizational outcomes. I shall indicate common misconceptions about selection tests, such as: Screening applicants for conscientiousness will yield better performers , then screening applicants for intelligence, screening applicants for their values will yield better performers , then screening applicants for intelligence, integrity tests are not ueful because job candidates misrepresent themselves on these typs of tests, unstructured interviews with candidates provide better information than structured assessment processes and using selection tests creates legal problems for organizations rather than helps to solve them.

There are numerous different types of formal assessments that organizations can use to select employees. The first step in developing or selecting an assessment method for a given situation is to understand what the job requires employees to do and what knowledge, skills and abilities individuals must posses in order to perform the job effectively. This is typically accomplished by conducting a job analysis . For job oriented job analysis recruitment example, providing test by stating fact and answer questions, gathering and reviewing information to obtain obtain evidence or develop background information on subjects, integrating diverse information to uncover relationships between individuals, events or evidences.

Other assessment methods focus on how measuring the best applicant who are required to perform job tasks effectively, such as various mental abilities, physical abilities or personality traits, depending on the job's requirements. If one were to assess whether candidates could solve decisive and communicate effectively. Alternatively, if one were selecting an administrative assistant, such as the ability to perform work conscientiously with speed and accuracy would be such more important for identifying capable candidates. Some worker-oriented or job analysis data are used as a basis for developing assessment method, that focus on a job candidate's underlying abilities to perform important work task.

In general, any organization interviews only divide either internal or external both selection. Internal selection refers to situations where organization is hiring or promoting from within, whereas, external selection refers to situations where an organization is hiring from the outside. When some assessent methods are used more commonly for external selection. ( e.g. cognitive ability tests, personality tests, integrity tests). There are numerous examples of organizations that have used one or more of the following tools for internal selection, external selection or both. I shall explain what the differences for these interview test methods as follow:

What is cognitive ability tests. These assessment measure a variety of mental abilities, such as verbal and mathematical ability, reasoning ability and reading comprehension. Cognitive ability tests have been shown to be extremely useful predictors of job performance and thus are used frequently in making selection decisions for many different types of jobs ( Hunter, J. 1986, Ree, M.J. & Teachout, M.S. 1984, Gottredson, L.S. 1982).

Cognitive ability tests typically consist of multipler choice items that are administered via a paper-and-pencil instructment or computer. Some cognitive ability tests contain test items that need various abilities, e.g. verbal ability, numberical ability etc. But then sum up the correct answers to all of the items to obtain a singl total score. The total score then represents a measure of general mental ability. If a separate score is computed for each of the specific types of abilities, then the resulting scores represent measures of the specific mental abilities.

Job knowledge tests mean these assessments measure critical knowledge areas that are needed to perform a job effectively. Typically, the knowledg areas measured represent technical knowledge. Job knowledge tests are used in situations m where candidates must clearly possess a body of knowledge prior to job entry. Job knowledge tests are not appropriate to use in situations where candidates will be trained after selection on the on knowledge areas who need to have. Like cognitive ability tests, job knowledge tests typically consist of multiple-choice items administered via a paper-and-pencil instrument or a computer , although essay items are sometimes included in job knowledg tests ( Hunter, J. 1986).

Personality tests that assess traits relevant to job performance have been shown to be effective predictors of subsequent job performance. The personality factors that are assessed most frequently in work situations include conscientiousness, extraversion, agreeableness, openness to experience and emotional stability ( Barrick, M.R. & Mount, M.K. 1991, Costa, P.T. Jr., & Mccae, r. R. 1982).

Research has shown that conscientiousness is the most useful predictor of performance across many different jobs. Although some of the other pesonality factors have been shown to be useful predictors of peformance in specific types of jobs ( Hough, L.M. 1992). It can consist of several multipe choice or true/false items measuring each personality factor. Like cognitive ability and knowledge tests, which are also administered in a paper-and-pencil or computer format.

Biographical data ( biodata) inventories, which ask job candidates questions covering their background, personal characteristics or interests have been shown to be effective predictors of job performance ( Stokes, G.S. & Owens, W.A. 1994, Shoenfeldt, L.F. 1999). Another form of a biodata inventory is an instrument called an " accomplishment stored". With this types of assessment, candidates prepare a written account of their most meritorious accomplishments in key skill and ability areas that are required for a job , e.g. planning and organizing, customer service, conflict resolution ( Hough, L.M. 1984).

Integrity tests measure attitudes and experiences that are related to an individual honesty, trustworthiness and dependability ( Sackett, P.R. & Wanek, J.E. 1996). It is typically multiple-choice in format and administered via a paper-and-pencil instrument or a computer.

Physical fitness tests are used in some selection situations. These tests require candidates to perform general physical activities to assess one's overall fitness, strength or other physical capabilities necessary to perform the job.

Situational judgement tests provide job candidates with situations that who would encounter on the job and viable options for handling the presented situations ( Mecichmann, D., Schmitt, N. & Harvey, V.S. 2001). depending on how the test is designed , candidates are asked to select the most effective or most and least effective ways of handling the situaton from the response options provided. Situational judgement tests are more complicated to develop than many of the other types of assessments. It is because more difficulty in developing scenarios with several likely response options that are all viable, but in fact, some are reliably rated as being more effective than others. Situational judgement tests are typically administered in written or paper-and-pencil test booklet or on a computer.

Assessment centers are a type of work sample test that is typically focused on assessing higher-level managerial and supervisory competencies ( Thornton, G.C III 1992). Assessment centers usually last at least a day and up to several days. They typically include role-play exercises in -basket exercises, analytical exercises and group discussion exercises. Trained assessors observe the performane of candidates during the assessment process and evaluate them on standardized rating. Some assessment centers also include other types of assessment methods, such as cognitive ability, job knowledge and personality tests. It should be noted selection purposes that assessment centers aren't only used for comprehensive development feedback to participants.

Physical ability tests are used regularly to select workers for physiclly demanding jobs, such as police officers and firefighters. These test are similar to work sample tests in that who typically require candidates to perform a series of actual job tasks to determine whether or not who can perform the physical requirements of a jobs. Physical ability tests are often scored in a pass/fail basis. To pass, the complete set of taks that comprise the test must be properly completed within a specified timeframe.

How to criteria for selecting and evaluating assessment methods in interview?

Properly identifying and implementing formed assessment methods to select employees is one of the more complex areas for HR department to learn about and understand. This is because understanding selection testing requires knowledge of statistics, measurement issues and legal issues relevant to testing.

I recommend any interviewers need to understand important criteria to decide to choose which kind of interview test is the suitable to test applicant individual abilities in every interview such as below:

The first criteria includes validity. Validity means the extent to which the assessment method is useful for predicting subsequent job performance. Adverse impact means the extent to which protected group members , e.g. minorities, females and individualds over 40 score lower on the assessment than majority group members.

The second criteria includes cost. Cost is both to develop and to administer the assessment. Applicant reactions means the extent to which applicants react positively versus negtively to the assessment method. For example, cognitive ability test. on the positive side, this type of assessment is high on validity and low on costs. However, it is also high on adverse impact, moderately favorable. Thus, when cognitive tests are inexpensive and very useful for predicting subsequent job performance, minoritie score significantly lower on them than whites. There is no simple, formulaic approach for selecting " one best" assessment method, because all of them have advantages and disadvantages.

However, the most important consideration in evaluating on assessment method is its validity. Validity refers to whether or not the assessment method provides useful information about how effectively an employee will actually perform once who is hired for a job. Validity is the most important factor in considerating whether or not to use an assessment method because identify who will doesn't accurately identify who will perform effectively on a job has no value to the organization.

There are two major forms of validity: criterion-related validity and content validity is a simple example will illustrate how criterion-related validity can be established. Assume that a sales job requires employees to have a high level of customer service orientation and an organization decides to implement a selection test that assesses prospective applicants on their customer service skills. In order to show that the client skills assessment is a valid predictor of peformance , it must be shown that individuals who score higher on the assessment perform better. On the job and individuals who score lower on the assessment perform less well on the job. Thus, validity in this case would be defined as a meaningful relationship between how well people performed on the assessment and how well who subsequently performed on the job. Content validity approach to validation involves demonstrating that an assessment provides a direct measure of how well candidates will actually perform to job. This type of validation requires analyzing the job to identify the tasks that are performed.

What are the differences between criterion related versus content validation. Criterion-related validity can be used to evaluate the validity of any assessment where individuals receive scores that reflect how well who perform on the test and these scores are subsequently shown to relate to how well who perform on the job. Content validation can only be used to validate assessments that provide a direct measure of how well candidates perform job tasks or the content of the jobs, such as work sample tests. Otherwise, criterion-related validity evidence or contect validity . Thus, it is more desirable to obtain if it is possible to conduct a successful unbiased performance measures must be available. Unfortunately, performance appraisal ratings, which are the most commonly used performance measures can be inaccurate and often fail.

Adverse impact is examined by comparing the proportion of majority group who are selected from a job to the protected group members who are selected. When organizations are and should be interested in selecting the higher quality work force possible, many are also concerned about selecting a diverse workforce ought not using measures that will systematically produce adverse impact against protected groups.

In conclusion, either if an assessment method is shown to produce adverse impact and the organization wished to continue the last of that assessment, there are legal requirements to ensure that the method must have demonstrated validity or if an organization uses an assessment that produces adverse impact that produces adverse impact without the validity evidence. The organization will encounter challenges against which it won't be able to prevail. When evidence of validity can be used to justify and defend the use of measures that produce an adverse impact many organizations nonetheless attempt to apply the adverse impact produced be their assessment methods to extent possible in order to minimize potential interview wrong recuritment decisions and lack of diversity concerns issues to recruit any the most suitable applicants to do any positions in any organizations.

Reference

Barrick, M. R. & Mount , M.K. (1991). The big five personality dimensions and job performance: A meta-analysis, personnel psychology, 91, 1-26.

Costa, P.T. & Jr., & McCrae, R.R. (1992). Four ways five factors are basic. Personality and individual differences, 13, 653-665.

Gottredson, L.S. (Ed). (1982). The g factor in employment, Journal of vacational behavior, 29(3).

Hough, L.. (1992) The big five personality variables construct confusion: Description versus prediction human performance, 5, 135-155.

Hough, L.M. (1984). Development and evaluation of the " accomplishment record" methods of selecting and promoting professonals. Journal of applied psychology, 69, 135-146.

Hunter, J. (1986). Cognitive ability, cognitive aptitudes, job knowledge and job performance, Journal of vacational behavior, 29, 340-362.

Meichmann, D., Schmitt, N., & Harvey, V.S. (20010. Incremental validity of situatinal judgement tests , Journal of applied psychology, 86, 410-417.

Ree, M.J. Earles, J.A., & Teachout, M.S. (1994), Predicting job performance: Hot much more than g. Journal of applied psychology, 79, 518-524.

Robserton, I. T., & Smith, M. (2001). Personnel Selection. Journal Of Occupational And Organizational Psychological Psychology, 74(4), 441-472.

Sackett, P.R. & Wanek, J.E. (1996). New developments in the use of measures of honesty, integrity, conscientiousness, dependability, trustworthiness and reliability for personnel selection, personnel psychology, 49, 787-829.

Schuler, Randalls, S: Personnel and human resources management. Third edition, 1987.

Shoenfeldt, L.F. (1999). From dustbowl empiricism to rational constructs in biodata. Human resource management review, 9, 147-167.

Steven, Kay Cynthia (1997). Effects of pre-interview beliefs on applicant's reactions to campus interviews. Academy of management journal, 40(4), 947-966.

Stokes, G.S. Mumford, M.D. & owen, W.A. (Eds.) (1994). Biodata handbook paloacto, CA: CPP Books.

Thornton, G.C. III (1992). Assessment centers in human resources management Addison-Wesley,

Whetton, D.A. & Cameron, K.S. (2002). Developing Management , Skill 5th edition, reading, MA: Addison Wesley Longman.

Developing a successful employee training program steps

To develop one successful employee training program, any employer must need to follow these steps to achieve to train employees to raise efficiencies and improving performance successfully. I recommend these steps to develop one successful training program as below:

The first step: Calculation to every training budget, its needs how much costs to implement. Because designing and arranging one successful training program. It needs expenditure to buy the training course materials, tutors employment and rent office or hotel hall to teach the organizational employees expenditure.

However, training has been proven an important part of continued growth and forward movement for both the employee and the organization as a whole. The organization needs to spend too much money and time to organize any training department programs justified and ensure return on investment. Hence, expenditure budget is needed to evaluate how to spend how much on trainers employment expenditure, courses teaching purchase expenditure, rent office or hotel hall for training teaching expenditure. For example, if the training program needs to spend long time to teach or train employees. It will cause too much training expenditure is needed for long time training period.

So, an absolute training program expenditure budget, e.g. every month, every quarter, every half year, even every year training program budget expenditure. It can avoid actual training expenditure which will exceed budget training expenditure for long time in order to organization's training department.

The second step: Deciding what type of training is needed? Training should be provided before problems or accidents occur. This step is to identify what is needed for people to do their jobs in a safe and productive way. New recruits may need basic training where more experienced workers only need refresher training. To avoid unnecessary training, it is equally important to determine wht kind of training, it is equally important to determine what kind of training is not needed.

The third step: Identifying goals and objectives for your every training program. Clearly stated goals and objectives will identify what your employer to do, to do better, or to stop doing. They don't necessarily have to be written, but in order for the training to be successful, objectives should be thought out before the training begins. Such as when should the training occur? Is it initial training or refresher? Will training include hands-on use of equipment? How much time will be required to training? How will training affect production? Will training be scheduled during work hours or using overtime?

So, when you ensure whether what goals or objectives are for you training program. Then, you will analyze whether you organization is really needed one training program to train your employees or not.

The fourth step: Conducting the training program. Training conducted is needed by professionals will knowledge and expertise in the given subject area is most successful. There are many different methods available to training. It should allow employees to participate in the training process and to practice their skills or knowledge.

The fifth step:Evaluating the effectiveness, testing and evaluating is necessary to measure the success of training. Testing at the ned of training helps determine the amount of learning achieved. providing a training evaluation worksheet following the training program will measure the comfort level and understanding of the training they received. The trainees will also tell the trainers if they feel the trainers are qualified. Also, employees should immediately use the skills they know.

How supervisors observe new and transfer employees to determine of they are doing the job right and they are using the new skills. If the employees don't understand the information they learned in training, they will not use it.

The sixth step: Improving the training program, if after evaluation, it is clear that the necessary to revise the training program. Employers need to ensure every employee has been given the necessary information and training that will enable them to perform their job duties safely. In addition, you might using a different method or facilitator. Asking questions of employees, other training peers and of those who conducted the training may be of some help in improving any of the organization's training programs.

The final step: Designing the suitable type of training. How to design the suitable type of training program, it is very important to train every trainee to achieve their learning aim effectively. The types of training program may include as below:

(1) On -the -job training by peers or group training by management. It's advantages include that questions are easily answered based on experience, trainees are production with less cost and time since training is on-the-job. Trainees hear the same thing from peers working in field. Usually, there is more training time since it is continue.

However it's disadvantges include that trainees learn habits that might be unsafe, there is less control over what traninee's learn, trainees require a good trainer to ensure information is communicated properly and trainees may be rushed and not get adequate training if time is limited. It will influence whose job performance if they can't get adequate training, but they need to do their jobs as the same time.

(2) Next is live instructor lead training by a outside professional. It's advantages include trainees are motivated to learn because of personal attention by outside trainer, the weaknesses or wrong vire points easily identified by professional and are corrected at the time of training, training content is more controlled and objective, job interruptions are limited. So, trainees can focus on training only.

However, it has also disadvantages include that the organization may require a good trainer. He/she may be ill-prepared or unfamiliar with your organization. It could be more costly. The live outside instructor may be difficult to coordinate with other departments and arrangement. The class schedue may be difficult.

(3) Finally, it is electronic instruction on video based/computer assisted training program. It's advantages include that the trainer doesn't need to go to school classroom or workplace or hotel hall or company training room to

teach his/ner trainees. He/she can be self directed or self controlled time from video face-to-face computer training channel contact. It is good for annual or refreshed training, virtual environment may be favorable to production , it can be cost effective, due to not need to pay too much prebooking school classrooms or hotel halls rent for training many employee number every time, e.g. 100 to 1000 trainee number.

In conclusion, all above steps are essential needed to follow to arrange for every training program to any organization. So, trainer must not neglect all any one of these steps if the trainer hope whose training program can be achieved to raise every employee performance and efficiency after they attend the training program.

● What kinds of organizations need training program

I believe innovative organizations need training program to assist whose organizations internal department. What is training and development mean? It means a function of human resource management and it concerns with organizational activity aimed at improving the performance of individuals and groups in organizational strategies. It has been known by human resource development and learning and development.

Why does innovative organization need training program? When an organization is felt that it needs to be innovated, then training and development will be also needed. Training and development is a subsystem of an organization. It ensures that unnecessary repeated or inefficient or unmeaning jobs are reduced and learning or behavioral change takes place in structured format.

So, training and development or learning and development is one of the most important organizations which have better performance or efficiency change to be designed to enhance the fulfillment and performance of employees. So, it brings training and development programs are needed to be offered by a innovative organization might include a variety or educational techniques and programs that can be attened on a compulsory or voluntary basis by staff.

Before any organization's innovation, in general, they never used to believe in training. They were holding the traditional view that managers have responsibilities and effort to do training activities and training is a very costly affair and not worth. But, now the scenario seems to be changed. The modern approach of training and development is that organizations have realized the importance of corporate training. The training industry has been changed to create a smarter workforce and active the best performance improvement and raising efficiency result.

Training and development includes three activities: training, education and development. Training is one activity is both focused upon, and evaluate against, the job that an individual currently holds.

(1) Education is one activity foucuses upon the jobs that an individual may potentially hold in the future, and is evaluated against these jobs.

(2) Development is one activity, focuses upon the activities the organization employing the individual, or that the individual is part of may partake in the future and is almost impossible to evaluate in long term plan.

When an organization is innovated by achieving training program. It will earn these benefits as below:

(1) Discovering or finding employee weaknesses: Most workers have certain weaknesses in their workplace. Training assists in eliminating those weaknesses by strengthening workers skills. A well organized development program

helps employees gain similar skills and knowledge ,thus bringing them all to a higher uniform level. It is simply that the whole workforce is reliable, so the whole company or one department doesn't have to rely only on specific employees.

(2) Improvement in workers performance: It is a properly trained employees become more informed about procedures for various tasks needs. The workers confidence is also boostes by training and development. This intangible confidence effort comes from the fact that the employee is fully aeare of his/her role and responsibilities. It helps the worker carry out the duties in better way.

(3) Consistency in duty performance a innovated organization gives the constant knowledge and experience. Consistency is very important when it cases to an change organization's procedures and policies and ethics during execution of duty to all different level of employees from top to down levels.

(4) Raising worker satisfaction: Training and development can drive the great ability to let employees to feel they belong to the company or the organization that they require for and the only way to reward, it is giving the best services they can after they attend any training programs to let they know, and they can judge whether their job degre and effort can achieve to satisfy their organization's demand.

(5) Raising employee individual productivity and improving quality of services: Employees can acquire all the knowledge any one of training program. When they can not learn or feel tasks. Workers can perform at a faster rate and with efficiency thus increasing overall productivity of the company as well as they also gain new duties of overcoming challenges when they face them.

Also, employees can gain standard methods to use in their tasks to maintain uniformity in the output they give. Even reduced cost in supervision, training and development can utilize resources and there is no wastage of resources reducing extra expenses which can caused by accidents occurrence changes during they are working.

Thus, considerately the expected innovative organizations ought choose to set up one training and development department to train trainers to teach trainees in order to raise whose efficiencies and improve performance for whole efficiencies and improve performance for whole organization's innovation aim achievement.

● Reasons of employee training fails and how to solve

In fact, if organizations can not apply corrective ways to facilitate training for employees. It won't improve engagement, productivity and staff retention effectively. The question is why training program can not guarantee any organizations to achieve performance improvement and efficiencies.

The reason is simply. Because these fail training organizations apply wrong training methods, so they can not achieve to improve efficiency and performance under the least budget expenditure spending. The reasons include as below:

(1) The traditional training method is not suitable or still effective to the organization, e.g. it can not help the organization to improve skills, boost morale and build good teams and work processes. I recommend that to maximum the impact of training investment. Organization leader needs to understand how to choose the right training programs, when they need to arrange training and how to select training for the future.

Training must be satisfied to the needs of the organization's staff. The perfect training program ought be excited, interest and engaged the trainees, which encourages them to make use of the training when they need to do their day-to-day jobs to deliver the right training is so important to trainees.

(2) The boring training presentation. Another reason is possible that the trainees feel the training program is bored. It is simply repeat what is being said by the presenter. The audiences feel all the training courses are similar and they are very attractive. So, the training presenter ought consider training time is precious time and organization is paying it, he/she ought not waste organization's precious time to attempt to train whose audiences. So, choosing the right training, it is the trainer's responsibility and he/she must sure that time and money is spent effectively and the organization must get the best return.

So, choosing what kinds of training fastor which is important to influence whether the training is successful or fail. The different kinds of training may include: 3 D virtual learning and video tuition, face-to-face training, self and paced learning and webiners , e-learning and social learning. For example, e-learning is becoming more popular organizations realize the potential of training staff at their own time and with the least impact to productivity.

It is one kind of skillsoft offer, a wide range of stimulating, engaging and effective learning option. It is different to traditional face-to-dce training. It is exciting, fun internet training tool to let every trainee to talk between them and trainer to discuss any training topic and it can let the trainer explains to them to let they listen and see them clearly by e-learning video tool at home conveniently.

The another training fail reason is that it is important to arrange training that repects that every trainee has different learning styles and rates. Not every trainee is going to want to lead a discussion or be led. A good training course is one that allows everybody to get involved through a range of different methods.

In response to these requirements, skill-soft offers a range of memorable and engaging video-based presentations is the best training to listen the trainer's presentation only, when he/she is watching the video. So, they do not need to discuss and the trainer doesn't need to lead them to listen every online training program. When the trainer arrange the date and time to let all trainees to turn on computer. Then, they can watch the trainer's face and listen whose presentation from onlin video attentively. The trainees will be attractive from the trainer's online training presentation.

This online training method is more better than traditional classroom or workplace training course because a boring class is often the sign of a training provider who has not put enough effort into winning trainees' attention. However, e-learning techniques give mployees access to wider range of trining resources than ever before . They can watch videos, interact with others on the same course and revise topcis at their leisure.

Finally, the training fail reason is that without good planning to a new training program. So, I recommend any one expected training organization nees to consider these factors are related to how to plan good training such as below:

What skills and competencies are required across the training preparation?

Are these skills gaps across the organization?

How to solve these softskills gaps before to achieve one training?

Has the organization developed a training strategy that will ensure training is invested in with the objectives of the company in mind?

Has the organization developed an similar training implementation plan?

How and when will training be delivered?

Can it deliver this training program efficiently, attractively, satisfactory to rais employee productivity efficiencies and improve performance absolutely?

Consequently, I recommend whole organization's top to down level employees who need to participate how to prepare the new training program planning in order to avoid its failure chance. The top level includes executive and senior level managers, the middle level includes middle managers and supervisors and the low level includes the trainers ot the training program. Because training course preparation is whole organization management duty. It is ont only training deparment duty. So, above all these staffs must need to consider how to plan to achieve the training program successfully.

● Prediction rewards and costs of training program

　　How to calculate every different kinds of training rewards and costs? How to evaluate the training whether it is worth to spend time and time to invest to train employees ( trainees)? Whether does the organization need to arrange one training program to let employees ( trainees) to be learn new skill knowledge? To answer these question: I shall assume one training program is such as one lotteruy, the lottery buyer will not know whether he/she will win ot lose the lottery, but he/she does not attempt to buy the lottery who won't have chance to win the lucky money.

So, one training program is such one lottery. Whether at the organization as part of a training department of the organization, the training time and money and teaching course material and trainers and training teaching method etc. arrangement must be dominated by the trainer and organization's time. It is determined by their moods. These factors will influence whether the training program can receive rewards or not after it is spent any expenditures are related to the training. Hence, the organization must not know whether how much rewards will be caused by the training program. It only know to plan how much expenditure budget will be spent to the training program. So, training seems to be one lottery game to be played by the player, he/she needs to spend money and time to participate the lottery game.

Training course is similar to lottery game, the organization needs to spend time and money to arrange trainer and trainees to participate the training program. Hence, whether the worth of training which can earn rewards or not, it needs time to wait. It is hard to predict training reward.

Indeed, economists tend to be unexpectedly indifferent to matters of money, such as cost of every training program. It is a complicating superficial distraction that can usually be assumed away without much harm being ( trainer and trainees, employees) done, such as waste or loss of the organization's time and money and human resource to prepare every training program.

It may be natural to look to economics for guidance about earnings, such as future every training program reward. However, when any organization expects to innovate its working environment, office politics, increasing truth, employee royalty, honestry and lies avoidance, raising every high management, middle management and low level working employee individual power and fair promotion, which must need to accept to choose to arrange any suitable training program to satisfy every high management, middle managers and low worker level skills and psychological needs in order to raise their efficiency and productivity and performance effectively. Hence, every organization's innovation aim is similar to playing one lottery game. When the organization can achieve its innovation intention or aim after every different kind of training program.

Then, if it can innovate all its policy, strategy, improving every employee work efficiency and performance, raising productivity etc. different aspects successfully. I believe the organization must earn more reward, due to it has one successful innovation after every different of training to be provided to satisfy all different levels of employee needs from top to low level in the organization.

One open organization is applied one free market principles to time management, such as how it encourages its trainer(s) and trainees ( employees) to arrange whose time to participate every different kind of training program efficiently and effectively. So the organization and its trainer(s) and trainee(s) must need time to learn how to arrange time to participate every different kinds of training to avoid to influence their performance or/and productivity efficiency to be worse during they also need time to do their day-to-day job, due to training participation influences their time arrangement spending ( opportunity cost) between their working hours/time and their training participation hours/time.

Thus, arrangement training program time can also give chance to let every trainee(s) and trainer to learn time management issue. Hence, I believe training reward is not only money reward (e.g. profit reward). It includes skill, knowledge upgrade, innovation strategy, policy changing, employee royalty, raising work efficiencies, improving work performance intangible reward. These reward must be the organizstion's future intangible reward. Hence, intangible reward must br more worth to compare tangible reward (profit) because the organization's employees will hav positive emotion or happy mood to serve whose organization if the training program can satisfy all of their psychological needs for long term.

Hence, a small company is arranging only one trainer may have a reasonable reason to require a quick training program decision, but larger firms are playing lottery game to need time spending to decide a training arrangement which is required or not. It is not to their advantage to withdraw the training program offer immediately. They must need spend time to decide whether one training program is required or not.

If they do wrong decision to reject the training program, it is possible to bring future serious economic loss. It can include intangible loss, such as loe efficiency, and low productivity, worse efficiency , waste working time, low employee royalty and bad mood, instead of money ( profit) loss. So, large companies must need to spend time to decide whether very training program is worth to be needed to train their employees.

● Can train employees raise efficiency ?

For robot society case, if future our society will be a robot society, based on high technology that high technology can fully replace human beings and workers. Hence, it brings this question: Do any robot manufacturing organizations or applying robot tools to assist productivity organizations need training courses to raise employee individual manufacturing effort to learn how to apply robot tools to assist them to manufacture any products or learn how to manufacture robots to sell ?

Hence, when all artifiacts discovery as well as new technology are created by human intellection. We will achieve outstanding results higher than we expected , such as organization's innovation expectation, if organizations lead and manage correctly their intellection. No one doubts knowledge can manage everything.

Knowledge is a competitive advantage at any level: individual, organizational and country. In today's more competitive society, employees should learn for better knowledge skills and better performance. So, such as (AI) artificial intelligent industry development cost. I believe every organization must need arrange suitable training programs to raise their employees' efficiencies, productivities and performance by any kinds of (AI) training courses knowledge.

Such as (AI) development case, it proves that employee training of (AI) learning apply knowledge is one of the best ways to accumulate knowledge , use knowledge , update knowledge as well as transfer it to other people in the either (AI) tool applying or (AI) product manufacturing development organization. It is essential to pay more attention to managing the (AI) training knowledge process.

Such as the (AI) development industry, by instilling knowledge is the best way to convert a manual worker into a white collar worker and into a knowledge work, such as one white collar accounting clerk who needs to learn how to apply robot tool to assist he/she raises whose accounting productive efficiency or one vehicle manufacturing worker needs to learn how to apply robot to raise whose efficiency to manufacture any kinds of vehicles for whose employers when their employers accep to adopt robot technology to assist their employees to work to achieve raising productivities and efficiencies aim. So, (AI) training courses may be needed to satisy the employers' innovation needs when they choose to apply (AI) technology to assist their employees to work efficiently to do their day-to-day jobs.

Considerately, training courses skills have the ability to help employees to learn how to manage themselves. The ability of problem solving and decision making, as well as continuing earning consciousness during they need to work with (AI) tools as the same time in every working day in habit. Hence, training courses must have economic worth when the organizations need to apply robots ( artificial intelligent tools) (AI) assistanc to raise whose every employee efficiency and productivity and work performance.

Consequently, when society accepts robots technology can be applied to assist any organization's employee to raise whose productivity, efficiency or performance. Then, I believe (AI) training courses will be accepted to be needed to every innovative orgaanization. It proves training can arise intangible and tangible rewards or benefits to every future innovative organization, when they accept (AI) tools assistance to their traditional inefficient worker production method. So, it seems training programs will have it's worth to assist any organization innovation or development to achieve long term benefits.

● Training Super Talent Human Methods
   Want a Superior Workforce? How to Develop a High-Performance Workforce ?
A superior workforce is one that is collectively better than an average workforce. It often includes employees who are smarter, faster, more creative, harder working, insightful, aware of the competition, and autonomous. They are daily contributors to a harmonious workplace that emphasizes accountability, reliability, and contribution.

If your goal is a superior, high-performance workforce that is focused on continuous improvement, you need to manage people within a framework that focuses on performance management and development.To achieve this, there are seven components you need to implement. They work together to create a superior, high-performance workforce. Create a checklist to implement these components and to make sure you are following through regularly.

1. Hiring

Create a documented, systematic hiring process. Ensure that you hire the best possible staff for your superior workforce:

· Define the outcomes desired from the people you hire.
   · Develop job descriptions that clearly outline the performance responsibilities.
   · Develop the largest pool of qualified candidates possible. Search via professional associations, social media networking sites such as LinkedIn, online job boards, personal contacts, employee referrals, university career services offices, search firms, job fairs, newspaper classifieds, and other creative sources when necessary.
   · Devise a careful candidate selection process that includes culture match, testing, behavioral interview questions, customer interviews, and tours of the work area.
· Perform appropriate background checks that include employment references, employment history, education, criminal records, credit history, drug testing, and more.
   · Make an employment offer that confirms your position as an employer of choice.

2. Defining Goals

Provide the direction and management needed to align the interests of your high-performance workforce with your organization's goals and desired outcomes:

· Provide effective supervisors who give clear direction and expectations, provide frequent feedback, and demonstrate the commitment to staff success.

· Company direction, goals, values, and vision should be communicated frequently and in memorable ways when possible.

· Provide a motivating work environment that helps employees want to come to work every day.

· Provide an empowering, demanding, commitment-oriented work environment with frequent mention of company goals to support your high-performance workforce.

## 3. Reviewing Progress

Hold quarterly performance development planning (PDPs) meetings to establish aligned direction, measurements, and goals:

· Performance and productivity goals and measurements that support your organization's goals should be developed and written.

· Personal development goals should be agreed upon with individual employees and written. These can range from attendance at a class to cross-training or a new job assignment.

· Most importantly, progress on the performance development goals is tracked for accomplishment. Central tracking by Human Resources ensures the development of the entire workforce.

## 4. Feedback

Provide regular feedback to employees that lets them know where they stand:

· Effective supervisory feedback means that people know how they are doing daily, via a posted measurement system, verbal or written feedback, and meetings.

· Develop a disciplinary system to help people improve areas in which they are not performing as expected. The system is written, progressive, provides measurements and timelines, and is regularly reviewed with staff members.

## 5. Employee Recognition

Provide a recognition system that rewards and recognizes people for real contributions:

· Provide equitable pay with a bias toward variable pay using such methods as bonuses and incentives. Whenever possible, pay above market.

· Develop a bonus system that recognizes accomplishments and contributions.

· Design ways to say "thank you" and other employee recognition processes such as company periodic anniversary remembrances, spot awards, team recognition lunches, and more. You are limited only by your imagination.

· Despite the rising cost of health care insurance, which you may need to share with your employees, provide a continually improving benefits package.

6. Training

Provide training, education, and development to build a superior, high-performance workforce:

.Employee retention and education begins with a positive employee orientation. Employee orientation should give new hires a complete understanding of the flow of the business, the nature of the work, employee benefits, and the fit of his or her job within the organization.

· Provide ongoing technical, developmental, managerial, safety, lean manufacturing, and/or workplace organization training and development regularly. The type of training depends on the job. Some experts recommend 40 or more hours of training a year per person.

· Develop a procedure-based, cross-training matrix for each position that includes employee skill testing and periodic, scheduled, on-the-job training and demonstration of capability, for most hands-on jobs.

· Provide regular management and leadership training and coaching from both internal and external sources. The impact of your frontline people on the development of your high-performance workforce is critical.

· Create jobs that enable a staff person to do all the components of a whole task, rather than pieces or parts of a process.

· Develop a learning organization culture through such activities as "lunch and learn," reading books as a team (book club), attending training together, and by making the concept of continuous learning an organization goal.

· Make a commitment to both providing and tracking the accomplishment of the developmental activities promised in the PDPs.

7. Employment Termination

End the employment relationship if the staff person is not working out:

· If you have done your job well—effective orientation, training, clear expectations, coaching, feedback, support—and your new staff person is failing to perform, termination of employment should be swift.

· View every termination as an opportunity for your organization to analyze its hiring, training, integrating, support, and coaching practices and policies. Can you improve any aspect of your process so the next new employee succeeds?

· Perform exit interviews with valued employees who leave. Debrief the same as you would a termination situation.


· Use an employment ending checklist to make certain you have wrapped up all loose ends.

Training method can be applied to employees. Similarity, training method can be also applied to super-athlete sport man.How to Grow a Super-Athlete ? I believe that training must need to grow a super-Athlete. I shall indicate how and why training is needed to grow a tennis super athlete sportman.

The future of tennis training?

A quick analysis of this talent map reveals some splashy numbers: for instance, the average woman in South Korea is more than six times as likely to be a professional golfer as an American woman. But the interesting question is, what underlying dynamic makes these people so spectacularly unaverage in the first place? What force is causing those from certain far-off places to become, competitively speaking, superior?

So even here, at the core of one of the globe's brightest talent blooms, the question of that talent's source remains enigmatically tangled, perhaps as much of a mystery to those who nurture these athletes as it is to the rest of us. It's enough to make you wish for a set of X-ray glasses that could reveal how these invisible forces of culture, history, genes, practice, coaching and belief work together to form that elemental material we call talent — to wish that science could come up with a way to see talent as a substance as tangible as muscle and bone, and whose inner workings we could someday attempt to understand.

However, basketball or tennis sport men, talent is not one main factor cause their super skill raising. Training is one important factor causes their super skill raising. "This is a new dimension that may help us understand a great deal about how the brain works, especially about how we gain skills."

Its very inertness is why the first brain researchers named their new science after the neuron instead of its insulation. They were correct to do so: neurons can indeed explain almost every class of mental phenomenon—memory, emotion, muscle control, sensory perception and so on. But there's one question neurons can't explain: why does it take so long to learn complex skills?

"Everything neurons do, they do pretty quickly; it happens with the flick of a switch," Fields said. "But flicking switches is not how we learn a lot of things. Getting good at piano or chess or baseball takes a lot of time, and that's what myelin is good at."

To the surprise of many neurologists, it turns out this electrical tape is quietly interacting with the neurons. Through a mechanism that Fields and his research team described in a 2006 paper in the journal Neuron, the little sausages of myelin get thicker when the nerve is repeatedly stimulated. The thicker the myelin gets, the better it insulates and the faster and more accurately the signals travel. As Fields puts it, "The signals have to travel at the right speed, arrive at the right time, and myelination is the brain's way of controlling that speed."

"What do good athletes do when they train?" George Bartzokis, a professor of neurology at U.C.L.A., had told me. "They send precise impulses along wires that give the signal to myelinate that wire. They end up, after all the training, with a super-duper wire — lots of bandwidth, high-speed T-1 line. That's what makes them different from the rest of us."

It also left me thinking about the clusters on the talent map. Specifically, wondering whether these places quietly possess myelin-accelerating factors: i.e., forces and conditions that promote what Fields would call "circuit optimization." Might those factors help explain the success of these superior athletes?
Hence, I feel that training is one important factor to manufacture super sport man and super employee. Talent is not the important factor to manufacture super sport man and super employee.

● The talent management skill
raises organizational development
and motivation of employees

When human primitive society is farming primary industry, farmers are only using hand to grow any kinds of plants, vegetable, fruit , rice to sell. Then, the farming work system was organized in primary forms using simple tools and with the least expertise and with division of duties in farm tasks. But in developed farming society, the farming work division is complicated, the farming duties are specialized, and the use of advanced farming technology, such as one farming vehicle can replace farmers' hand to grow any kinds of plants on farms.
The science of growing technology can help any plants to grow in fast speed and kill any animals, they can hurt plants to grow easily. This is good example of human talent technique development in farming industry. It can increase any kinds of plants growing of efficiency in fast speed and short time growing in order to raise plants, fruit food productivies.
If human talent technique can be applied to our business society. Can human talent technique help any organization job characteristics raising efficiency and intrinsic motivation is more for the employees that are satisfied with their growth, and the employees with more experience were more satisfied with supervisor and collegues.
How can organizations apply talent management technique to raise work quality of the employees and their attempts? If any organizations hope to raise employee motivation. They need to concern how to change any job forms of content, job process to be more attractive. In order to achieve employees motivation more efficiently. For example, if the organization's employees can be motivated by more payments, fewer work hours, and suitable work condition. This kind of organizational talent management method ought bring employees motivation can be increased through providing independence and responsibility of the employees. The question concerns: Which factor or which factors motivate each employee in any organizations? Because every organization has different characteristics and different job title and duty. Some every organization factors motivate employees, they ought be different. Every organization

ought focus on why individuals choose certain behavioral alternatives for satisfaction of needs in order to seek what factor(s) can increase its employees' motivation. Hence, if the organization has high degree of job motivation and satisfaction. The organization can predict the organizational commitment positively. So, it seems that one high degree of job motivation an satisfactory organization can bring high employee productivities turnover.

Organizational strategic talent method aims to create an accessible source of talents for adapting the right individuals with the right jobs and the right time based on the strategic purposes of business. Because the lack of talent is the biggest obstacle on the lack is a kind of major strategic advantage. Hence, any organization managers must need to know how to manage talents. How to use the individuals and how strategically to place them in proper position. Managers must design the situation to have the maximum knowledge and information, innovation and effort. And identify and discover whom are talents scarce and underdeveloped resources, how to seek talented employees. Such as talent labor market, it has key factors influence the efficiency of entering the labor market. These factors are the analysis of the current labor market situation and the rational preference of specialization. The active search and the talent employees interviewing, talent employees labor market search, these components are any organizations' talent recruitment essential method, if they hope to recurit any talented people to serve their organizations absolutely. Instead of talent recruitment factor, the other factors influence organizational success. They may include: Whether the organization has implemented feedback surveys, sensitivity training, management network, practical research, and training the techniques of improvement of intrapersonal relationships. So, those soft skills will be any successful organizations' essential talent management methods. So, organizations can not neglect any one of these factors in order to employee talented people to serve their organizations effectively.

● What is strategic talent management skill?

Strategic talent management skill can maximize the competitive advantage of an organization's human capital, this talent management is even more significant to be needed in nowadays organizational management, e.g. how to develop a talent pool of high potential and high performance to fill the organizatons' any roles as well as how to develop in differentiated human resource strategy to facilitate filling these positions with competent and to ensure all employees are talent to continue commitment to the organizations.

It is important to note that key positions are not necessarily restricted to the top management team ( TMT), but also include key positions at levels lower than the TME and many vary between operating units and time. The reason is because any organization ought not need a stable top position, and this top position ought may be variable any time. For one bank organization example, it ought not only CEO top position. It ought follow its market need to change CEO position, e.g. sometimes the bank may have more than one CEO position, e.g. share selling division CEO, housing loan division CEO, investment division CEO. Moreover, the lower position , such as manager can also increase to two or more, e.g. house loan division can have one CEO manager two housing loan department managers, even more. If the house loan division needs to increase staffs number to do any loan administration, loan applicaion and loan confirmation tasks in the house loan clients number busy time. So, bank top management CEO and lower management manager positions number can not ought keep only one. It is one wrong talent management strategy. It ought follow the client number to decide how to increase the right employees number in order to decide whether the bank's any department ought employ one CEO or manager position or more in order to solve the bank clients need number. Because if the bank only have one CEO and manager to manage their department. They will feel difficulty, if employees and bank clients number are increasing suddenly. They will feel busy and feel stressful. So, the bank ought need to decide whether the only one CEO and one manager to every department in busy time. It is suitable to its any departments to cooperate efficiently. Because if its any one department's management is inefficient, then it will influence employee performance and client dissatisfaction. So, the bank talent management method is that any time changes CEO and manager number to any department. Hence, organizational talent management depends on employees, clients number , market need, labor market supply factors.

● Talent in the world of work meaning

   Talent in the world of work concerns talent management , high performers, high potentials and talent workforce segmentation. Talent should refer to a person's recurring patterns of thought, feeling or behavior that can be productivity applied. The sum of a person's abilities, his or her intrinsic gifts, skills, knowledge, experience, intelligence, judgement, attitudes, character and drive. Talent can be considered as a complex employees' skills, knowledge, cognitive ability and potential. Employees' values and work preferences are also of major importance, a select group of employees, those that rank at the top in terms of capability and preference, rather than the job, times commitment, willing to do the job, times contribition finding meaning and purpose in their work.
Hence, a talent person or worker who ensures the competitiveness, and future of a company as specialist or leader, through his organizational job specific qualification and knowledge , his social and methodical competencies, ans his characteristic attributes , such as eager to learn or achievement oriented. A talent person or worker has these characteristics: competence, knowledge, skills and values required for today' and tomorrow's job, right skills, right place, right job, right time and contribution , finding meaning and any nowadays talent person's characteristics.
Does talent refers to people ( subject) or to the characteristics of people ( object) ? Is talent more about performance, potential , competence, or commitment? Is talent a natural ability or does it relates more to further improving through practice? Talent is typically associated with athletes ( e.g. Olympians, exceptional coaches, extraordinary teams, musicians of extraordinary ability, singers with incredible voices). It is commonly understood as above-average ability for a specific function or range or functions. Rather than corresponding to " normal" ability, talent is considered a special ability that makes the people who posses, develop and use it in the specific area of their talent.
Consequently, talent is often meant to excellent performance in a given performance domain. But in working society, talent has another meaning, i.e. people posses special skills or abilities. For job advertisement in which talent refers to potential applicants ( e.g. talent wanted).
Talent s as a kind of natural ability, more than training to own personal skills capacity. In general, talent person owns a unique mix of innate intelligence or brain power, and a certain degree of creativity or the capacity to go beyond

estabished stereotypes and provide innovative solutions to problems in his everyday life more easily to compare common people.

In general, common people or student or worker can be taught to own skills and knowledge to learn easily. But , talent has characteristics much more unique. Therefore, talent is impossible to learn or teach easily. It is the person innate nature owns, talent can not really managed by any persons or organizations easily, because talent is always a function of experience and effort, e.g. an excellent sport person can be trained to be one excellent sport skillful talent person, even he has not one talent sport skillful person to any kinds of sport, e.g. riding bicycle, sport. If the sport person is not excellent in riding bicycle sport, but if he has a good trainer, he can teach good riding bicycle method or skill to be trained him to be one riding bicycle sporter. Then, for a long time riding bicycle learning perios, he will have possible to be one talent riding bicycle sport person. So, in some situaton, one non-talent learner will be trained to be one talent learner, if the trainer has good skills and methods to teach the trainee, such as riding bicycle sport case, it is not all riding bicycle sport person is one talent sport man. Their excellent riding bicycle skills need to be trained to raise their riding bicycle skills. Then, their talent on riding bicycle skills will be raised to be performed in possible. So, for sport man case, talent is not natural, talent sport man ( trainee) is trained by trainer.

Hence, creating a talent person, it depends on these factors: The right place, the right position, and/or the right time. Such as the riding bicycle sport trainee case, he needs have right riding bicycle learning school , e.g. riding bicycle facility, good quality bicycle and large bicycle indoor spor place to let the bicycle sport trainee to learn. Then, he also needs a good trainee to learn. Then, he also needs a good bicycle teaching trainer , he can teach good riding bicycle skill and fast speed riding and safe riding knowledge to let him to ride his bicycle in the riding bicycle competitive games in the fastest speed safely in order to win his riding bicycle competitors.

Finally, right time is also important factor, if in the time, the riding bicycle trainee has physical body hurt challenge or poor emotion psychological challenge. These factors will influnce his riding bicycle learning performance or abilities in order to achieve the best performance level. So, he needs to wait the time, he has good physical health and good emotion psychological time, then he can learn his riding bicycle trainer's riding bicycle knowledge and skill easily. Hence, one talent sport man needs have above these thress basic requirements: right place, right position, right ime in order to achieve the talent sport man training in success.

Training Super Talent Human Methods


● Non-training method creates talent young people

Want a Superior Workforce? How to Develop a High-Performance Workforce ?

A superior workforce is one that is collectively better than an average workforce. It often includes employees who are smarter, faster, more creative, harder working, insightful, aware of the competition, and autonomous. They are daily contributors to a harmonious workplace that emphasizes accountability, reliability, and contribution.

If your goal is a superior, high-performance workforce that is focused on continuous improvement, you need to manage people within a framework that focuses on performance management and development.To achieve this, there are seven components you need to implement. They work together to create a superior, high-performance workforce. Create a checklist to implement these components and to make sure you are following through regularly.

## 1. Hiring

Create a documented, systematic hiring process. Ensure that you hire the best possible staff for your superior workforce:

· Define the outcomes desired from the people you hire.
· Develop job descriptions that clearly outline the performance responsibilities.
· Develop the largest pool of qualified candidates possible. Search via professional associations, social media networking sites such as LinkedIn, online job boards, personal contacts, employee referrals, university career services offices, search firms, job fairs, newspaper classifieds, and other creative sources when necessary.
· Devise a careful candidate selection process that includes culture match, testing, behavioral interview questions, customer interviews, and tours of the work area.
· Perform appropriate background checks that include employment references, employment history, education, criminal records, credit history, drug testing, and more.
· Make an employment offer that confirms your position as an employer of choice.

## 2. Defining Goals

Provide the direction and management needed to align the interests of your high-performance workforce with your organization's goals and desired outcomes:

· Provide effective supervisors who give clear direction and expectations, provide frequent feedback, and demonstrate the commitment to staff success.
· Company direction, goals, values, and vision should be communicated frequently and in memorable ways when possible.
· Provide a motivating work environment that helps employees want to come to work every day.
· Provide an empowering, demanding, commitment-oriented work environment with frequent mention of company goals to support your high-performance workforce.

## 3. Reviewing Progress

Hold quarterly performance development planning (PDPs) meetings to establish aligned direction, measurements, and goals:

· Performance and productivity goals and measurements that support your organization's goals should be developed and written.
· Personal development goals should be agreed upon with individual employees and written. These can range from attendance at a class to cross-training or a new job assignment.
· Most importantly, progress on the performance development goals is tracked for accomplishment. Central tracking by Human Resources ensures the development of the entire workforce.

4. Feedback

Provide regular feedback to employees that lets them know where they stand:

· Effective supervisory feedback means that people know how they are doing daily, via a posted measurement system, verbal or written feedback, and meetings.
· Develop a disciplinary system to help people improve areas in which they are not performing as expected. The system is written, progressive, provides measurements and timelines, and is regularly reviewed with staff members.

5. Employee Recognition

Provide a recognition system that rewards and recognizes people for real contributions:

· Provide equitable pay with a bias toward variable pay using such methods as bonuses and incentives. Whenever possible, pay above market.
· Develop a bonus system that recognizes accomplishments and contributions.
· Design ways to say "thank you" and other employee recognition processes such as company periodic anniversary remembrances, spot awards, team recognition lunches, and more. You are limited only by your imagination.
· Despite the rising cost of health care insurance, which you may need to share with your employees, provide a continually improving benefits package.

6. Training

Provide training, education, and development to build a superior, high-performance workforce:

.Employee retention and education begins with a positive employee orientation. Employee orientation should give new hires a complete understanding of the flow of the business, the nature of the work, employee benefits, and the fit of his or her job within the organization.

· Provide ongoing technical, developmental, managerial, safety, lean manufacturing, and/or workplace organization training and development regularly. The type of training depends on the job. Some experts recommend 40 or more hours of training a year per person.

· Develop a procedure-based, cross-training matrix for each position that includes employee skill testing and periodic, scheduled, on-the-job training and demonstration of capability, for most hands-on jobs.

· Provide regular management and leadership training and coaching from both internal and external sources. The impact of your frontline people on the development of your high-performance workforce is critical.

· Create jobs that enable a staff person to do all the components of a whole task, rather than pieces or parts of a process.

· Develop a learning organization culture through such activities as "lunch and learn," reading books as a team (book club), attending training together, and by making the concept of continuous learning an organization goal.

· Make a commitment to both providing and tracking the accomplishment of the developmental activities promised in the PDPs.

7. Employment Termination

End the employment relationship if the staff person is not working out:

· If you have done your job well—effective orientation, training, clear expectations, coaching, feedback, support—and your new staff person is failing to perform, termination of employment should be swift.

· View every termination as an opportunity for your organization to analyze its hiring, training, integrating, support, and coaching practices and policies. Can you improve any aspect of your process so the next new employee succeeds?

· Perform exit interviews with valued employees who leave. Debrief the same as you would a termination situation.

· Use an employment ending checklist to make certain you have wrapped up all loose ends.

Training method can be applied to employees. Similarity, training method can be also applied to super-athlete sport man.How to Grow a Super-Athlete ? I believe that training must need to grow a super-Athlete. I shall indicate how and why training is needed to grow a tennis super athlete sportman.

The future of tennis training?

A quick analysis of this talent map reveals some splashy numbers: for instance, the average woman in South Korea is more than six times as likely to be a professional golfer as an American woman. But the interesting question is, what underlying dynamic makes these people so spectacularly unaverage in the first place? What force is causing those from certain far-off places to become, competitively speaking, superior?

So even here, at the core of one of the globe's brightest talent blooms, the question of that talent's source remains enigmatically tangled, perhaps as much of a mystery to those who nurture these athletes as it is to the rest of us. It's enough to make you wish for a set of X-ray glasses that could reveal how these invisible forces of culture, history, genes, practice, coaching and belief work together to form that elemental material we call talent — to wish that science could come up with a way to see talent as a substance as tangible as muscle and bone, and whose inner workings we could someday attempt to understand.

However, basketball or tennis sport men, talent is not one main factor cause their super skill raising. Training is one important factor causes their super skill raising. "This is a new dimension that may help us understand a great deal about how the brain works, especially about how we gain skills."

Its very inertness is why the first brain researchers named their new science after the neuron instead of its insulation. They were correct to do so: neurons can indeed explain almost every class of mental phenomenon—memory, emotion, muscle control, sensory perception and so on. But there's one question neurons can't explain: why does it take so long to learn complex skills?

"Everything neurons do, they do pretty quickly; it happens with the flick of a switch," Fields said. "But flicking switches is not how we learn a lot of things. Getting good at piano or chess or baseball takes a lot of time, and that's what myelin is good at."

To the surprise of many neurologists, it turns out this electrical tape is quietly interacting with the neurons. Through a mechanism that Fields and his research team described in a 2006 paper in the journal Neuron, the little sausages of myelin get thicker when the nerve is repeatedly stimulated. The thicker the myelin gets, the better it insulates and the faster and more accurately the signals travel. As Fields puts it, "The signals have to travel at the right speed, arrive at the right time, and myelination is the brain's way of controlling that speed."

"What do good athletes do when they train?" George Bartzokis, a professor of neurology at U.C.L.A., had told me. "They send precise impulses along wires that give the signal to myelinate that wire. They end up, after all the training, with a super-duper wire — lots of bandwidth, high-speed T-1 line. That's what makes them different from the rest of us."

It also left me thinking about the clusters on the talent map. Specifically, wondering whether these places quietly possess myelin-accelerating factors: i.e., forces and conditions that promote what Fields would call "circuit optimization." Might those factors help explain the success of these superior athletes?

Hence, I feel that training is one important factor to manufacture super sport man and super employee. Talent is not the important factor to manufacture super sport man and super employee.

● The talent management skill
raises organizational development
and motivation of employees

When human primitive society is farming primary industry, farmers are only using hand to grow any kinds of plants, vegetable, fruit , rice to sell. Then, the farming work system was organized in primary forms using simple tools and with the least expertise and with division of duties in farm tasks. But in developed farming society, the farming work division is complicated, the farming duties are specialized, and the use of advanced farming technology, such as one farming vehicle can replace farmers' hand to grow any kinds of plants on farms.

The science of growing technology can help any plants to grow in fast speed and kill any animals, they can hurt plants to grow easily. This is good example of human talent technique development in farming industry. It can increase any kinds of plants growing of efficiency in fast speed and short time growing in order to raise plants, fruit food productivies.

If human talent technique can be applied to our business society. Can human talent technique help any organization job characteristics raising efficiency and intrinsic motivation is more for the employees that are satisfied with their growth, and the employees with more experience were more satisfied with supervisor and collegues.

How can organizations apply talent management technique to raise work quality of the employees and their attempts? If any organizations hope to raise employee motivation. They need to concern how to change any job forms of content, job process to be more attractive. In order to achieve employees motivation more efficiently. For example, if the organization's employees can be motivated by more payments, fewer work hours, and suitable work condition. This kind of organizational talent management method ought bring employees motivation can be increased through providing independence and responsibility of the employees. The question concerns: Which factor or which factors motivate each employee in any organizations? Because every organization has different characteristics and different job title and duty. Some every organization factors motivate employees, they ought be different. Every organization ought focus on why individuals choose certain behavioral alternatives for satisfaction of needs in order to seek what factor(s) can increase its employees' motivation. Hence, if the organization has high degree of job motivation and satisfaction. The organization can predict the organizational commitment positively. So, it seems that one high degree of job motivation an satisfactory organization can bring high employee productivities turnover.

Organizational strategic talent method aims to create an accessible source of talents for adapting the right individuals with the right jobs and the right time based on the strategic purposes of business. Because the lack of talent is the biggest obstacle on the lack is a kind of major strategic advantage. Hence, any organization managers must need to know how to manage talents. How to use the individuals and how strategically to place them in proper position. Managers must design the situation to have the maximum knowledge and information, innovation and effort. And identify and discover whom are talents scarce and underdeveloped resources, how to seek talented employees. Such as talent labor market, it has key factors influence the efficiency of entering the labor market. These factors are the analysis of the current labor market situation and the rational preference of specialization. The active search and the talent employees interviewing, talent employees labor market search, these components are any organizations' talent recruitment essential method, if they hope to recurit any talented people to serve their organizations absolutely. Instead of talent recruitment factor, the other factors influence organizational success. They may include: Whether the organization has implemented feedback surveys, sensitivity training, management network, practical research, and training the techniques of improvement of intrapersonal relationships. So, those soft skills will be any successful organizations' essential talent management methods. So, organizations can not neglect any one of these factors in order to employee talented people to serve their organizations effectively.

● What is strategic talent management skill?

Strategic talent management skill can maximize the competitive advantage of an organization's human capital, this talent management is even more significant to be needed in nowadays organizational management, e.g. how to develop a talent pool of high potential and high performance to fill the organizatons' any roles as well as how to develop in differentiated human resource strategy to facilitate filling these positions with competent and to ensure all employees are talent to continue commitment to the organizations.

It is important to note thait key positions are not necessarily restricted to the top management team ( TMT), but also include key positions at levels lower than the TME and many vary between operating units and time. The reason is because any organization ought not need a stable top position, and this top position ought may be variable any time. For one bank organization example, it ought not only CEO top position. It ought follow its market need to change CEO position, e.g. sometimes the bank may have more than one CEO position, e.g. share selling division CEO, housing loan division CEO, investment division CEO. Moreover, the lower position , such as manager can also increase to two or more, e.g. house loan division can have one CEO manager two housing loan department managers, even more. If the house loan division needs to increase staffs number to do any loan administration, loan applicaion and loan confirmation tasks in the house loan clients number busy time. So, bank top management CEO and lower management manager positions number can not ought keep only one. It is one wrong talent management strategy. It ought follow the client number to decide how to increase the right employees number in order to decide whether the bank's any department ought employ one CEO or manager position or more in order to solve the bank clients need number. Because if the bank only have one CEO and manager to manage their department. They will feel difficulty, if employees and bank clients number are increasing suddenly. They will feel busy and feel stressful. So, the bank ought need to decide whether the only one CEO and one manager to every department in busy time. It is suitable to its any departments to cooperate efficiently. Because if its any one department's management is inefficient, then it will influence employee performance and client dissatisfaction. So, the bank talent management method is that any time changes CEO and manager number to any department. Hence, organizational talent management depends on employees, clients number , market need, labor market supply factors.

● Talent in the world of work meaning

Talent in the world of work concerns talent management , high performers, high potentials and talent workforce segmentation. Talent should refer to a person's recurring patterns of thought, feeling or behavior that can be productivity applied. The sum of a person's abilities, his or her intrinsic gifts, skills, knowledge, experience, intelligence, judgement, attitudes, character and drive. Talent can be considered as a complex employees' skills, knowledge, cognitive ability and potential. Employees' values and work preferences are also of major importance, a select group of employees, those that rank at the top in terms of capability and preference, rather than the job, times commitment, willing to do the job, times contribition finding meaning and purpose in their work.

Hence, a talent person or worker who ensures the competitiveness, and future of a company as specialist or leader, through his organizational job specific qualification and knowledge , his social and methodical competencies, ans his characteristic attributes , such as eager to learn or achievement oriented. A talent person or worker has these characteristics: competence, knowledge, skills and values required for today' and tomorrow's job, right skills, right place, right job, right time and contribution , finding meaning and any nowadays talent person's characteristics.

Does talent refers to people ( subject) or to the characteristics of people ( object) ? Is talent more about performance, potential , competence, or commitment? Is talent a natural ability or does it relates more to further improving through practice? Talent is typically associated with athletes ( e.g. Olympians, exceptional coaches, extraordinary teams, musicians of extraordinary ability, singers with incredible voices). It is commonly understood as above-average ability for a specific function or range or functions. Rather than corresponding to " normal" ability, talent is considered a special ability that makes the people who posses, develop and use it in the specific area of their talent.

Consequently, talent is often meant to excellent performance in a given performance domain. But in working society, talent has another meaning, i.e. people posses special skills or abilities. For job advertisement in which talent refers to potential applicants ( e.g. talent wanted).

Talent s as a kind of natural ability, more than training to own personal skills capacity. In general, talent person owns a unique mix of innate intelligence or brain power, and a certain degree of creativity or the capacity to go beyond estabished stereotypes and provide innovative solutions to problems in his everyday life more easily to compare common people.

In general, common people or student or worker can be taught to own skills and knowledge to learn easily. But , talent has characteristics much more unique. Therefore, talent is impossible to learn or teach easily. It is the person innate nature owns, talent can not really managed by any persons or organizations easily, because talent is always a function of experience and effort, e.g. an excellent sport person can be trained to be one excellent sport skillful talent person, even he has not one talent sport skillful person to any kinds of sport, e.g. riding bicycle, sport. If the sport person is not excellent in riding bicycle sport, but if he has a good trainer, he can teach good riding bicycle method or skill to be trained him to be one riding bicycle sporter. Then, for a long time riding bicycle learning perios, he will have possible to be one talent riding bicycle sport person. So, in some situaton, one non-talent learner will be trained to be one talent learner, if the trainer has good skills and methods to teach the trainee, such as riding bicycle sport case, it is not all riding bicycle sport person is one talent sport man. Their excellent riding bicycle skills need to be trained to raise their riding bicycle skills. Then, their talent on riding bicycle skills will be raised to be performed in possible. So, for sport man case, talent is not natural, talent sport man ( trainee) is trained by trainer.

Hence, creating a talent person, it depends on these factors: The right place, the right position, and/or the right time. Such as the riding bicycle sport trainee case, he needs have right riding bicycle learning school , e.g. riding bicycle facility, good quality bicycle and large bicycle indoor spor place to let the bicycle sport trainee to learn. Then, he also needs a good trainee to learn. Then, he also needs a good bicycle teaching trainer , he can teach good riding bicycle skill and fast speed riding and safe riding knowledge to let him to ride his bicycle in the riding bicycle competitive games in the fastest speed safely in order to win his riding bicycle competitors.

Finally, right time is also important factor, if in the time, the riding bicycle trainee has physical body hurt challenge or poor emotion psychological challenge. These factors will influnce his riding bicycle learning performance or abilities in order to achieve the best performance level. So, he needs to wait the time, he has good physical health and good emotion psychological time, then he can learn his riding bicycle trainer's riding bicycle knowledge and skill easily. Hence, one talent sport man needs have above these thress basic requirements: right place, right position, right ime in order to achieve the talent sport man training in success.

● Building high performance culture
talent management method
to organizations

Any human decision making can influence our organizations value. How our culture causes may influence how we can fall serve to our organization? Our organization culture can influence how we bring energy, creativity and enthusiasm to our organization value. So, it brings these questions concern how our organizational culture can bring high performance to our organization productivity , such as:

How can our talent management to our organization culture can bring consequence on increasing profits and shareholder value, attracting and keeping talented people, building brand loyalty, ensure that ethic corporate culture to achieve high performance. Also, how out talent management to our organization culture can help we deliver high quality , cost effective services and a sustainable society service. The key questions concern how building a high performance culture to our private and public sector organizations. We need to know that the culture of an private organization's source comes from its competitive advantage and brand differentiation, as well as the culture of an public organization source comes from its cost effectiveness and quality of services.

Hence one successful public and private organization cultures may bring these performance effects: values and behaviors drive cutlure, culture drives employee fulfilment, employee fulfilment drives customer satisfaction and mission achievement. Because any organizational staff's cultural behavior, their principles, ideas, or briefs that people ( staffs) can influence organizational operation. For example, similarly, if the organization has potentially limiting value of bureaucracy, that it can cause rigidity and limit the free idea expression from any staffs. This organization cultural value will limit employees' personal value and poor financial peformance because it's organizational cultural value is not " open mind" or let employees have chance to share their opinions to discuss their company any issues very easily.

So, bureaucracy cultural value will be weakness to any organizations, e.g. some countries' government organization is bureaucracy cultural value. It can not innovate or raise or improve its government internal organization different departments' efficiencies very easily. But, it needs lone time to do any decisions . It is a bureaucracy organization's weakness or easy cooperation between the values of the culture of the organization and the personal values of employees, the final effect is low performance, which can further resultin low levels of staff engagement and poor quality of products and services. All these bureacucracy organization's long time decision making and messages need long time delivery factors can have a significant impact on the financial performance or low efficiency ( inefficiency) of the organization or its ability to deliver services of low quality.

Hence, if the organization's culture is able to attract and retain talented individuals. This gives organizations a significant commercial advantage, especially when talent is in short supply. Strong brand values are always those with the strongest internal cultures. So, it has relationship between high cultures, brand differentiation, or retaining talented individuals and the successful is highly dependent on the culture that the leaders create.

Also, the culture that leaders create is highly dependent on the behaviors of the leaders and their relationship to other leaders in the organization, and their relationships with their employees. It explains that why organizations with strong , high performing cultures tend to replace their leaders by promoting from within, whereas low -performing cultures tend to replace their leader's with external candidates. The reason is because that by promoting from within, organization's good cultures are also to retain their successful leadership styles. However, organization's culture and desired leadership styles is one kind of management feeling from all employees and managers working behavior and attitude. Any organizations must need spend time to research what their organization culture is and what leaders desired leadership styles are.

How can we know our organization culture is suitable to let our low level and high level employees accept to work together? We can follow those change to judge whether our organization's culture is suitable organization culture. The change may include: A different way of doing. Doing what we do now, but doing it in a more efficient, productive, or quality -enhancing way, a different way of being. Transformation involves changes at the deepest levels of beliefs, values and assumptions. Transformation occurs when we are also be learnt from our mistakes, are open to a new future, and can let revise of the part mistakes.

Hence talent retension is critically important for all organizations for two main reasons: Turnover is expensive and top performers drive business performance. Turnover costs arise from the direct replacement costs of talent acquisition, the opportunity costs of vacant positions and time to productivity, in the result costing of business performance. Hence, one organization has good cultural value, it may have characteristics: The organization can have confidence to recruit the right people in the first place, it can improve the line manager's ability to manage, it can give employee's constrant feedback about clear, meaningful goals, it can empower employees to manage their own careers, it can continuously measure and improve retention strategies easily. All of these are any good cultural organization's characteristics.

Hence, talent managemen may a key aspect of human resources management strategy in any organizations? In this age of the rapily expanding knowledge-based economy, the quality of human resources has assumed crucial importance. This complex and demanding market environment has a demand for outstanding and talented with high development potential, being the lever of growth in shareholder value. The organization talent leader has attitude, a performance -oriented approach, the ability to persuade, teamwork, emotional intelligence, flexibility, a high tolerance to change, and highly developed specialist technical skills. However, it has relationship between developing talent people and good organizational culture. Because developing talent people and good culture, then it can develop talent people easily.

How can we know that the organization has good culture. Similarly, if we discover that the organization has many talent people are working, then we may assume that the organization has good organizational culture . We can follow how many employees' talent level, they own and they are working in the organization. The talent level can consist of these several points: Extraordinary intellectual skills ( general and specialist), a creative attitude ( originality, flexible thinking and acting, solving unconventional problems easily, and a high tolerance to risk, change , uncertainty) and a commitment to work ( self-disciplined, persistent in pursuing goals, and hard-working). Hence, if the organization has many employees, who own extraordinary intellectual skills, a creative attitude, a commitment to work attitude. Then, I believe that the organization owns many talent suitable to let them to feel to work.

Hence, what is talent management cultural organization? A talent management cultural organization can ensure that talent people are attracted, retained, motivated and developed in line with the needs of the organization, i.e. the most valuable staff memebers, by creating conditions conducive to their potential development. So that they can be put to use for the company's operations for as long as possible, talent management is a set of activities taken vis-a vis personnel with outstanding talents to ensure their development and increase their operational efficiency, when immediately achieve corporate goals easily. A talent management cultural organization consists of searching for talents inside or outside the organization, undertaking special activities to enable their development, training and career path planning and ensuring that their remuneration is competitive with that of other organizations, talent management involves implementing a set of key activities as part od human resource management , when immediately applying more advanced methods and techniques.

Hence, one talent management cultural organization ought own above all these characteristics. A talent management cultural organization can reduce employee turnover number, they can keep talent people continue stay to work in their organization for long time. So, when the organization's workforce ( employee leaving) turnove rate reduces, in special talent employees, then its high performers and employees with hard-to-replace skills, these group employees will continue work in their present employers for long time.

Similarly, any talent management cultural organization really can prove itself is one successful organization , it must need long time to learn or improve itself strategy in order to attract many talent employees choose itself organization to work. Hence," learning how to attract talent employee method", which is a important factor to influence whether the organization can be one talent management cultural organization in success.

How can a digital platform one online talent platform assist organizations to recruit talent people? Online talent platforms can ease a number of these dysfunctions by more effective connecting individuals with work opportunities. Labor markets are arriving in the form of digital platforms, the very same technologies that have reshaped the businesses and consumer environment in areas , such as e-commerce.

Online talent platforms are marketplaces and tools that can connect individuals to the right work opportunities. The size of their user networks expand the pool of possibilities, and their powerful search capabilities in an efficient and personalized way. These digital platforms are rapidly popular, acceptable to apply on online talent recruitment method for any organizations.

Talent online recruitment platforms can help companies transform or change the traditional recruitment way or method. They hire, train and manage their employees. All this online talent recruitment method can give better-informed decisions about human capital produce better business results. In additions, online talent recruitment platform could improve signaling about the skill that are actually in demand across the economy. As this information shapes decisions about education and training, the entire skills mix of the economy could adjust more accurately over time.

Online talent recruitment platforms can take form of websites mobile apps, or proprietary corporate systems. They gather a huge volume of information regarding both individual workers and employers or work projects, then synthesize this data to match individuals with job opportunities and produce better work outcomes.

One online talent recruitment platform is a digital tools that enable users ( organizations) to post full time or part time jobs, create online resumes of individuals, search for talent or work opportunities, based on extended matching attributes, provide personal working experience and qualification data into company or worker reputations, skills, assess candidates' attributes, skills or fit, personalize onboarding, training and talent management optimize team formation and internal matching, determine the best options for training and skill development.

Hence, online recruitment talent management platform will be a good tool to any organizations' human resource department talent employee choice method to help them to select the most talent employee(s) to work in the right position and in right time. It can replace the traditional newspapers applicant recruitment method or outsoucing job agent applicant recuriment method or government labor department post recruitment method. When one organization has many employees, e.g. 100, even 1000, 10000 or more employees number. Online talent recruitment platform can help it to reduce to spend much time to choose whom are the right applicatns to apply the job position, because ( artificial intelligence ) AI technology can replace human's judgement ability, it's judgement accurate level may exceed to human judgement level to choose the right applicants to enter the next interview stage. So, it explains that why online talent recruitment platform can replace any organization's human resource department's CV sceening process. It is one good (AI) online recruitment platform to help any recruiters' CV sceening process to be avoided, when (AI) online recruitment CV screening platform method is invented to assist any large organizations' human resource department to reduce time and staff nervous to do every applicant's CV screening activity. This is one good talent management application and recruitment and selection method to any large organizations' large human resource recruitment process.

Among young people are potential philosophers, artists, writers, entrepreneurs, whether training method is one important factor to create or manufacture any one of young peole to be super talent person successfully in our society. Some psychologists or behavioral scientists or doctors believe that formal educational (school) training is only the important method to train super talent young people. But, other some psychologists or behavioral scientists or doctors , they argue that formal educaiton ( school) training is not the main method to create any one super talent young person in our society.Otherwise, they also feel that non-formal educaiotn method will be easily to create or manufacture one real super talent person in our society nowadays.

I agree the later professional groups' view point any more. I believe that the young person himself/herself free learning
atitude factor is the most influential method to attract any one capacity within the young person to be one super talent person in society in possible more. The super talent young people can discover or seek whether what the real capability, they own
in success. They have these same characteristics: They can spend time to attempt to seek whether what their talent capability may own in order
to develop their talent capabilities. Moreover, they do not need any teachers to teach how they may discover their talent capabilities in success in classrooms. Otherwise, they accept to spend their extra non-schooling time to seek whether what kind of talent capabilities , they may own in habit. Because when they feel what kind of talent capabilities that they may own in possible, then they will have habitual behaviors to be creative and innovative to their specialized talent undiscovered capabiliities often. Due to their accumulative time creates and innovates and concentrate on learning their one kind of talent capability, then they can enhance their the ability of non-formal education learning experience method to create or upgrade or raise the kind of their talent capabilities easily.

The question concerns: How do these common young people not need training method to create or innovate or raise
their talent capabilities to become one super talent young person in success? In fact, any one super talent person, he/she
must be common person in past long time before. It depends on whe he/she can discover or seek whether what the real talent capability that he/she may own in order to upgrade or raise himself/herself this kind of talent capability

in success. Even, when he/she knows or ensures that this kind of talent capability , he/she has owned really. He/she also needs long time to learn in order to upgrade or raise this kind of talent capability. SO, any one super talent young person must need long time to learn the kind of capability in order to be the kind of capability super talent young person.

Hence, it explains why school formal educaiton can not train any super talent students focus on one kind of capability in success. Schools can only provide one group students classroom learning environment to train any one common lazy student to be hard student to attempt to earn high grade to each subject in order to graduate to seek any kinds of occupation in achievement in our society. Otherwise, any one super talent owning one kind of capability at least person, who will not need school learning training method.

They need to spend time to discover any one kind of talent capability , that they own in possible in order to attempt to learn how to upgrade or raise their this kind of themselve owning capability to be raised to super talent capability level, e.g. some super talent pinano music tool player, when he/she feels interest to play pinano music tool, then he/she will spend extra time to learn how to play this kind of pinano music
tool in order to create many good pinano music to let audiences to listen. They do not feel formal education training method can
raise their playing pinano music tool skill. They choose to learn from themselves at home in their extra time. So, non formal education learning method has more successful chance to train one common pinano music player to be one super talent pinano music player to compare formal education learning method consequently.

Hence, young people need know how to create and innovate their capacities by themselves. This positive attitude is important in enhancing young peoples' innovative and creative potential in ways that are relevant to employability. It seems that non-formal learning method can support innovation and creativity in young people to their undiscovered capabilities to be upgraded or raised. Any countries government need to spend time to invest non-formal
education method to raise young people to discover and learn what their talent capabilities are. The non-formal eduational talent young capabilities plan aims and strategies and outputs may include as below:

It's goals is investment in non-formal learning , leadning to increased capacity for innovation and creativity in young people in ways relevant to employability,
enhancing user-freindly and efficient procedures and methods for recognition of non-formal learning in the development of innovation and creativity skills.

Targets set with indicators to provide signs of progress achievement. The implementing strategies can support non-formal education workers, especially youth workers, who work directly with young people, to raise the quality of provision, such as improving the recognition and validation of non-formal learning, providing (AI) artificialintelligent , robust and accessible tools and resources to support the talent young people capabilities discovering work. Developing partnership working relationship
between business and the formal education and non-formal sector, closing the gap between requirements of the

labour market and

the contribution of no-formal school learning, enhancing entreprensurial skills in young people.

In conclusion, non-formal school or non-formal training learning method or student himself/herself learning method can bring outputs to manufacture or create super talent young peron more easily to compare formal school learning method, e.g. one school teach 100 students, it won't create any one super talent capability of student easily. Otherwise, 100 young people who can spend extra time to learn how to upgrade or raise themselves owning capabilities at home. Any of one or more than one these

100 young people will have more chance to learn to become one super talent person who owns this kind of capability by himself/herself in success when he/she can accept to spend long time to learn by himself/herself. The reaons is that teachers can not persuade they discover to learn themselves capabilities more easier from themselves. So, one non-formal learning method can achieve these outputs, such as improved procedures and better use of non-formal learning method to measure and accredit non-formal learning, better use of methods to measure and access formal learning , improved provision of training and support for non-formal education workers, effective partnership between labour market and education ( formal and non-formal ) sectors, promotion of non-formal learning through financial support , technical advice, networks and databases, experiments to develop specific areas of practice. However, instead of young people need to spend time to discover what themselves interests or

capabilities are and learn them, the another most importance to achieve non-formal education method successful factor is that the expert group will assist itself country

government to work with formal and non-formal partners to ensure that ideas from social scientific research, literature, practice wisdom, policy and discovering any kind of capability consultation processes, inform understandings of any individual young person problems, situations and issues, as well as ideas about work that can enable desired outcomes and ways of monitoring and evaluating any individual young person himself/herself " capability discovery work" in order to create talent young person mission in success.

Psychological Research

Employee satisfaction measurement

● How to measure employee satisfaction ?

It has close relationship between employee satisfaction and work motivation. The right staff can work in the right position which can affect the effective productivity of the company. Also, if employees feel satisfactory , then the company can have more chance to raise (increase) productivity, responsiveness, quality amd good customer service performance. However, if any company want employees to work efficiently, then which needs to know that one of the biggest internal strength of the organization is the relationship and communication between employees and the managers. Besides, the biggest improvement is also needed in the field of the financial rewards, because most of the employees are not showing high satisfaction to them.

Whether how to measure what the level of employee satisfaction is accepted to achieve the stable productivities? The main subjects will be leadership and motivaton to answer this question. For example, supermarket organization, whether which factors could be improved in the target work in supermarket organization every day? I shall assume it has perhaps to cause job dissatisfaction if the supermarket has only the power of money as motivator in supermarket organization. Any organization has its culture. As supermarket organization has also itself culture. However, I believe that cultural traits that can affect the employee satisfaction in any supermarket organizations. Although, any supermarket organization has usually different departments to cooperate work together. Hence, if it has good organizational culture to make different departments, e.g. store, food, wine, stationery, clerical, counter etc. departments staff who can have good communication to work in comfortable cultural supermarket environment together, then its staff can have more ability to achieve the best work performance. How to solve this department cultural difference of challenge, I suggest any supermarket needs have good HRM plan to control its department's employee behaviors.

Human resource means the staff who work in a organization and the contribution who make with whose skill, knowledge and competence. The most important successful factor of knowledge based economy in which intelligent organizations are the key aspects of economic growth in the global economy. Why does organization need to satisfy employee needs? Because any staff trend to change working places often, any staff can change their workplaces to gain more respect and to feel more valued in their jobs. So, it can avoid staff turnover ( leaving) whose organization very easy if the employer can satisfy whose staff needs. Thus, human resource plan is needed to achieve policies, recruiting and selecting work force, training and development, workplace planning, ensuring fair treatment of employees, ensuring equal opportunities, assessing the performance of employees, managing employee welfare, providing a counseling service for employees, managing the payment and rewards systems, supervising health and safety procedures, disciplining individuals, dealing with dismissal or promotion, negotiation, ensuring the legality of organizations etc. concerning about managing employees' positive psychological issues, in order to build positive emotion to them.


● How can leaders satisfy employee needs?
Any organization needs have good leaders because leaders act to provide satisfaction or more likely to offer means of satisfaction to whose team members. Leaders don't necessarily motivate. A successful leader understands the needs of the others and persuades them to act in a certain way. A good leaders can make whose workers see that following the views of the leader's workers will get the most satisfaction out of their work. However, a person can be motivated without leadership. But leadership, however, can't succeed without the motivation of the follower's side. If a staff has the feeling that who can perform a higher level job, himself/herself who have the motivation to attend courses or train in another way to be able to perform at the required higher levels.

Douglas Mc Gregor's famous classification of theory x versus theory y is applicable for leadership approaches. In general, any staff has two kinds of psychological characteristics of either theory x person or theory y person.

Theory x assumes that in general most staff find working distasteful and usually avoid doing it if it is possible . That is why most staff must be controlled and directed, even threatened to perform the way the organizational goals will be reached. Theory x also assumes that staff want to be controlled and directed rather than take responsibility and that staff lack ambition. Otherwise, theory y on the other hand, is more likely to have roots in the recent knowledge of human behavior. It assumes that physical and mental effort in work is as natural as play or rest. So, leaders need to judge whether whole managing staffs ( team members) who belong to theory x or theory y kind of staff. Then, who will have more accurate method to lead whose team members easily.

What level of satisfaction to the organization's staff can achieve the best performance. I feel that when the organization can reach the willingness level to be told the extent to which any one of staff has motivation and commitment or self-confidence to accomplish a certain task. So, the willingless level is the most satisfactory maturity level to achieve the best performance psychological factor to any organization. Because of the maturity satisfactory level of employees is high, the employees are both willing and able to do the tasks given more efficient. Otherwise, if the maturity satisfactory level is moderate, leaders can concentrate on the relationship and participate in the decision making and willing processes as workers are able but may be unwilling to complete their tasks. Only a little bit of enouraging is needed. Otherwise, if the maturety satisfactory level is low, workers are willing but may be unable to complete the tasks, so leaders must push to sell the tasks and let the workers do the rest or leaders must tell workers what to do.

In this supermarket organization case, if supermarket's gocery department and logistic department and clerical or cashier departments and fishing/meet etc. department whose employees' maturity satisfactory level is low, then it is possible that who are unable and unwilling to complete whose individual department daily tasks efficiently and these different department managers need to concentrate on both relationship and task aspects to raise whose maturity satisfactory level to be moderate level, even the high level in order to achieve the best performance.

Leaders also need to concern staff job satisfaction issue. Job satisfaction is the reflection of a good treatment. It also can be considered as an indicator of emotioned well being or psychological health, even job satisfaction can lead to behavior by an employee that affects organizational functioning. Furthermore, job satisfaction can be a reflection of organizational functioning. Why can job satisfaction influence any organizational performance? The reason is some people like to work and who find working is an important part of their lives. Some people on the other hand find work unpleasant and work only because who have to do support their lives. However, job satisfaction tells how much people like their job. Job satisfaction is the most studied field of organizational behavior. It is important to know the level of satisfaction at work for many reasons and the results of the job satisfaction studies. In the workers' point of view, it is obvious that feel repected and satisfied at work, it could be a reflection of a good treatment. In the organization's point of view good job satisfaction can lead to better performance of the workers which affects how the result of the organization to achieve its productivities for long term.

So, any employer or leader can not neglect whose staff what job satisfaction level to whose staff in any time. In general, if whose staff can not feel job satisaction, who will choose to leave whose current employer more easily.

Raising employee efficiency

● How does one company raise employee efficiency

What makes one company more successful than another? It is possible to conern better products, services, strategies, technologies or perhaps a better cost structure. However, the final source is the best staff performance of good productive factor, because it can cause these result, also employees who are engaged significantly outperform work group and who are tangible asset to raise the company's competitive advantage where employees are the differentiator, engaged employees are the ultimate goal. What factors can affect job satisfaction. I find that agency theory might be helpful to explain how organizations need to think of their human resource responsible in producing the output needed by organizations to meet shareholders value. Agency theory is concerned with issues related to the ownership of the firm when that ownership is separated from the day-to-day running of the organization. It assumes that in all but owner managed organizations, the owner or owners ( known is agency theory as the "principle" of an organization must best authority to an agent -corporate management to act on their behalf) Shenkel, R. Gardner, C. ( 2004, pp. 57-59).

The principle recognises the risk, here and act on the assumption that any agent will look to serve its own as well as the principle interests as it fulfills it contract with that principal. However, this is not the situation in real life situation. As all agents are perceived to be opportunistic. Agency theory is therefore used to analysis this conflict in interest between the principal ( shareholders of organizations) and their agents ( leaders of these organizations). The agents in keeping with the interest of the shareholders and organizational goals turn to use financial motivational aspects like bonuses, higher payrolls, pensions, sick allowances, risk payments to reward and retained their staff and enhance their performance. However, given this perception, the principal in an organization will feel unable to predict an agent's behavior in any given situation and so brings into play various measures to do with incentives in other to tie employee's needs to those of their organization. However, the fundamental problem, dealt with is that drives or induces people to exploit their potential resources in the way they do in organization. The issue of motivation and performance are who positively related. By focusing on the financial aspect of motivation problem likes bonus system, allowances perks, salaries etc. I believe financial motivation and trying to Mallow's Basic needs non financial aspect why comes in when financial motivation has failed. So, employers need to evaluate the methods of performance motivation in whose organization in organizing some motivational factors like satisfies and dissatisfies will be used to evaluate how employees motivation is enhanced other, than financial aspects of motivation. I believe that with the changing nature of the work force, recent trends in development, information and technology, the issue of financial motivation becomes consent on one of the most important assets in an organization. The potential role of money is as conditioned reinforce and an incentive which is capable of satisfying needs and an anxiety reducer and serves to erase feelings of dissatisfaction.

In general, any organization can use performance or efficiency to measure its productivities. Such as, performance means the act of performing; of doing something successfully; using knowledge as distinguished from merely possessing it; a performance comprises an event in which generally one group of staff ( the performer or performers) behave in a particular way for another group its staff.

Efficiency means the ratio of the output to the input of any system. Economic efficiency is a general term for the value assigned to a situation by some measure designed to capture the amount of waste or friction or other undesiable and undesirable economic feature present. It can also be looked as a short run criterion of effectiveness that refers to the ability of the organization to produce outputs with minimum use of inputs.

Why does employer need to know how to motivate whose staff? What is meaning of motivation? Motivation means as the psychological process that give behavior purpose and direction to behave in a purposive manner to achieve specific unmet needs, an unsatisfied need, and they will to achieve respectively. So, salary, job satisfaction, job goal , reward will be task -related motivation since goals direct staffs' thoughts and action. So, motivation to staff needs have these factors expected. For example, phychological needs are the bottom of the staff, such as foods, air, water and shelter. Any staff needs a salary that enable then to afford adequate living conditions. Then, staffs need safety, psychological needs. They need to work for a secure working environment free from any threats or harms and organizations can provide these need by providing employees, with safety working equipment e.g. hardhars, health insurance plans, fire protection etc. Next, staffs need social needs and the needed to be loved and accepted by other people. Esteem includes the need for self-respect and approval of others. Finally, self actualisation is the top psychological need, it is capable of being to develop the staff himself/herself full potential. The rationale holds to the point that self actualised employees repect valuable assets to the organization human resource.

Why do employers need to concern flexible working arrangement? Employers need to concern flexible working arrangement if who hope employees can raise productivities and efficiencies to achieve the best work performance. Flexible working describes any types of working arrangement that gives some degree of flexibility on how long, where and when employees work. Because employees need time to learn a familiar phase with workplaces, flexible working arrangements have been an option in many employment sectors for a long time, helping employment meets the changing needs of their customers and staff. The reasons include customers expect to have products and services available outside of the traditional 9 to 5 working hours; employees want to achieve a better balance of between work and home life and organizations want to meet their customers and employees needs in a way that enables them to be as productive as possible. Organizations need to produce any products and services of the right quality and at the right price, under constant pressure. To meet customers' demands, sometimes new ways of working have to be found to make the best use of staff and resources. Flexible patterns of work can help to solve those pressures by maximising the available labor and improving customer service.

At employers, organizations also have a duty of care to protect whose staff from risks to their health and safety, e.g. stress caused by working long hours or feeling pressure to need to balance work and home life. However, flexible working can help to improve the health and wellbeing of employees and by extension, reduce absenteeism, increase productivity, and enhance employee engagement and loyalty. Flexible working time includes per time works often used in hotels, restaurants, warehouses etc. flexitime. Mostly used in office based environments for staff below managerial level in public and private sector service organizations; annualised hours often used in manufacturing and agriculture where there can be big variations in demand throughout the year.

Thus, I feel the flexible working and work life balance benefits can include a more efficient and productive organization, a more motivated workforce, better retention of valuable employees, a wider pool of applicants can be attracted for vacancies, reduced levels of absence and increased customer loyalty and working hours that the best suit the organization, its employees and its customers applications of knowledge about how people as indicators and groups, act within the total organization, analyzing the external environment's effect on the organization and its human resources, missions, objectives and strategies. So, it concerns how to predict staff psychological feeling to learn how to motivate who to work efficiently.

Why does manager need to concern employee's individual diversity need? Also, manager needs to know each person is substantially different from all others in terms of their personalities, needs, demographic factors and past experiences and/or because who are placed in different physical settings, time periods or social surroundings. This diversity needs to be recognized and viewed as a valuabe asset to organizations. Selective perceptions may lead be misinterprectation of single event work or create a barrier in the search for new experience. Managers need to recognize the perceptual differences aiming the the employees and manage them accordingly. These whole person effects between the work life and life outside work and mangagement's focus should be in developing not only a better employee but also better person in terms of growth and fulment. If the whole person can be developed, then benefits will beyong the firm into the larger society in which each employee lives. Because individual's behavior are guided by their needs and the consequences that results from their acts. In case of needs, people are motivated not by what others think who ought to have but by what who themselves went. However, motivation of employee is essential to the operation of organizations and the biggest challenge faced by managers. Organizations ought give more opportunities to let employees who can contribute their talents and ideas because many employees actively seek opportunities at work to become relevant decisions the stay or leave the organization, also managers ought concern any employee's individual skills and abilities and to be provided with opportunities to develop themselves.

Organizational behavior theory
● What is system approach?
What is system approach? All parts of an organization interact in a complex relationship. Systems approach takes an across, the board view of people in organizations and analyses issues in terms of total situations and as many factor as possible that may effect people's behavior. Three theoretical frameworks, the cognitive behavioristic and social learning frameworks, the basis of any organizational behavior model. The cognitive approach is based on the staff and organization expectancy, demand and incentive concepts. Because staff behavior on the basis of the connection between stimulus and response in any organization. The social learning approach incorporates the concepts and principle of both the cognitive and behavioristic frameworks. In this approach, staff behavior is explained as a continuous interaction between cognitive is explained as a continuous environmental determinants.

In the organizational behavioral model, there are some dependent variables like productivity, absenteeism turnover, job satisfaction, deviane absenteeism, turnover, organizational citizenship behavior etc. The reason of which staff try to understand. The cause of these outcomes like with some variables of individual, groups and individual level, these variables are called independent variables.

It seems different organizational workplace environments will influence staff's different variable causes to decide how to do whole daily behaviors, how to fit to work in the organization. So, any manager needs to know what every staff is individual characteristics to judge how to manager himself/herself. For example, if the staff is thoery x person, who will dislikes work and will avoid it if possible, who lacks responsibility, has little ambition and seeks security above all who must be controlled, threatened with punishment to get who to work. So, the manager's attitude is needed to control whom. Otherwise, if the staff is theory y person, who will feel work is as natural as play as rest. People are not inherently lazy,who have become the way is as a result committed, the staff has potential, under proper condition who learn to accept and seek responsibility, who has imagination creativity that can be applied to work, so manageer who is to develop the potential to the staff and help who release that potential toward common objectives.

Any organization depends on the external environment for two kinds of into outputs, which it transforms into outputs and then releases in the hope that external environment will accept them. First, human input, employees and natural resources. Second, non human inputs, e.g. equipment, information, raw materials. However, organization needs to adjust to environmental demands, e.g. customer complaints, market research, financial reports, in order to keep to improve performance easily.

How to raise organizational efficiency? As systems theory indicates organizational effectiveness and time is considered as one element of a larger system of number of elements. The organization takes resources ( inputs) from the external environment, processes these resources and returns them in changed form ( output). According to system theory, effectiveness criteria must reflect the entire input process, output cycle, not simply output and must also reflect the interrelationships between the organization and its outside environment. In relation to environmental circumstances organization passes through different phases of lifecycle like forming, developing , maturing and declining and the appropriate criteria of effectiveness must reflect the stage of the organization's life cycle.

The criteria of effectiveness are also time based short run ( results of actions concluded in a year or less), intermediate run ( when effectiveness of individual, group or organization is considered for a longer period, perhaps five years and long run for this the time frame is indefinite future. The four short run effectiveness criteria are quality, productivity, efficiency and satisfaction. Three intermediate criteria are quality, adaptiveness, efficiency amd satisfaction. The two long run criteria are quality and survival. So, any organization needs have effectiveness criteria because effectiveness criteria can reflect the stage is of the organization's life-cycle ( which includes stages of growth, maturation and decline) and short, intermediate and long term perspectives. Quality means the total quality control rank among the most used programs to meet customers' changing demand. Hence, employee's indiviaual satisfaction will influence productivity. Because productivity reflects the relationship between the organization's inputs and outputs and measures of productivity include profit, sales, market share. For example, patients released, clients served concerns the relationship between employees' satisfaction and clients' overall satisfaction. When the employee feel more satisfactory, then who will work more efficient or who will serve the clients more pleasant. Then, the customers will have more chance to feel more satisfactory from the staff's individual service.

Efficiency is the ratio of outputs to inputs. It focuses on the entire input process output cycle, emphazing inout and progess. Measures of efficiency include rate of return on capital, or assets, unit cost, waste, downtime, occupancy rates and cost per patient/student etc. customers. Satisfaction meets employee needs. It recognizes the organization is as social system that benefit its participants. Measures of satisfaction include turnover, absenteeism and employee attitudes. Adoptiveness means the degree to which the organization can and does respond to internal and external changes. It relates to management's ability to sense environmental changes and changes within the organizaton. There are no specific measure of adaptiveness, but certain progress, e.g. employee training and career counseling increase its capacity to deal with it. Finally, development means the ability of the organization to increase its capacity to deal with environmental demand. So, if the organization hope to be survival in the long term, then it needs to achieve training programs and organizational development to be represent the organization's investment in survival.

Employee satisfaction methods

● How can satisfy to employees' needs ?

How can satisfy to employees? Because a high rate of employee is directly related to a lower turnover rate. Thus, keeping employees' satisfied with their careers should be a major priority for every employers. Reasons why employees can become discourages with jobs and design, including high stress, lack of communication within the organization, lack of recognition, or limited opportunity for growth. So, management need actively seek to improve these factors to avoid if who hope to lower turnover rate. However, some employee will often be feel bored with the work because there is no intrinsic motivation to succeed. Finding the daily same job duties can reduce the individual's motivation to succeed to raise desire to show up to work and to do the job well. In this case, the employee may continue to come to work, but whose efforts will be minimal.


Stress is another factor to cause low performance. Branham (2005) indicates that " it seems clear that one quarter to one half of all workers are feeling some level of dysfunction, sue to stress, which is undoubtedly have a negative improve on their productivity and the probability that they will stay with their employers."
However, stress can be caused by these factors, e.g. in the situation, when a company can't or won't supply the tools necessary to produce or work efficiently on the job. This produced higher stress levels because these workers are expected to perform at certain rates, yet who are unable to do so. This results in lower productivity and higher turnover because quotes can't be met by the employees. On staff knowing that management is able to provide the tools essential for the position is important to employee trusting the intentions of their employer.


Dissatisfaction with the job many come from sources other than stress or poor fit between employee and the job. Employers that are deemed unethical by workers because who appear to care about company revenues, rather than the employees that are working for them. In the result, the employer may lead to job dissatisfaction, and raise the company's turnover rate.

Lack of communication in the workforce is another major contributor to dissatisfaction. Bad communication leaves employees feeling disconnected from the organizations. This is detrimental to wellbeing of the company because when an employee feels neglected, who will trend to perform at a lower level because who feels unsure of whose position within the company and wonders what whose purpose is within the workplace. Also, employees may be unaware of how whose performance measures up to that of their co-workers and have no sense of who can improve. So, without communication, it becomes difficult for employees to make any progress in their efficiency. The employee may feel uncomfortable in the workplace, of who feel rarely be praises for the quality of whose performance. Finally, those factors cause the failure to provide employees with opportunities to grow within the company results in employee frustration to cause whose poor performance and low productivity.

Whether can bonuses increase raise employee satisfaction and team performance? In some occupations, I feel bonuses can raise staff performance, such as bonuses lead to happier and it can be used in the form of donations to charity organization or bonuses in the form of expenditures to pharmaceutical sales teams and sport teams organizations. However, employees are becoming more and more unhappy, more and more of time at work, hardly a formula for a healthy and productive workplace. In this increasingly negative environment, how can employers incentivize their employees to increase their happiness, job satisfaction, and job performance? Certainly, designing effective incentive schemes is a central challenge for a wide range of organizations form multi-national corporations to academic departments. Identifying the most effective strategies, a variety of incentive schemes and are suggested such as bonuses from fixed salaries to pay-performance from commission to end-of-year bonuses. It is based to assume that the best way to motivate employees is to reward them with money that who then spend on themselves. In general, existing methods of increasing workplace performance, including individual-based and team based bonuses schemes, which trend to reveal both benefits and unexpected cost. Whether the benefits of improving social life in the work phase can increase employee citizenship behaviors to satisfy the organization actual needs from these bonuses compensation schemes.

What is the effect of money on employee's job satisfaction and performance? On one hand, monetary bonuses have been found to have positive effects, increased productivity effort, performance and job satisfaction. Individual bonuses increase job satisfaction in part. On the other hand, individual incentives, such as large bonuses are often surprising ineffective increasingly employee morale and productivity. In an effort to prevent such negative competitive dynamic that can result from individual based-bonuses, organizations often change to incentivize employees for their collective performance, encouraging cooperation and teamwork rather than competition. Otherwise, in some cases, team based compensation schemes have been shown to raise this sense of cooperation between team members, inducing them to exert additional effort toward helping another worker to work together linked to employee morale and performance.

Whether bonuses can have a causal impact on employee. In fact, individual incentives, such as large bonuses are often surprisingly ineffective in increasingly employee morale and productivity. Also, rewarding individual employees can produce negative outcomes, as employees become reluctant to share information with others even at the expense of reduced output. In an effort to prevent such negative competitive dynamics that can result from individual based bonuses. Importantly, such increased cooperation due to interdependent rewards has been shown to improve team performance, suggesting that team based bonuses may be an effective means of improving employee social life. As with individual based bonuses, however team based bonuses offer important advantages, but also potential drawbacks. I suggest that prosocial bonuses can have a causal impact on employee satisfaction and performance, such that providing employees with money to spend on themselves.

How effective organizational communication can affect employee attitude, happiness and job satisfaction. Communication has been studied with regard to performance and job satisfaction, but the relationship with employee attitude and happiness has not been done in a higher education setting. The value of communication in an employee's choice to be happy is explained as it affects the individual, team and overall organizational culture. Attitude and happiness have been recognized by communication examination of organizational culture and emotion in the workplace. For example, for frontline employees are needed have cheerful and positive in the face or any situation. So, it requires the owners, managers and supervisors communicate to whose team efficiently.

Communication with telecommuting or remote workers is a consideration that organizations must take seriously more than 24 million people were working remotely in 2008 year ( World at work, 2009) and that number is steadily rising. Teleworkers report feelings of isolation, uncertainty, a lack of trust and lower organizational commitment with lower job satisfaction. Managers may not communicate the save way with remote workers as who do with employees who are in the workplace each day. Improve communication is important to hold employee engagement initiatives together, particularly in government public sector organizations must communicate throughout the entire cycle of planning, conducting and acting on engagement. So, I suggest some effective communication method to raise productivity and improve performance. Such as ensuring that employees understand their work expectation between their jobs and the organization's mission, meeting regularly with staff members, providing feedback as performance , as well as opportunities to grow and developing , even fail as a way to learn and holding employees accountable for performance, including with poor performance.

How to make a difference at work be more meaningful and purposeful workplaces. The workplace provides a wealth of opportunities and possibilities through which anyone can make a difference every day. Whether it's one person, one team or one organization, everyone has the capacity to create positive and meaningful change in their workplace in both small and large ways. How to foster the work motivation of individuals and team? Nowadays, some evidence supports claims that motivational programs can increase the quality and quantity of performance from 20 to 40 percent. Moreover, motivation can solve three types of performance challenges: first, staff are refusing to change often, second, allowing themselves to be distracted and not persist at a key task and/or third, treating a task as familiar, making mistakes but not investing mental effort and taking responsibility because of overconfidence.

Imagine that more than 50% of staff in your organization decided that from this point, who would work one extra day a work without an extra day of rest. What impact would their decision have on your organization's bottom line? What is the value of a 50% increase in performance by 100% of the workforce? Assuming that you may know some of the 50% , who do the minimum and a few of the 80% who could work much harder, do you think that there is anything that would convince people to work harder than who are now? Is it possible that half of your staff who admit that who could work much harder might actually decide to increase whose performance by 20% or more if they were adequately motivated? The best evidence suggests that highly significant performance increases are possible when motivational strategies are implemented ( Clark & Estes, 2002).

● How to achieve work motivation strategy ?

Work motivation is the process that initiates and maintains goal-directed performance. Without motivation , even the most capable person will refuse to work hard. Thus, motivational performance gaps exist whenever staff avoid starting something new, resist doing something familiar, stop doing something important or attention to a less valued task, or refuse to work smart on a new challenges, instead use old familiar, but inadequate solutions to solve a new problem ( Clark, 1998).

How can we make sense of such variety and get benefits as performance technologies? Is any given situation where we want to increase work motivation, we must determine what will convince staff to start doing something new or different increase their persistence at an important task and investment mental effort. The staff must believe that the motivator driving their enhanced performance will directly or indirectly contribute significantly to what who need to feel successful and effective. The motivator's work has to cost less than the value of the increased performance and it must meet both ethical and legal requirement. When it might appear that solutions have to be tailored to the different demands of individuals in a team. In the absence of a clear vision leading to work defined business and performance goals, people substitute their own goals and whose goals may not support the organization. So, it is important to ask about evidence for the benefit of all work rules and what might be cost of the rules more eliminated. What is gained by rules that staff can't take or eat in certain areas? Why can't they decorate their work space in ways that suit them? How much of staff's behavior must you control to achieve business goals? One way to motivate and staff and simplify organizational work processes is to eliminate all unnecessary rules, policies and procedures.

To learn how to motivate staff, we need to learn how to predict staff's individual psychological behavior. Organizational behavior is a scientific discipline in which large number of research studies and conceptual developments are constantly adding to its knowledge base. It is also an applied science, in that information about effective practices in one organization is being extended to many others. Organizational behavior is the systematic study of human behavior, attitudes and performance within an organizational setting, drawing on theory methods and principles from such disciplines as psychology, sociology and cultural anthropology to learn about individual perceptions, values, learning, capacities and actions when workings in groups .

Nowadays, why employees hope employers can give them to enjoy well life balance. The reasons may include care commitments to children or elderly relatives, education commitment that limit availability at times of the week/month/year, duties and/or interests outsid of work, needing to be available for people making a greater sense of well being and reduced stress levels. How to arrange flexible working in organization? For example, an employer may be thinking about introducing annualised hours in order to increase productiom levels to meet infrequent rises in demand because who can work well where, there are peaks in works, the workforce is required to be available with little notice. The employer could decide to meet these increases in demand by introducing overtime because it provides flexibility to meet fluctuations and it could be a smaller change to the organization than annualised hour. However, there are many different forms of flexible working. Flexible working can cover the way working hours are organised during the day, week or year. It can also describe the place of work, such as homeworking or the kind of contract, such as a temporary contract. Anyway, flexitime can operate in different ways depending on business need. On the one hand, there may be a system to allow employee to build up additional hours, which can be used to leave early, come in late, or take longer periods off with early, come in late, ot take longer periods off, with approval from line management. An example of this might be an assembly line or call centre where staffing must be scheduled to meet customer demand. For example, an employer needs to extend the hours that whose business is open to 8 AM to 8 PM, but can't afford the extra overtime. how to manage flexitime approach could help provide the additional hours, reduce staff numbers at quiet times and minimise the need for overtime. Employer may benefit from the opportunity to travel outside of peak hours and/or accommodate personal responsibilities, such as the school runs part time work is the must common types of flexible working. It's potential benefits include customer demands on be met and machinery can be caused more efficiently if part time workers cover lunch breaks/evening shifts and weekends, the working day can be arranges around caring responsibilities and/or other commitments, employees can continue to work increasing whose own leisure time. But part time work also have potential challenges, such as increase in training, increase in administrative and recruitment costs, e.g. recruiting two part timers could longer than one full times and providing a continuous level of service may be difficult.

Overtime is normally hours that are worked over the usual full time hours. It can be compulsory or voluntary . A recognized system of paid overtime is more common with hourly paid staff than salaried staff. Potential benefits include that employer can provide flexibility to meet fluctuations in demand, short term labor shortage without having to recruit extra staff overtime. Even with premium payments, is often less costly than recruiting and training extra staff or buying extra equipment. However, overtime work has also potential challenges, include when working excessive overtime can affect an employee is performance health and home life. It can result in higher absence levels and unsafe working practices.

Job sharing is a form of part time working where two or more people share the responsibility for a full time job. They share the pay and benefits in proportion to the hours each works. They share the pay and benefits in proportion to the hours each works. Job shares may work split days, split weeks or alternate weeks. it's potential benefits include that if one job sharer is absent, due to illness or holiday, the other can carry on with at least half the work, who can help meet people demand , e.g. both shares being present when workloads are heavy, a wider range of available, who can help people with caring responsibilities and/or other commitments to continue working. It is potential challenges also include extra induction, training and administration cost, replacement may be difficult if one job sharer leaves, added responsibility on supervisors/managers, who must allocate well fairly and ensure that the job shares communicate effectiveness. If the shared role involves managing on supervising staff can find it is difficult working for two managers.

Shift work is a pattern of work in which one employee replace another doing the same job within a 24 hour periods. Shift workers normally work in crews, which are groups of workers who make up a separate shift team. it's potential benefits include it can reduce costs by using equipment more intensively and taking advantage of cheaper off peak. It's potential challenges include it can increase wage and labor costs, it can disrupt employees' social and domestic lives, it can upset employees' body and affect an employee's performance and health.

Employers ought concern employee engagement issue. Different professions have their own specific, which need to be addressed during the engagement building process. For example, for hospital workers, safety issue is of a high importance as who deal with different kinds of sicknesses, whereas for teachers or conselors, ths issue of stress and emotional exhaustion many be of more importance.

To learn how to satisfy employees, content with their work experience, was a good formula for success, as a satisified employees, who wanted to stay with a company, contributed to the workforce stability and productivity. However, satisfied employees may just meet the work demands, but this won't lead to higher performance. In order to compete effectively, employers need to go beyond satisfaction. Therefore, modern organizations expect their employees to be full of enthusiasm to work. Other researchers state that employee engagements is the best fool in the company's efforts to gain on competitive advantages and stay competition. Though, the notion of engagement is relatively new, and it is already a hot managerial topic and it is rare to find an HR or managerial related acticle that doesn't mention employee engagement. These researchers agree that engagement creates the prospect for employees to attach closely with their managers, co-workers and organization in general and engaging environment is the environment when employees have positive attitude toward their job and are willing to do high quality job.

It seems that how to develop good engagement workplace environment can influence employees' satisfaction, then it can influence whose performance or productivity. So, they have close relationship. however, it is even harder to build engagement within the specific group of employees in the situation, when the knowledge about the specifics of their work-life is missing. Different occupations need have different engagement workplace environments and engagement methods to let employees to feel satisfaction. For example, engagement of administrative workers in the educational organizations is rarely studied and poorly understanding, even though these employees have a significant influence in the institution and the quality of their performance contributes to the quality of relationships with faculty students and the public. So, understanding the administrative personnel work life perception is important to educational organizations. How schools can implement engagement to achieve target to improve administration employees ( administrative workers) whose performance, students, faculty public satisfaction and other organizational outcomes. Because whose performance is not save to factory workers to cause how many product quantities manufacturing per hour to calculate, whose need to use service quality to measure performance.

I feel it is better in the situation when organizattions have a better understanding of the administrative personnel work-life perceptions, it is easier for them to create appropriate engagement building tools. Such as, administration employees working at small sized education organizations are more engaged, and this might be due to the reason that they have better relationships with colleagues and experience a greater sense of belonging than their colleages from larger education organizatins. Futhermore, Johnsrud and Rosser ( 1999) also suggest that the smaller the institution, the more positive administrative workers moral and consequentially the higher chances for their engagement. Therefore, result of this study can be applied only to the educational institutions of the similar size. Furthermore, results of this study can't be used for similar organization in order contributions.

What factors can influence the engagement of administration staff. I feel that significant variables factors include: working conditions, job fit, role fit, time spent interacting with students and length of employment on campus. As some researchers working conditions were found to be a significant and positive factor influencing engagement, this means that better working conditions increase the chance that the employee will shoe in higher level of engagement person job fit was defined by Edwards ( 1991, as referenced in Kristof, 1996, p.8) as " the fit between the abilities of a person and the demands of a job , i.e. demands-abilities or the desires of a person and the attributes of a job needs supplies". Job fit also focuses more on the formal aspects of the work, when role-fit includes both established and new tasks, which core out in teams, as team members' roles include formal tasks as well as informal socially defined tasks. The only factor , which was found to have a negative influence on the engagement of administrative workers was employment history, meaning that the higher level of employees were working within an educational organizaton, the lower level of engagement who showing.

I shall recommend to measure the engagement level of employees and to find out the specific engagement that need to be improved, the quantitative research with questionnaires as the main source collecting data was needed to choose to any educational organizations. Because questionnaires can produce numberical data, which is a quantitative approach. The educational administrative workers can be compared with each other within the category of engagement and can point out the factors driving engagement, which need to be improved. These numbers are the basis for further analysis and recommendations. The factors, which can be chosen for the investigation, include meaningful job autonomy at work, performance feedback, institution development opportunities, organizational support, procedural justice, social support from colleagues, supervisory support, social climate etc. The reasons to choose these factors to investigate because the meaningful job can increase psychological meaningfulness for the employee and therefore increases engagement.The above factor meaningful job has been included in the list. Besides, job characteristics can increase meaningfulness for the employee and are positively rarely to job engagement. However, educational administrative workers' moral has an influence on their perception an attitude to the job. The same study pointed out that the moral of administrative workers in educational organization is influenced by number of factors, such as working atmosphere, relations with colleagues and supervisors. For example, social support from colleagues and supervisory support is concerned to moral issue. Social climate factor is concerned to reward and recognition issue.

Why employers need to concern employee moral issue. For example, any clinic organization has complex interpersonal relationships within the clinical domain and the critical issues are faced by nurses on a daily basis, indicate that morale, job satisfaction and motivation are essential components in improving workplace efficiency, output and communiction amongst staff. Drawing on educational , organizational and psychological research, that the ability to inspire morale, staff morale which is a fundamental indicator of sound leadership and managerial characteristics. These includes role preparation for managers, understanding internal and external motivation, how internal motivation to nursing staff and the importantce of attitude when investing in relationships. Because this factors can influence nurse performance. As the field of nursing, amongst money others, the concepts of developing emotional self-awareness in staffs, self-control, adaptability in initiating in management, and organization teamwork in social networks have been poorly applied. Despite this, it has been suggested that nurse and physican collaboration is one of three strongest predictors of psychological empowerment of nurses ( Larrabee et. 2003).

Relationships on the ward can influence to nurse satisfaction and personal professionals are closely linked to self-esteem or person's own morale. So, morale of nurse occupation can influence performance to serve patients. In health care industries, how to create healthy working clinical environments and encourage nursing staff for leadership and management roles, the issues of morale and motivation need to become primary concerns in the ward setting. Because any nurse service will fill with dread, fear and anxiety to whose patients if who neglects to concern care morale. So, nurses need to concern motivating behavior and discourages pessimistic feelings and performance. The reality is that some people naturally posses a high level of this internal motivation, these who focus on the internal feelings of satisfaction who will attain despite any difficulties who face along the way. Exceutives are coached, athletes are coached, why not health care professionals? The nature of helping others through clinical care provision may preclude staff from asking for help themselves.

Has it relationship between boosting morale and improving performance in the nursing occupation? For example, healthy working environment and system may be assisted through the regularity of coaching key staff, e.g. nurses in hospitals need to create any clinic ward organizations. Clinical will environments with good retention, work satisfaction and high quality measures. Nurses can also learn how to self-coach be more self aware and develop themselves. In the nursing occupation, linking nurses' daily work to long term ambitions will impose their motivation, boost their self-confidence and assist them to function at a higher performance level. Coaching will also help staff recognise their own management styles, and identify their leadership strengths and areas for improvement. Because nursing work is frequently rewarded by patients' gratitude. Nurses within clinical settings often comment on the patients' capacity to say thank you and their appreciation of how nurses contribute to their well being. So, the success of their health care service. In fact, performance appraisal is ideally about recognising the direction an individual nurse wishes to pursue concern how health care moral behavior to nurses to achieve to satisfy patient's individual need to reduce complaint occurrences to build healthy clinic environment to let nurses to work enjoyable.

Why absenteeism will influence performance? Unscheduled absenteeism is a popular problem for U.S. employers, conservatively costing $3,600 per hourly employee per year and $2,650 per salaries employee per year, the majority of employers have limited ability to accurately and regularly track how much absenteeism is reducing their bottom line earning, effective absence management systems can track absenteeism, manage absence policies and work schedules, and control overtime, allowing management to reduce lost earnings, also reducing absenteeism will also help employers better meet production and service demands without requiring an increase in headcount. Commonly, the unschedules absenteeism rate in the U.S. hourly workforce is approximately 9% almost one in ten workers is absent when who woud be at work. There are considerble direct and indirect costs are increasing. Not only should managers be motivated to reduce absenteeism because of the excss costs, but without absence tracking tools, employers can't adequately estimate their accurated liabilities. However, absenteeism causing is probable due to poor health to the individual employee. So, who will perform poorly to influence whose productivity to be worse. Why is there such little focus on absenteeism, compared to other costs, health care or low productivity or poor service performance costs for example? So absenteeism can raise much different workforce related costs. The excess costs arise cause disruption to the business, make it difficult to deloy the workforce, and have a profound effect productivity, profit margins and poor employee morale.

However, improving employee health can at most, only reduce absenteeism by one-third, as two-thirds of absenteeism is caused with non-sickness ( personal reasons, feeling of entitlement, family issues). In the result, the direct impact is reduced or poor delayed production or customers are not being served. How to solve absenteeism challenges? Generally, the employer was using a five day schedule, but demand was such that employees were asked to come in on the weekend on a regular basis. The employees disliked working, so many consecutive days with no time off, which led to very high absence rates. The shortages of employees results in demand not being met and customers were dissatisfied. The organization has to replace missing workers with other employees or contractors and pay overtime or higher rates. Overtime levels are 28% higher in facilities with low absenteeism. Excess staffing plan, such as headcount is higher than necessary in order to cover unplanned absences. For example, the employer routinely increased headcount by 13% on weekends to copr with extra absenteeism on a Saturday and Sunday. It is less usual for a salaried employee to be replaced when absent. Instead, the demands of customers (internal or external ) are not met and depending on the employee's position in the company, the ability to create revenue may be affected. Excess absenteeism can also lead to increased health care cost, greater safety issues and accidents, high turnover, and poor morale or performance. To achieve significant reductions in the excess costs with absence, the manager must reduce the rate of absenteeism and the subsequent effect that absenteeism hasno the business. The first step is accuratey and efficiently tracking absenteeism rates and pattrens on a regular basis. The majority of organizations don't hae an automated means to track every instance of absence in one system and therefore lack the visibility necessary to address this business problem. Once the root causes of the problem are known. The manager can consider what steps need to be taken. There may include using rules engines and process automation to consistently enforce absence policies, compliance with union, state and rules, improving absence management technology and increasing employee satisfaction with the workplace, reducing overtime costs by selecting employee to cover for absence based on their competence, training and hours worked during the week, accurate reports of absenteeism , patterns over time and root causes.

In order to take full advantage of opportunities for business expansion and growth. Human assets investment strategy is very important to any organizations. For example, airport organization, it needs good employees serve to provide excellent customer services to satisfy the increase flight slots at airports. So good human assets investment strategy can drive focus on safety, innovation and globalization and create programs for motivating employees to enable them to fully demonstrate their abilities. Such as airport training is needed to be given by lecturers, include rank based and elective training to airport service industry. Methods are such as on site courses, supporting the career development to any airport different rank of staffs to promote on environment where individual employees can display their capabilities to the maximum possible extent in their repective roles. In special, giving women career training establishing a mentor system under which senior employees provide ongoing direction and support for junior and new employees and introducing role models through an intranet, supporting for working includes holding seminars for woman who are pregnant or on maternity leave and introducing a system or partical employment. As a result, the number of employee and nearly all of tem return to the workforce. Because airport service industry needs have a large female workforce, including cabin attendants and airport passenger service staff. Besides, airport service industry also needs to hire women for career track administrative and maintenance positions and flight crews and working to increase the percentage of women in management positions.

Better work life balance is also needed to satisfy airport service industry staff. Besides, airport service industry also needs to hire women for career track administrative and maintenance positions and flight crews and working to increase the percentage of women in management positions. Because airport job duty is common needed to be shift duty. Hence, the working time is flexible time to work when new employees decide to attribute to airport service career. However, due to many passengers need, so airport service workers need to work overtime hours. But, commonly, who do not hope to work overtime often. So, airport management needs to create an comfortable and enjoyable working environment in which each new or old employee can rethink whose own working style to contribute will help vitalize society, companies and individuals.

How to leverage technology to improve employee engagement? Nowadays, employee engagement has evolved from a relatively unknown trend to a term in common usage, which leads itself to a variety of forms and levels of understanding. Employee engagement is about the ability of leaders to inspire their people around the way forward at the desired pace, involving a planned communication effort that is integrated with all the other leadership and change activites. Employee engagement is the emotional commitment the employee has to the organization and its goals. However, technology can play an important role in making engagement a practical part of everyday work. As companies move towards a digital workplace, understanding the impact of technology on employee engagement is critical.

What is the digital workplace? The digital workplace is the digital environment in which staff work, and a place to find corporate knowledge. It includes a collection of election tools that enable productive, effective, work from anywhere. In the future, according to the workplace of the future survey by Teknion corporation predicted 88% of companies offer their workforce personal devices, such as smartphones and tablets. Nearly 90% of companies plan to increase their investment in productivity enabling technologies, such as voice activation and video conferencing by 20 15 year. Organizations are seeking the difital workplace as which search for ways to be more efficient, more collaborative and reduce their physical workplace to realizing higher levels of productivity with their workforce. So, it seems digital workplace can assist to raise performance. Two important reasons why new technology tools will be represent great return on investment for internal use with employees.

The first reason is technology helps us comment with and engage remote or disconnected employees, those with little or no computer or internet access during their work time . The second reason is peer-to-peer engagement and using technology can drive the generation of more ideas, which drives innovation and improvement to produce in any workplace. So, creating an actionable roadmap that fully technology in sny organization's staff engagement initiatives can improve bottom line performance. So, technology can assist organization to measure employee engagement, connect disconnected workers, envourage collaboration and social interaction.

I assure engagement lies in sound decision making and action, then driving good decision making and action should be a communicator's core strategy. Many communicators are already doing good work to drive action. Then, good decision making is driven, in part, by the availability f good information. Even employees who are less digitially connected at work can contribue great ideas that improve that work situation and organizational productivity. Examples, of ways technology helps to that such as: one employee posts about a project who is working on, another employee in an office on the other side ot the world sees the post and realizes who is working on a similar project. If the two teams combine their effort, who can solve the problem and the company gets a globl solution. So, corporate internet is a new digital workplace tools. To effectively solve challenge as making the right information available to the right people at the right time. Organizations must begin by clearly identifying the core types of information that must be shared to engage employee and bring about maximum organizational benefit.

What critical organizational information should all employees access? What types of knowledge are suitable for collaboration? What informational exist today and how are these pockets of information affecting business performance? When analyzing your environment for knowledge sharing, take the time to understand knowledge sharing objectives and how to get employees on information that empowers them to be more successful and therefore more engaged. Remember, anyone can serve in this knowledge management role as long as who are contributing relevant and engaging information.

When looking at any new technology to improve organization knowledge transfer and employee engagement for your employees you should conside the following questions: How does the proposed technology create for information sharing? Are they create for information sharing? Are they easy to use for people of all levels of the organization? How does the technology solution you are examing help employees get work accomplished? This is especially important when examining enterprise social technologies. How can the technology provide more information about company vision, people, business processes. How effectively does the technology support key organizational scenarios, such as identifying the best talent for a particular department or initiative? For example, hospital environment can give conversation about the patient benefits of a new in-room online information display at a hospital.

● How can influence organizational positive behaviors ?
Nowadays, there are key forces are affecting daily organizational behaviors and continuing challenges, such as staff structure ( work relationship), technology ( resources inputs )are needs to transform to with people work and affects the tasks that who perform, environment ( internal and external) factors influence the attitudes of staff, affect working conditions and provide competiton for resources and power. So, based on these four forces, managers need to face the different challenges, such as managing chances in a global environment, managing ethical issues at work.

How to raise staff performance to satisfy clients' needs? Customer service and satisfaction is not limited to the private sector, public sector also needs , e.g. education reform, privatizatin, managed case. So, staff need have excellent performance to raise quality of service to satisfy students, patients etc. needs. Why organizations focus on customer satisfaction. Business monitor customer satisfaction in order to determine how to increase customer base, customer loyalty, revenue, profit, market share and survival. Besides, government needs to monitor monitor customer satisfaction to achieve citizen needs. What is customer satisfaction? Customer satisfaction can be experienced in a variety of situations and connected to both products and services. It is a highy personal assessment that is greatly affected by customer expectations, satisfaction also is based on the customer's experience of both contact with the organization , the moment of touth and personal outcomes. Private sector means it is as one who receives significant added value as well as public sector means it is to whose bottom line. However, customer satisfaction differs depending on the situation and the product or service. A client may be satisfied with a product or service on experience, a purchase decision, a salesperson, store, servicce provider or an attitude. So, staff performance can influence or client's decision to choose to buy the product or consume the service indirectly. For example, in hospital organization , patient surveys often ask customers to rate their providers and experiences in response to detailed questions, such as " How well did your physicians keep you informed?" These surveys provide "actions" data that reveal obvious steps for improvement.

Client satisfaction is highly personal assessment that is greatly influenced by individual expectation. In the public sector, the definition of client satisfaction is often linked to both the personal interaction with the service provider and the outcomes experiences by service users. For example, satisfaction with client worker interaction whether in person, by phone, or by mail or by email communication, satisfaction with the support payment , e.g. its accuracy and timeliness ans satisfaction with the effect of child support enforcement on the child. For hospital organization, staff performance need have these service quality factors to raise or improve whose service satisfaction experience to whose patients ( clients), e.g. timeliness and convenience, personal attention, reliability and dependability, employee competence and professionalism, empathy, responsiveness, assurance, availability and tangible, such as physical facilities and equipment and the appearance of the personnel.

Satisfaction and engagement are two important distinct mesurements that provide valuable and actionable insights into the workforce. The problem is that how many organizations still view them as one and th same thing. As a result, they may be missing critical opportunities to foster the kind of workforce engagement that drives innovtion, boosts performance and increases competitive success. However, some organizations think which don't have to worry about engagement because turnover is how and employees seem satisfied when employee satisfaction is important to matintaining a positive work environment. Is it enough to help you retain top performers and drive bottom line impact? Probably not, by focusing more employee engagement, organizations are more likely to maintain a strong, motivated workforce that is willing to expand extra effort, drive business goals and deliver a return on HR's talent management investment. How to acheve actionable strategies for maximizing workforce engagement and subsequently, driving higher perfomance across the organization. It addresses critical questions, such as: Do you want satisfied employees or engaged employees? Which has a greater impact on the organization's bottom line? What are some proven techniques for addressing both satisfaction and engagement? Employee satisfaction can typically measued through surveys to gsther opinions about HR related issues like bonus programs, benefits and work/life balance. Som employee satisfaction can refer to how employees feel, that happiness about their job and conditions, such as compensation, benefits, work environment, career development opportunities. On the other hand, engagement refers to employees commitment and connection to work as measured by the amount of discretinary effort, who are willing to expand discretionary effort, who are willing to expand on behalf of their employer. High engaged employees go above and beyond the core responsibilities outlines in their job descriptions, innovating and thinking outside the box to move their organizations forward, much like volunteers are willing to give their fine and energy to support a cause about which they are truly passionate.

Can an organization have a satisfied employee who isn't engaged? Chances is an engaged employee is also a satisfied employee. However, it is certainly possible to have a satisfied employee a with a low engagement level. That's why focusing on satisfaction without addressing engagement is unlikely to foster the kind of expectional workforce performance that drives business results. Why do organizations need to care about their workforce engagement level? The primary goal of a business is to make money, even non profit organizations exist to fund their specific causes. Many studies have linked organizations need to get employees at all levels focused on driving revenue. Also which indicates to link employee engagement to workforce preference, customer satisfaction, productivity absenteeism, turnover. Employee engagement is a concept that is rooted in science and at the most fundamental level reflects the human condition itself.

It makes sense that this human motivation process would apply in the workplace just as in other areas of life. By motivating employees beyond basic satisfaction to achieve higher levels of engagement. HR professionals have more significantly impact business outcomes and drive bottom line results. Top-performing organizations understand that measuring employees' contentment levels and emotionl commitment to the organization on a regular basis can put them at a competitive advantage. Since satisfaction measures on employee happiness with current job and security opportunities to use skills and abilities, the organiztion's financial stability, relationship with immediate supervisor, compensation and benefits. In general, these factors can contribute to job satisfaction, such as job security, opportunities to use skills and abilities, organization's financial stability, relationship with immediate supervisor compensation and benefit, communication between employees and senior management, the work itself, autonomy and independence, management's recognition of employee preformance. However, fact engagement condition can have these difference with job satisfaction, such as relationship with co-workers, opportunities to use skills and abilities relationship with immediate supervisor, contribution of work to organization's business goal, meaningfulness of job, variety of work, overll corporate cultures. In general, staff tend to receive more pleasure and satisfaction from what who do if who are in jobs or roles that match both their interests and skills if staff feel who are making meaningful contributions to whose jobs, thei organizations do society as a whole, they tend to be more engages. Staff want to be recognized and rewarded for their contributions. Rewards and recognition come in many forms, including competitive compensation packages, a healthy work/life balance, or sales trips etc. benefits. So, lack of motivation will affect productivity. In addition, a number of point to low morale: declining productivity, higher incidence of absenteeism and friendness, increasing defective products higher number of accidents or a higher level of waste materials and scrapes. How much money ( salary) will you give to your employee to satisfy whose needs? However, staff's needs differ some can be motivated by opportunity for growth and development, job security, good working condition moew than high salary.

In conclusion, as a manager, if you want to develop and encourage good employee performance, and good performance comes from strong employee motivation. But managers can't motivate employee. Motivation is an internal state, like emotions and attitudes, that only the individual can control. Managers can however, create a workplace environment to attempt to motivate staff. Nowadays, workplace is affected by a number of factors, includng a decreasing emphasis on money, an increasing amount of work, an increasing need to work together in teams. Hence, employers concern to consider these above different psychological factors which can influence employee's individual behavior to perform efficiently in any organization.

Reference
Branham, L. (2005). The 7 Hidden Reasons Employees Leave: How To Recognize The Subtle Signs And Act Before Its Too Late. New York, NY: Amacom.
Clark, R.E. (1998). Motivating Performance, Performance Improvement, 37 (8), 39-47.
Clark, R.E. & Estes, F. (2002). Turning Research Into
Results: A Guide To Selecting The Right Performance Solutions. Atlanta, G.A: CEP Press.
Johnsrud, L.K. and Rosser, V.J., 1999. College and
University Midlevel Administrators:
Explaining and improving their morale. The

review of higher education, 22(2), pp. 121-141.

Kristof, A.C. 1996. Person-organization fit: An

Integrative Review of its conceptualizations, measurement and implications. Personnel psychology, 49(1), pp.1-49.

Larrabee J.H. Janney M.A., Ostrow C.L., Withrow M.L.,

Hobbs G.R. And Burant C. (2003) Predicting

registered nurse job satisfaction and intent

to leave., Journal of nursing administration,

33 (5), 271-283.

Shenkel, R. & Gardner, C. (2004), " Five ways to retain good staff", Family Management, Now-Dec. , pp.57-59.

World at work (2009). Telework trend lines. Retrieved from http://www.workingfromanywhere.org/

News/Trend lines_2009.pdf

# CHAPTER NINE

# Human resource strategy to medical organization

England NHS public hospital patient price structure of marketing strategy

1. What do you understand by the concept of a pricing model? Critically discuss their relevance to a public sector service ,such as the NHS.

A price model reflects the fact that companies can generate revenue through a variety of combination of the basic price and prices charged for optional additional items. Some price models may be sustainable by giving away a product at very low price initially, but then charge higher prices for essential items that are needed to make the product function. Sometimes, the dominant pricing model in a market is challenged by a new entrant, with the result that consumers' expectations are changed. The price model can occur in perfectly competitive market or non perfectly competitive market. A perfectly competitive market characteristics include there are many producers supplying the market, each with similar cost structures and each producing an identical product. No single supplier on its own influence the market price because it is not monopoly, water and electricity is managed by government to control the public utility company which can not charge high fee to every householder user at the reasonable price ; both buyers and sellers are free to enter or leave the market and there are no barriers to entry or exit and there is a ready of information for buyers and sellers, for example about competing alternatives, e.g. oil products and stock markets where shares are bought and sold are exist in perfectly competitive market. In perfectly competitive markets, firms are price taker and their ability to set prices is limited by the level of demand and supply within the market they serve. If the total demand go up, all other things being equal, the going rate of prices in the market for their product will rise. Likewise, if there is a drop in total supply for whatever reason ( e.g. because of bad weather, there will be further pressure for prices in the market to rise. The final price paid in the market will reflect the balance between supply side and demand side factors.

The model of perfect competition presented the forces of competition may be ideal for consumers because the tendency of market forces to minimize prices and/or maximize firms' outputs. But in such markets, suppliers are forced to be price takers rather than price makers. in a perfectly competitive market, firms are unable to use marketing strategies to affect the price at which they sell. At a higher price, buyers will immediately substitute identical products from other suppliers. Lower prices would be unsustainable in an industry where all firms had similar cost structures. Otherwise, an non perfectly competitive market, firms are able to use marketing strategies to affect the price at which they sell. Such as UK medical service market , private hospitals and public hospitals and clinics which can raise their service fee to their patients to follow their patients demand due to their doctors and nurses service performance, medicines quality and price and patient beds supplies factors to influence their service charges to their patients in UK. Hence, NHS needs to provide different and excellent medical service to its patients to make them to feel it's service is better to other private hospitals and clinics if it wanted to apply price model to its car parking or hospital phone system service charge to its patients because it is a public sector medical service organization. It ought not charge extra service fee to its patients in its hospitals. If it charged extra service fee, such as car parking and hospital phone system service which are same or higher or lower than other private hospitals or clinic , which need to ensure which medicine quality, doctors and nurses performance which are better than private hospitals and clinics and its patient beds need have enough supply to any patients when who feel need to sleep in its hospital. Because NHS image is a non profit medical organization to any UK poor patients, who choose NHS medical service are due to its medical service charge is cheaper than private hospitals and clinics and who feel it can provide free car parking and free hospital phone system service.

A market is defined here need not be a physical location where exchange takes place ( as happens in retail and wholesale grocery markets). A market in the economist's sense refers to all individuals and firms who wish either to buy or sell a specific product. A market is defined in terms of products or service and geographic description, so the UK soft drinks market refers to all individuals in the UK who seek to buy soft drinks and the suppliers to that market. The UK medical service market structure can describe as the number of consumers, such as patients and medical providers , such as private hospitals and public hospital , such as NHS ( National health service) and clinics; the barriers that exist to prevent new private hospitals or clinics or public assistance hospitals from entering the UK medical service market ( or prevent UK patients do not prefer to choose NHS medical service ); the extent to which the supply medical services is concentrated in the UK small number patients normally and the degree of collusion that occurs between patients and/or private or public hospitals or clinics medical service providers in the UK medical market. Governments often seek to regulate the prices of key products and service, such as electricity and telephones and public hospitals medical services, so it is important to understand how firms can reconcile the sometimes conflicting approaches of market forces and regulation, such as NHS public sector medical service in United Kingdom. Of course, if NHS public sector medical service planned to charge some non major service fees, such as car parking and hospital phone calling service to its patients and hospital visitors and staffs which are same to private hospitals, it needs to consider pricing model should never be seen as an isolated element of hospital's marketing decision making. It needed to consider its service performance of its doctors and nurses, its social responsibility of public medical service image whether it is better or worse than private hospitals that it had created and NHS 's distribution strategy whether it's patient beds supply numbers are enough to patients and whether it's medicine quality and supplies and prices which are reasonable to compare to private hospitals or clinics in this medical service market in United Kingdom. Private business organization with a broad range if products or services are often price different with their portfolio in quite different ways. They may have developed a price model, which describes the way that it uses pricing of its portfolio to maximize its overall revenue. Hence, one product or service may be charged at a very low price, on the assumption that it can raise higher price if many clients choose to buy its product or consume its service. In some sectors, a number of different pricing models co-exist. For example, in the emerging multi-channel television broadcasting market, some channels are provided free of charge to users, but make revenue from selling advertising space, when others charge to users, either on a monthly/annual basis or a pay to view basis. The idea of a pricing model is familiar to private sector organizations, but do they have a role to play in the public sector? In the UK, pricing models are increasingly being discussed and developed for services which have previously been considered a vital service and available freely to all.

Adrian, P.( 2012) showed that the National Health Service ( NHS) has a long and proud tradition of providing health service to all, according to an individual's need, paid for out of general taxation, according to individuals' means. Pricing has historically had very little role to play in the NHS. However, from the mid-1990 year, individual NHS trusts began exploiting charges for ancillary services as a means of boosting their revenue. One of the first targets for charging was users of hospitals' car parks. Trusts argued that providing car parks was not central to the mission of NHS trusts, and conveniently, government was encouraging more people to use public transport and leave their cars at home. Critics argued that patients were essentially captive and public transport was not a realistic alternative for most people. However, it showed that at one hospital in London, a patient who attended A&E on the advice of her GP, was charged UK$3.75 for the first two hours' use of the hospital car park and UK$7.5 thereafter. She was ten minutes over the two hour period and therefore had to pay higher charge. She also questioned the fact that charges were reduced to UK$1 per hour after 6:00 PM, when many hospital departments were closed. For private sector service, a lower evening price, when there is not much demand from customers, and plenty of spare capacity, it quite common. But is it right that a hospital should only charges lower prices at the not busy time when much of the hospital itself is closed? If lower prices are designed to stimulate additional demand, it this a realistic prospect when many hospital departments are only available between 9:00 AM to 5:00 PM? Another source of revenue exploited by many hospital trusts from the use of bedside telephones by patients. Many trusts entered agreements with private telephone service providers which allowed incoming and outgoing patient calls only through the officially appointed system, which used a premium rate number.

A proportion of the revenue was retained by the hospital. Conveniently, hospital trusts pointed to evidence that mobile phones could harm sensitive medical equipment , and therefore used this to eliminate competitive pressure from patients' mobile phones, forcing them to use the hospital's own telephone system. The ethic of hospital telephone pricing was challenged by the House of Commons Health Select Committee, which accused some trusts of using excessively outgoing call, adding to patients' costs, and boosting hospital revenue. It cited a hospital in Essex where people wishing to telephone patients were being charges 49p per minute at peak time and 39p off peak. By comparison , a typical household rate for a long distance phone call was around 7p in the peak and 2p in the off peak. The select committee also expressed doubts about whether a ban on mobile phones in hospitals was actually a result of possible interference with medical equipment and recommend visitors should be able to use mobile phone within certain areas of hospitals. So, it seems that UK private hospitals patients phone calling service fee is below than householder phone calling service fee and it is not every patient must need to use phone when who stays in hospital as well as the visitors should able to use mobile phones and who should not use hospital phones within certain areas of hospital, who will not interference with medial equipment. Otherwise, by banning mobile phones, had private hospitals been more concerned about creating a monopoly environment for pricing their telephone service, than any possible risk to their equipment? However, I think National health service (NHS) which is one public government assistant hospital, it can not be same to private hospital to charge unreasonable car parking fee or hospital phone service fee to its patients, due to these ancillary services is not hospital main income source and it is one non profit hospital, it needs to provide the fair and non expensive medial charges to its poor patient segment because who are not rich, so who will prefer to choose NHS medical service to compare to choose private hospital services in United Kingdom.

National health service (NHS) is a privatization, fragmentation and market competition of health care provision supposedly to cut costs and improve the efficiency of the health service in England. The NHS was set up in 1948 year to be a free and accessible care, publicly owned and funded sector service in England. NHS needs to consider to redefine its relationship with health service, limiting the quality and quantity of care it can expect to receive, how it access that care, who is delivering if and even how it is paid for. The result will be poorer, fragmented services with larger differences in quality and access. Services/treatments will cost more and the public will increasingly have to pay for aspects of its care that used to be free at the time of treatment. Traditionally privatization has been through the sale of public assets and services to private owners through the mass sale of shares, e.g. the sale of telecoms, railways, energy or water services. These companies than own the services and are able to make profits from them like any other are able private businesses. In the NHS until now, this model of privatization is taking place through a combination of the reduction of the role of government in regulating health provision, the transfer of services to the private sector through commissioning from any qualified providers, such as independent sector treatment care centers, outsourcing of parts of services to the private sector, the creation of market mechanisms for the distribution of funding within the NHS ( e.g. commissioning, payment by results mechanisms, the purchaser-provider split and so called patient choice policies). The use of private finance initiatives that use private money to build new buildings and infrastructure and then the state has to pay, the creation of foundation trusts that are run much more like private businesses and have the ability to raise funding through private patients that pay for services, allowing services to become not for profit organizations, such as social enterprises, cooperatives or mutual and thus leave public ownership, limiting access to certain services previously provided by the NHS. Provided healthcare tends to cost more. It requires a large bureaucracy to operate, with huge transaction costs that come with contracts, billing and litigation. In general, as the proportion of private spending on health care rises, so does the overall cost.

The creation of healthcare market can also impact upon the continuity of care people receive. There is always the threat that the private sectors or other providers who take on a service that doesn't secure the expected financial returns may cut losses and withdraw from the provision of that service. NHS is under increasing financial pressure. For example, surgery like hip and knee replacements are more expensive areas of care, the results cause the loss of training opportunities for junior doctors expenditure spending and other health professionals as ever large shares of routine surgery and medical procedures are diverted away from the NHS. Centers for research and medical innovations are also threatened. This can lead to service being out. NHS hospitals will therefore fail financially and be pushed into greater debt. This could lead to hospital mergers, closure or the private sector coming in to run the service on profit making contracts. NHS will bring poor health care service if it will not increase its service charge price to patients. The poor service will be caused, such as permanent damage may have been inflicted on patients with serious conditions due to the lack of follow up care after treatments. In a second worrying example dangerous delays affected the patients of a privatized out of hours. A competitive market system leads to greater rationing and gradually drives patients to take on more responsibility for funding their own care. It seems this already in the privatization of long term care and dentistry. Patients may soon have to top up the cost of their hospital care in the same way that many already do for community health services. The concern is that the NHS will provide a less comprehensive range of treatments. For the private sector, the aim is to make a profit from every contracts, which is not the same as providing the best service . For example, Southern Cross, where the need to make profit lead to the rapid closure of care homes, leaving old people with no home. Hospital people with learning disabilities and challenging behavior were subject to physical and psychological abuse. Privatization will lead to fragmentation of the health services. This is a process on a commercial footing and redesigning the system along market lives. With different organizations delivering different service in different locations, it is also likely to lead a new health service with some area receiving much better care than others, hardest, leading to greater health inequalities. Fragmentation of services leads to worse clinical outcomes as staff have less opportunity to work in a fully integrated dynamic multi disciplinary team. Patients with complex needs can be particularly considerable.

The impact of privatization on current NHS staff, who are transferred from NHS employment to non NHS organizations would be changed terms and conditions at the time of transfer. These terms and conditions could be changes at some time in the future, staff would no longer be covered by the national negotiating arrangement in the NHS, meaning they would not be entitled to any future pay uplifts or agreed charges to the change terms and conditions of service . If staff moved from this employer to another outsourced community service, who would lose their entitlement to access the NHS pension scheme and would be treated as new staff rather then former NHS staff, the new service provider could argue that the service who will be providing is so different that they will not be requiring staff to transfer. Those staff will than be made redundant. In conclusion, NHS is one public medical service non profit organization. It's pricing model ought be public service price model, such as no price discrimination and non competitor based pricing aim. It may be difficult or undesirable to implement a straightforward price-value relationship with individual of public services for a number of reasons: Such as NHS public sector medical service pricing can be actively used as a means of social policy, subsidized prices are often used to favor particular patient segment groups, such as car parking fee charges to visitors or hospital staffs only as well as hospital phone system service charges to visitors only or prescription medical service charges favor the very ill and unemployed patients and low income patients and students patients.

2. What factors should influence the level of charges at an NHS car park?

Principles for fair hospital car parking, such as NHS is important because its car park service represents the hospital reputation. Charging for car parking is often necessary, but needs to be fair, providing a travel plan for users of all types of transport, controlling parking fairly, with concession for those whose health conditions or work commitments mean they have to park frequently or at anti social hours, showing car park and transport costs and how charges are invested, thinking about the environment and how transport can reduce the NHS 's impact , being open and involve patients and the public. It is important to get car parking and transport policy and it is communication, right to ensure fair access, good patient and staff experience and to protect hospital organization , such as NHS reputation. Clinical and social changes as car ownership to patients, staff and visitors to hospital sites has increased. For services with rural or urban , as public transport infrastructure is less convenient and reliable . When for specialist treatment, some patients need to travel greater distance and modern hospitals have often been located on the edge of population centres.

Car parking is also a factor in patient's experience of using healthcare. When much progress has been achieves to improve the patient environment inside the hospital, including cleanliness and new buildings, patients frequently report dissatisfaction with transport and parking arrangement. Visitors concerns both cost of car parking and also the availability of space for people with an essential need, illustrating the competing demands that managers need to balance. Patient experience is an important objective for hospitals; poor experiences can undermine confidence in clinical quality and stress can be worsened by poor transport and parking policies. Car parking can have a major impact on the local and national reputation of the NHS hospital . As patient choice increases, reputation and loyalty will be key drivers for provider's commercial sustainability. It seems car parking is one important factor to influence patients who choose hospital more than location/ transport/ easy to get to/ reputation of consultants factors. Ensuring that patients can access hospital when they need to is an important part of healthcare delivery. Many patients who need to travel to hospital by car, either because of mobility or illness, a lock of alternatives or through choice. However, providing a car park is not the only component of a travel plan. Access to healthcare should be considered in terms of service planning, decisions on location of services, building design, access routes and the other transport modes. One of the factor of the current changes to the way that NHS hospital services are delivered is that healthcare should be localized where possible. In many cases, people who used to have to travel to hospital are being treated in community health centers. The NHS hospital can also ensure services are accessible. Most notably, ease of access has recently been improved by reducing waiting times and by enabling patients to choose and book their appointment at a time and location that is convenient to them. Another of factor is whether NHS hospital had or had not ran a bus service from a nearby park and ride car park that runs every 15 minutes. The service has proved popular and is now run by the UK country council.

The hospital is been to extend the shuttle service to the other three park and ride car parks which serve the city. The other factor influences NHS hospital charge includes the control parking fairly with concessions for those whose health conditions or work commitments mean they have to park frequently or at anti-social ours. In order to ensure that those patients who really need to access hospital by car are able to NHS often need to ensure that car parking space is available on site. Space is usually constrained, NHS hospital is in city or town center with high land costs and planning constraints. Charging some patients, visitors and staff to park can manage demand for space when ensuring that those who really need to park are able to access services. Where charging is required to manage demand, the overriding principle should be to ensure that where possible those patients who have the greatest need to park are prioritized. Where managing demand is a reason for charging for car parking, there may be scope for varying rates for different times of the day and the week, for example, increasing charges for non essential users in peak hours but applying a minimal charge at night when there is less reason to ration space. As well as prioritizing car access for those with greatest needs restrictions on car parking may also be required to deter non hospital traffic, particularly where NHS hospital is located in controlled parking zones, near shopping centers or other facilities that might need to illegitimate required use of NHS hospital grounds. In these cases , NHS hospital may be required to be charge the same as local car parks to avoid abuse by non visitors. However, alternative arrangement could also be explored, including day permits for people with appointment. NHS car parking fair policies should need to be fair application. This is often a cause of concern for patients and visitors.

Concessionary schemes and season tickets should be well publicized and available, since a patient may not known in advance low frequently who will need to attend a clinic in the next month. Penalty charges, or towing away should only be applied extreme circumstances with a presumption of good faith that no patient or visitor chooses to stay in hospital longer than necessary and may how on arrival how long who will have to wait for treatment. Running a car park can be expensive. These are maintenance, security, insurance and running costs and the NHS hospital has to pay for the space the car park uses. Costs are particularly high where land prices are high or there is increased risk of crime. At the same time, patients and the public rightly don't expect healthcare to suffer to pay for parking. The transport costs of non car owners are not subsidized by the NHS budgets to provide subsidized free car parks . To make car parking fee would be to penalize those using public transport. Therefore, fair charging is often the most sensible answer to adopt these two demands. Climate charge and pollution and congestion factor also have health impacts. Reducing car dependency is also a public health objective in order to reduce traffic accidents and increase physical activity.

These NHS organizations have a number of environmental and health reasons to seek to encourage people to use other modes of transport. Parking charge together with the expansion of alternative bus an cycling options to encourage a modal shift from cars to alternative transport. Patients , visitors and staff need to be made aware of these aims. NHS hospital can achieve a travel plan to develop to its car parking with the aim of during a period of busy time reducing single occupancy car journeys by 15% over three years, ensuring tat patients and visitors do not have to search for a space for more than ten minutes at peak times, encouraging the number of direct bus routes to the site to increase reducing staff parking spaces per employee by 10% as staff numbers grow. Car parking charges were introduced as part of the plan with certain categories of staff on exempted from charges ( night and weekend staff, disabled staff, volunteers, car sharers and tenants of residential accommodation. From an environmental perspective, NHS travel plan supposed to reduce numbers of cars arriving at the site and the numbers of bus car raise. It aims to improve bus services to cause air pollution at the busy car parking period and cycle parking spaces and improved cycle facilities have encouraged staff to commute by bike. Additionally, a park and ride scheme aims to reduce car traffic of the NHS hospital in the busy time.

Moreover, it is absolutely wrong to charge cancer patients regardless of income, for unavoidable parking costs. From a staff point of view, NHS hospital car parking is an indirect tax on healthcare. However, most unions also support the aim of reducing car usage, as long as policies are fair. Because NHS hospital needs to develop transport policies for patients requiring regular cancer treatment. This approach has potentially negative publicity into a positive image to public. These ought be free parking for the duration of a cancer patient treatment or as often as is needed. So, price structure strategy will be needed to this UK hospital to solve nowadays challenge.

Service-line strategies for medical organizations

● Strategies to Provide Patients With Superior Customer Service

Any hospitals or medical health service organizations , if they can consider patients are they asset or capital principle. Then, I believe that their patients number won't be influenced to reduce by poor health service performance in possible. Due to medical is one kind of service industry, so learning patients psychology how to let they feel health service performance satisfaction is one important factors to influence any kinds of medical service organizations in success, such as dentist, doctor, facial, hospital, etoc. different medical organizations.I believe that these patient service performance factors will influence their patients number to be increased or decreased as below:

1. Start seeing patients as customers. Taking care of patients is what healthcare is all about. It may be hard for some people to think of patients as customers, but they definitely are. Their choices bring thousands and even millions of dollars into a hospital's coffers. In most cases, they don't necessarily need to use your hospital, even though you have Dr. Brightstar on staff. They may end up at the institution down the street that treats patients better.

2. Be courteous and respectful. Always, always, make sure patients are treated with courtesy and respect. I know executives who pretended to be patients inside their own institutions and were shocked by the lack of focus and concern they received. Treating patients has become simply a job for many healthcare professionals. They manifest boredom with their jobs by treating patients indifferently. That's not professional and it's bad business!

3. Never show indifference to patients. It can be quite disappointing at some urban hospitals and even at some suburban settings. If the illness is not life-threatening, patients are virtually given a number and told to sit down and wait. Many otherwise competent and even brilliant healthcare professionals give patients the feeling they are an inconvenience and a bother. Patients should not be made to feel inferior and misinformed.

4. Don't contradict, argue . Telling patients they are wrong about anything is just plain rude. Even when they have incorrect information, they still should be accorded respect. If you disagree with them, politely explain why their point of view isn't necessarily correct. Your goal should be to explain and communicate, and then to continue to explain and communicate. Help patients understand what is going on as treatment is being given. Patients should feel they are just important, in the scheme of things, as you are.

5. Tell patients you appreciate their business. Everybody likes to be thanked when purchasing an item in a retail store, but in all too many healthcare venues, saying "thank you" is seen as inappropriate. You know as well as I do that saying "thank you" has magic vibes for any kind of relationship. Go ahead and try it! It's a great way to receive your customers' repeat business.

6. Use plain terms and simple explanations. It may be fun to throw around complicated jargon, but it results in misunderstandings and sometimes errors. Nobody wants errors in today's healthcare environment. Always make sure your explanations are not clouded with excessive and complicated verbiage. Be brief and to the point. True professionals go out of their way to explain things in simple, declarative sentences.

7. Good manners are part and parcel of confidence and competence. Don't hide the truth even if it creates problems for you. Treat patients the way you'd want to be treated. Saying the appropriate words can show respect. Establishing eye contact is also part of good manners. Go way out of your way to show respect to others! It's what being civilized is all about, isn't it?

8. Keep seeing healthcare as a calling. Too many professionals begin to see healthcare as a job rather than a calling. There's a big difference between the two. When healthcare becomes a job, mistakes are not far behind. Today there are so many complicated variables in healthcare that it is easy to get off track. Remember who you are and what your core business is. It might help to recall what brought you into the healthcare field. Was it to take care of people or was it to make a lot of money?

9. Stay in touch with patients. Many healthcare professionals don't think they have the time to stay in touch with patients after care is rendered. They tend to think it's unnecessary and creates too much stress. That rationale should never be tolerated. Staying in touch with patients, even if it's an e-mail or a phone call, will pay off.

10. Keep your promises. Many promises made to patients are never kept. Things like, "You'll get the best care here" and "We treat each individual who comes to us with dignity and respect" and also, "You'll be just fine in a week or so." The difference between empty talk and promises is that promises must be kept. And if it turns out you overpromised, own up to it. Being honest will pay off later. Any quality business must keep its promises.

● Service-line strategies for hospitals

For hospitals battered by competition, trying to be all things to all patients is no longer a viable strategy. One way hospitals can more effectively compete with smaller, more focused competitors is to organize themselves by service line, focusing on building world-class capabilities in just a few clinical areas. Hospitals that succeed with this strategy can achieve fiscal benefits while enhancing their ability to serve their communities. But as three disguised case studies show, the successful implementation of a service-line strategy is no mean feat.

Choosing the right service lines to emphasize requires a superior understanding of a hospital's economics and competitive environment. Hospitals also need to overhaul the management of both strategic and nonstrategic service lines. The full-service, general hospital—still the mainstay of acute-care delivery—is under attack. Immense clinical complexity; the advent of performance transparency for evaluating quality, service, and costs; and growing competitive intensity are challenging the notion that any hospital can excel across a broad spectrum of clinical service lines.

Consider a small or large size hospital of average size, with roughly 100 to 200 staffed beds and a mean daily patient census of about 100. On any given day, it might admit only a handful of patients with similar conditions. Contrast this with the current crop of sophisticated, focused, multispecialty institutes for heart, cancer, or neurological care: they treat up to several hundred patients each day. "Pure play" specialty hospitals and outpatient centers with low-cost structures, limited complexity, and focused, high-quality service are also emerging. Competitors like these are raising the performance bar for general acute-care hospitals and, in some cases, posing serious questions about their sustainability.

● Changing traditional medial service to innovative medical service front line service method

While traditional general hospitals are unlikely to disappear anytime soon, a new approach—a commitment to clinical service lines as an organizing paradigm, much as many corporations organize themselves by business unit—is becoming a necessity for many such organizations. Specializing in a few service lines allows hospitals to build a critical mass of patients in select areas and to enjoy economies of skill and scale. In some doctor and nurse past service experience, hospitals that make the leap to a service-line orientation become more productive, improve their quality of care, recruit physicians more effectively, and build market share. By developing a focused service-line strategy, hospitals can also limit their investment in nonpriority areas, with savings to be found in areas ranging from marketing to new technologies. Some hospitals may even choose to take facilities off-line if they are unlikely to reach minimum effective scale in any individual service or combination of service areas.

The transition to service lines is about much more than introducing a new vocabulary or high-level concepts into business planning and strategy. Full implementation of a service-line approach requires real changes in organizational structure, incentive plans, physician relationships, and business development, as well as in many support functions, including IT and human resources. To make wise decisions about which service lines to emphasize, hospitals must have a deep understanding of their own economics and competitive environments. Furthermore, running a hospital with a service-line orientation requires new approaches for recruiting the clinical staff, for aligning its interests with those of the hospital, and for measuring success. Hospitals that succeed—whether or not they are nonprofit institutions—can reap tremendous quality, cost, and service benefits and avoid turning themselves into specialty hospitals, closing their emergency rooms, or lowering the level of care they offer their communities. They will become far more effective competitors as well.

Three portraits few medical service organizations have captured the full potential of a service-line transformation.

Issues complicating the transition include : the effort required to reorient a hospital's structures and systems, the leadership commitment needed to shepherd the change process, the difficulty of assembling the high-quality data needed to support good decision making, and the risk aversion of many staff members and physicians. Patience is also necessary—many changes won't yield results for months or even years.

As three disguised case studies show, full-service hospitals face a range of challenges and opportunities when developing a service-line focus. Like many general hospitals, these three organizations have been caught in a vicious cycle of declining resources and patient volumes, as well as a diminished ability to offer high-quality care and to serve those members of their communities most in need. The cycle of decline often begins when transparent information about the quality and pricing of hospitals becomes available—making payers and patients more value conscious and fueling the rise of focused competitors that can attract the most valuable patients. For example, competition is raised for skilled physicians, who see investing and working in specialty and pure-play facilities as an increasingly attractive career option. At a recent gathering of 250 cardiology practice managers, roughly 70 percent reported that their practices had either been purchased by pure-play or specialty hospital groups or had entered into discussions for purchase. Meanwhile, reimbursement rates for Medicare, Medicaid, and commercial patients aren't rising as quickly as a hospital's costs for treating them.

For example, a small size hospital served one million residents across three separate hospital campuses and had a 55 percent share of its city's inpatient cases . Each of the hospitals determined what services it would provide, and the result was duplication and subscale programs. All three facilities offered open-heart surgery programs; as a result of this overlap, each hospital performed fewer than 100 such procedures a year, far from the 300 to 400 needed to keep surgeons and staff clinically competent. Complications and mortality were 40 percent above average. Maintaining three separate subscale programs was also expensive, and the open-heart service line operated at a loss of $1 million a year.

However, when one hospital can attempt to innovate its medical service. Within four years, it may successfully raise its market share to 25 percent, from 20 percent. But it hadn't scrutinized the demographics or payer-reimbursement dynamics—and therefore the profitability—of the new patients it attracted.

Medical equipment must be important to influence patients service feeling, e.g. surgen service. So, any hospital must need to pump money into its loss-generating emergency department, if it was failing to invest in upgraded operating-room and imaging equipment for its highly profitable spinal-surgery unit. This new equipment would have raised productivity significantly and helped to attract and retain valuable physicians. Instead, some hospitals neglect market share in spinal surgery service and they can not spend much money to buy the new medical equipment to serve their patients and in a number of other profitable specialized service lines , they won't increase surgeon patients number, due to they can not own the innovative medical equipment to serve their patients in hospitals.

One hospital was trying to compete across a range of transplant services, including heart, kidney, liver, and bone marrow transplants. Fierce local competition sent the hospital into a downward spiral; it took on unprofitable cases and performed too few procedures to maintain clinical expertise or even the recommended safety standards. When it discovered poor clinical outcomes were the result. Liver transplant surgeons and hepatologists began taking their cases to other hospitals, where heavier case loads and experienced support staff helped ensure a higher quality of care. The less patients hospitals recognized that to improve its clinical quality it had to attract more transplant patients. But its efforts yielded disappointing financial results because the hospital focused on disciplines where revenues were highest, without regard to profit margins.

● calculation the medical cost and charge to patients service fee

However, to execute a service-line approach, hospitals must first gain a strong understanding of their economics—down to the level of specific clinical activities—and of the growth potential of various service lines. This change of focus involves learning more about the competitive environment, referral patterns, and the possibility of cross-selling other hospital services to current patients.

Understanding current economics Hospitals should aim to understand their profitability by diagnosis-related groups, payers, physicians, and service lines before they undertake a new service-line strategy. Standard billing approaches usually make revenue numbers straightforward, but costs—and hence profit margins—are another thing. For many hospital services, each patient and procedure is different; therefore allocating costs is far more complicated and expensive for them than for manufacturers or retailers. An accurate cost-accounting system is a prerequisite for effective service-line planning. Simply relying on surrogates (such as volume, payer mix, or revenues) can be deceptive and leads, in many cases, to incorrect conclusions.

When the hospital realized that the expansion of its emergency department was shrinking its profit margins, the hospital began analyzing cost-accounting data to determine the profitability of patients and service lines. When a hospital understands where its true profitability lies, it can also negotiate contracts more effectively. When one hospital implemented a service-line strategy, its ought make negotiations with payers involved simply pushing for higher per-diem reimbursements. Armed with the new service-line-specific economics, the hospital greatly improved its strategy for negotiating with the managed-care plan that provided 65 percent of its commercially insured volume. By projecting cost trends on a procedure-by-procedure basis, the hospital learned that for certain cases (where resources used and lengths of stay were more predictable), it would derive greater benefit from per-case reimbursements. It pushed the payer to make the switch, and the new contract soon increased profits by more than $10 million—a 16 percent jump in the annual yield. Estimating growth potential Deciding where and how to focus also requires an understanding of the growth potential for different service lines. An analysis of competitors and referral patterns, as well as a comprehensive clinical understanding of disease pathways (the biological mechanisms that allow diseases to progress), can all uncover growth opportunities.

● Learning similar medical service competitors service attitude and medical service provision method to compare difference

Competitive factors and referral patterns. Understanding the competitive footprint of a service line requires knowing whether community needs are currently being met. Although information about the number of potential local patients and market share is available through public sources , data from these sources often lag by up to two years. To develop more current growth forecasts, hospitals should gather their own demographic data, including the number of underinsured and uninsured patients in an area.

The referral patterns of physicians are another key to estimating a hospital's market potential, since their preferences, together with those of patients and insurance plans, play a major role in a patient's choice of hospital. Moreover, physicians help determine whether cases are referred for treatment, thereby limiting the effective size of the market when cases are indicated but not referred.

For each geographic area that the similar medical service organizations served, the hospital's business-development office mapped referral volumes of key physicians—from primary-care doctors to specialists to doctors affiliated with the hospital—to better understand shifts in market share. Hospital analysts, in contrast to their previous approach, which relied on rarely codified anecdotal evidence, interviewed staff and physicians, much as medical-device and pharmaceutical sales forces commonly do. Learning how rival hospitals influence physician referrals offered insights that helped develop countermeasures to gain market share. Hospital administrators responsible for building relationships with physicians started reaching out to them, and the hospital enhanced its continuing medical-education programs for certain strategic service lines. In addition, a revamping of the Web site, direct-mail system, and advertisements of the hospital raised awareness of it both among referring doctors and prospective patients.

Well-prepared hospitals evaluate the growth potential not just of initial care episodes in a given clinical area but also of related services. To do so, they must understand how patients typically flow within and between service lines. Such an understanding requires hospitals to study disease pathways, likely treatment regimens, and relevant treatment technologies. For example, along with a local physician group, the hospital then invested in a heart failure clinic and began making more regular contact with patients. It turned out that many of congestive heart failure patients could benefit from device therapy (such as implanted defibrillators or ventricular resynchronization). The hospital's focus on its long-term relationship with heart failure patients was critical to its success. Just as retailers and financial-services companies use customer data to their advantage in building enduring relationships, providers increasingly recognize the value of advanced customer-relationship-management techniques. When and where changes are necessary Identifying the most competitive service lines is only half the battle; hospitals also need to change the way they operate these service lines. Rewards for success can be substantial. For example, one hospital have purchased many new medical equipment, if it increased its annual profits by about $15 million within two years of undertaking an ambitious service-line reorientation. I believe that its medical equipment can let many surgeon patients feel medical service satisfaction.

● Calculation of salary level by performance measurement

Changing people processes Implementing a service-line strategy requires changing how a hospital manages human resources. Hospitals may need to recruit more people for critical service lines and fewer for others. Not least important, the professionals and staff of each service line must understand the new strategy and accept the plan so that they will be willing to change the way they work. Incentives that encourage the staff, particularly physicians, to act like owners—including more formal joint-ownership structures, such as equity sharing, investment partnerships, or even full employment—are typically necessary to align the physicians' interests with those of the hospital.

When on hospital changed its personnel processes to support its advanced cardiovascular service line and its elective general-surgery program, which focused on breast cancer. The hospital filled talent gaps by recruiting new physicians (including, for instance, a radiologist with experience and interest in mammography) and increased training to ensure the clinical competency of the operating-room support staff. Before updating an existing joint business plan to improve the alignment between the new goals and the interests of the relevant specialists, the hospital conducted extensive conversations with them. Measuring progress When it comes to performance, most hospitals track only gross patient volumes, net revenue, and, sometimes, hospital-wide profit margins. But to ensure that a service-line strategy is working, they must also track patient-level performance.

For every patient admitted and diagnosed, a hospital might assign a score indicating the clinical outcome and monitor both the cost to treat the patient and the patient's total charges. These cost-accounting figures, plus yields from managed-care contracts, are vital to tracking a hospital's progress. Furthermore, because service-line strategies may take years to implement and show results, it is important to track process milestones (such as the recruitment of key physicians) and traditional measures such as profit margins or the total volume of cases. Like many hospitals, Springfield General found that quarterly performance scorecards helped it track both its financial and nonfinancial performance at a greater level of detail than had previously been possible.

Measuring performance with this degree of precision is challenging, so hospitals should consider taking interim steps. A hospital might use the ratio of costs to charges from each department to gauge a service line's performance. Knowing how every patient is admitted (through the emergency department, electively, or by referral from a specific physician group) can help the hospital to uncover patterns of unusually high or low profitability or possible sources of additional volume.

In addition, tracking how much a hospital actually collects for a service line (after writing off bad debt) can help to judge its true profitability and inform future contract negotiations with payers.An added benefit of detailed performance metrics is that their use often generates a virtuous cycle of improved clinical outcomes. Hospitals should track outcome-specific patient-level data (for example, the time from the arrival of a postsurgery coronary-bypass patient in the intensive-care unit to the point when the patient no longer needs the help of a ventilator to breathe) rather than more generic measures (such as whether discharge instructions were delivered). The more specific approach allows hospitals both to pinpoint areas of care that need improvement and to reward effective performance by the administrative, managerial, and clinical staff.

Managing service lines that aren't a priority In most cases, service lines that are not a strategic priority will continue operating at some level to help hospitals meet basic community needs and cover fixed costs. Hospitals should avoid investing large amounts of capital, their physicians' management time, or executive leadership in nonpriority service lines. But such clinical areas often employ dedicated nursing staff, support personnel, and physicians, most of whom have a vested interest in the status quo. Hospital leaders must develop an effective communication plan to lay out the rationale for change and to set the staff's expectations. The hospital should tell its employees that it will maintain high safety and quality standards but probably won't be an early adopter of expensive technologies in these service lines and won't respond to competitive forces.

For the emergency department, when the hospital choose to limit capital investments, marketing budgets, and efforts to reach previously unaffiliated physicians, as well as to reallocate a portion of the department's expanded space to a gastrointestinal diagnostics unit. The initial reaction of the emergency department's physicians was predictably negative, but by communicating the strategy effectively and sharing the data underlying the decision-making process, the administrative team eventually gained the confidence of the medical professionals, including those in the emergency department. It also used this transparent approach to reassure the broader community that the new strategy was in its best interest as well. Although the emergency department was scaled back, the community benefited from expanded colorectal-cancer-screening outreach programs and gastrointestinal-disease seminars for both the public and the primary-care community. So, emergency department medical equipment need is essential to any hospital service improvement if the hospital hopes to innovate its medical service to let any emergency service patients feel satisfactory.

● What 4 Factors Should Determine a Hospital's Service Line Strategy?

These include the hospital's mission, market growth, margin and the likelihood of the service line's success, as well as the following factors:

• Hospital mission: Type of patient care (secondary, tertiary, quaternary); types of education; and types of research.

• Market growth: Growth by service line; payor mix by service line; ability to feed into other key profitable service lines; and the ability to partner with payors and/or employers and shift share.

• Margin: Payor mix by service line; impact of reimbursement changes; and ability to partner with physicians to control costs.

• Likelihood of success: Necessary investments, such as physician recruitment and capital expenditures; internal capabilities; and competitors' capabilities.

The rate at which these lines are expected to grow is not directly correlated with their profitability, however. For instance, out of those five specialties, orthopedics is generally third in terms of profits and General surgery is the most profitable. Hospitals will need to cross-examine each specialty's expected market growth and its profitability, as service lines across hospitals and geographies can present different clusters of performance. While this data can help hospitals prioritize their service lines, some qualitative factors also need consideration, such as competitors' capabilities. Do competitors offer any specific services within their service line? Do they provide key feeder services for your hospital? Also, what is physicians' perception of competitors? How aggressively do they market their service lines? These questions can help bring a greater understanding to how likely a hospital service line is to succeed.

Service-line strategies for medical organizations
● Strategies to Provide Patients With Superior Customer Service

Any hospitals or medical health service organizations , if they can consider patients are they asset or capital principle. Then, I believe that their patients number won't be influenced to reduce by poor health service performance in possible. Due to medical is one kind of service industry, so learning patients psychology how to let they feel health service performance satisfaction is one important factors to influence any kinds of medical service organizations in success, such as dentist, doctor, facial, hospital, etoc. different medical organizations.I believe that these patient service performance factors will influence their patients number to be increased or decreased as below:

1. Start seeing patients as customers. Taking care of patients is what healthcare is all about. It may be hard for some people to think of patients as customers, but they definitely are. Their choices bring thousands and even millions of dollars into a hospital's coffers. In most cases, they don't necessarily need to use your hospital, even though you have Dr. Brightstar on staff. They may end up at the institution down the street that treats patients better.

2. Be courteous and respectful. Always, always, make sure patients are treated with courtesy and respect. I know executives who pretended to be patients inside their own institutions and were shocked by the lack of focus and concern they received. Treating patients has become simply a job for many healthcare professionals. They manifest boredom with their jobs by treating patients indifferently. That's not professional and it's bad business!

3. Never show indifference to patients. It can be quite disappointing at some urban hospitals and even at some suburban settings. If the illness is not life-threatening, patients are virtually given a number and told to sit down and wait. Many otherwise competent and even brilliant healthcare professionals give patients the feeling they are an inconvenience and a bother. Patients should not be made to feel inferior and misinformed.

4. Don't contradict, argue . Telling patients they are wrong about anything is just plain rude. Even when they have incorrect information, they still should be accorded respect. If you disagree with them, politely explain why their point of view isn't necessarily correct. Your goal should be to explain and communicate, and then to continue to explain and communicate. Help patients understand what is going on as treatment is being given. Patients should feel they are just important, in the scheme of things, as you are.

5. Tell patients you appreciate their business. Everybody likes to be thanked when purchasing an item in a retail store, but in all too many healthcare venues, saying "thank you" is seen as inappropriate. You know as well as I do that saying "thank you" has magic vibes for any kind of relationship. Go ahead and try it! It's a great way to receive your customers' repeat business.

6. Use plain terms and simple explanations. It may be fun to throw around complicated jargon, but it results in misunderstandings and sometimes errors. Nobody wants errors in today's healthcare environment. Always make sure your explanations are not clouded with excessive and complicated verbiage. Be brief and to the point. True professionals go out of their way to explain things in simple, declarative sentences.

7. Good manners are part and parcel of confidence and competence. Don't hide the truth even if it creates problems for you. Treat patients the way you'd want to be treated. Saying the appropriate words can show respect. Establishing

eye contact is also part of good manners. Go way out of your way to show respect to others! It's what being civilized is all about, isn't it?

8. Keep seeing healthcare as a calling. Too many professionals begin to see healthcare as a job rather than a calling. There's a big difference between the two. When healthcare becomes a job, mistakes are not far behind. Today there are so many complicated variables in healthcare that it is easy to get off track. Remember who you are and what your core business is. It might help to recall what brought you into the healthcare field. Was it to take care of people or was it to make a lot of money?

9. Stay in touch with patients. Many healthcare professionals don't think they have the time to stay in touch with patients after care is rendered. They tend to think it's unnecessary and creates too much stress. That rationale should never be tolerated. Staying in touch with patients, even if it's an e-mail or a phone call, will pay off.

10. Keep your promises. Many promises made to patients are never kept. Things like, "You'll get the best care here" and "We treat each individual who comes to us with dignity and respect" and also, "You'll be just fine in a week or so." The difference between empty talk and promises is that promises must be kept. And if it turns out you overpromised, own up to it. Being honest will pay off later. Any quality business must keep its promises.


● Service-line strategies for hospitals

For hospitals battered by competition, trying to be all things to all patients is no longer a viable strategy. One way hospitals can more effectively compete with smaller, more focused competitors is to organize themselves by service line, focusing on building world-class capabilities in just a few clinical areas. Hospitals that succeed with this strategy can achieve fiscal benefits while enhancing their ability to serve their communities. But as three disguised case studies show, the successful implementation of a service-line strategy is no mean feat.

Choosing the right service lines to emphasize requires a superior understanding of a hospital's economics and competitive environment. Hospitals also need to overhaul the management of both strategic and nonstrategic service lines. The full-service, general hospital—still the mainstay of acute-care delivery—is under attack. Immense clinical complexity; the advent of performance transparency for evaluating quality, service, and costs; and growing competitive intensity are challenging the notion that any hospital can excel across a broad spectrum of clinical service lines.

Consider a small or large size hospital of average size, with roughly 100 to 200 staffed beds and a mean daily patient census of about 100. On any given day, it might admit only a handful of patients with similar conditions. Contrast this with the current crop of sophisticated, focused, multispecialty institutes for heart, cancer, or neurological care: they treat up to several hundred patients each day. "Pure play" specialty hospitals and outpatient centers with low-cost structures, limited complexity, and focused, high-quality service are also emerging. Competitors like these are raising the performance bar for general acute-care hospitals and, in some cases, posing serious questions about their sustainability.

● Changing traditional medial service to innovative medical service front line service method

While traditional general hospitals are unlikely to disappear anytime soon, a new approach—a commitment to clinical service lines as an organizing paradigm, much as many corporations organize themselves by business unit—is becoming a necessity for many such organizations. Specializing in a few service lines allows hospitals to build a critical mass of patients in select areas and to enjoy economies of skill and scale. In some doctor and nurse past service experience, hospitals that make the leap to a service-line orientation become more productive, improve their quality of care, recruit physicians more effectively, and build market share. By developing a focused service-line strategy, hospitals can also limit their investment in nonpriority areas, with savings to be found in areas ranging from marketing to new technologies. Some hospitals may even choose to take facilities off-line if they are unlikely to reach minimum effective scale in any individual service or combination of service areas.

The transition to service lines is about much more than introducing a new vocabulary or high-level concepts into business planning and strategy. Full implementation of a service-line approach requires real changes in organizational structure, incentive plans, physician relationships, and business development, as well as in many support functions, including IT and human resources. To make wise decisions about which service lines to emphasize, hospitals must have a deep understanding of their own economics and competitive environments. Furthermore, running a hospital with a service-line orientation requires new approaches for recruiting the clinical staff, for aligning its interests with those of the hospital, and for measuring success. Hospitals that succeed—whether or not they are nonprofit institutions—can reap tremendous quality, cost, and service benefits and avoid turning themselves into specialty hospitals, closing their emergency rooms, or lowering the level of care they offer their communities. They will become far more effective competitors as well. Three portraits few medical service organizations have captured the full potential of a service-line transformation. Issues complicating the transition include : the effort required to reorient a hospital's structures and systems, the leadership commitment needed to shepherd the change process, the difficulty of assembling the high-quality data needed to support good decision making, and the risk aversion of many staff members and physicians. Patience is also necessary—many changes won't yield results for months or even years.

As three disguised case studies show, full-service hospitals face a range of challenges and opportunities when developing a service-line focus. Like many general hospitals, these three organizations have been caught in a vicious cycle of declining resources and patient volumes, as well as a diminished ability to offer high-quality care and to serve those members of their communities most in need. The cycle of decline often begins when transparent information about the quality and pricing of hospitals becomes available—making payers and patients more value conscious and fueling the rise of focused competitors that can attract the most valuable patients. For example, competition is raised for skilled physicians, who see investing and working in specialty and pure-play facilities as an increasingly attractive career option. At a recent gathering of 250 cardiology practice managers, roughly 70 percent reported that their practices had either been purchased by pure-play or specialty hospital groups or had entered into discussions for purchase. Meanwhile, reimbursement rates for Medicare, Medicaid, and commercial patients aren't rising as quickly as a hospital's costs for treating them.For example, a small size hospital served one million residents across three separate hospital campuses and had a 55 percent share of its city's inpatient cases . Each of the hospitals determined what services it would provide, and the result was duplication and subscale programs. All three facilities offered open-heart surgery programs; as a result of this overlap, each hospital performed fewer than 100 such procedures a year, far from the 300 to 400 needed to keep surgeons and staff clinically competent. Complications and mortality were 40 percent above average. Maintaining three separate subscale programs was also expensive, and the open-heart service line operated at a loss of $1 million a year.

However, when one hospital can attempt to innovate its medical service. Within four years, it may successfully raise its market share to 25 percent, from 20 percent. But it hadn't scrutinized the demographics or payer-reimbursement dynamics—and therefore the profitability—of the new patients it attracted. Medical equipment must be important to influence patients service feeling, e.g. surgen service. So, any hospital must need to pump money into its loss-generating emergency department, if it was failing to invest in upgraded operating-room and imaging equipment for its highly profitable spinal-surgery unit. This new equipment would have raised productivity significantly and helped to attract and retain valuable physicians. Instead, some hospitals neglect market share in spinal surgery service and they can not spend much money to buy the new medical equipment to serve their patients and in a number of other profitable specialized service lines , they won't increase surgeon patients number, due to they can not own the innovative medical equipment to serve their patients in hospitals.

One hospital was trying to compete across a range of transplant services, including heart, kidney, liver, and bone marrow transplants. Fierce local competition sent the hospital into a downward spiral; it took on unprofitable cases and performed too few procedures to maintain clinical expertise or even the recommended safety standards. When it discovered poor clinical outcomes were the result. Liver transplant surgeons and hepatologists began taking their cases to other hospitals, where heavier case loads and experienced support staff helped ensure a higher quality of care. The less patients hospitals recognized that to improve its clinical quality it had to attract more transplant patients. But its efforts yielded disappointing financial results because the hospital focused on disciplines where revenues were highest, without regard to profit margins.

- calculation the medical cost and charge to patients service fee

However, to execute a service-line approach, hospitals must first gain a strong understanding of their economics—down to the level of specific clinical activities—and of the growth potential of various service lines. This change of focus involves learning more about the competitive environment, referral patterns, and the possibility of cross-selling other hospital services to current patients.Understanding current economics Hospitals should aim to understand their profitability by diagnosis-related groups, payers, physicians, and service lines before they undertake a new service-line strategy. Standard billing approaches usually make revenue numbers straightforward, but costs—and hence profit margins—are another thing. For many hospital services, each patient and procedure is different; therefore allocating costs is far more complicated and expensive for them than for manufacturers or retailers. An accurate cost-accounting system is a prerequisite for effective service-line planning. Simply relying on surrogates (such as volume, payer mix, or revenues) can be deceptive and leads, in many cases, to incorrect conclusions.

When the hospital realized that the expansion of its emergency department was shrinking its profit margins, the hospital began analyzing cost-accounting data to determine the profitability of patients and service lines. When a hospital understands where its true profitability lies, it can also negotiate contracts more effectively. When one hospital implemented a service-line strategy, its ought make negotiations with payers involved simply pushing for higher per-diem reimbursements. Armed with the new service-line-specific economics, the hospital greatly improved its strategy for negotiating with the managed-care plan that provided 65 percent of its commercially insured volume. By projecting cost trends on a procedure-by-procedure basis, the hospital learned that for certain cases (where resources used and lengths of stay were more predictable), it would derive greater benefit from per-case reimbursements. It pushed the payer to make the switch, and the new contract soon increased profits by more than $10 million—a 16 percent jump in the annual yield. Estimating growth potential Deciding where and how to focus also requires an understanding of the growth potential for different service lines. An analysis of competitors and referral patterns, as well as a comprehensive clinical understanding of disease pathways (the biological mechanisms that allow diseases to progress), can all uncover growth opportunities.

● Learning similar medical service competitors service attitude and medical service provision method to compare difference

Competitive factors and referral patterns. Understanding the competitive footprint of a service line requires knowing whether community needs are currently being met. Although information about the number of potential local patients and market share is available through public sources , data from these sources often lag by up to two years. To develop more current growth forecasts, hospitals should gather their own demographic data, including the number of underinsured and uninsured patients in an area.

The referral patterns of physicians are another key to estimating a hospital's market potential, since their preferences, together with those of patients and insurance plans, play a major role in a patient's choice of hospital. Moreover, physicians help determine whether cases are referred for treatment, thereby limiting the effective size of the market when cases are indicated but not referred. For each geographic area that the similar medical service organizations served, the hospital's business-development office mapped referral volumes of key physicians—from primary-care doctors to specialists to doctors affiliated with the hospital—to better understand shifts in market share. Hospital analysts, in contrast to their previous approach, which relied on rarely codified anecdotal evidence, interviewed staff and physicians, much as medical-device and pharmaceutical sales forces commonly do. Learning how rival hospitals influence physician referrals offered insights that helped develop countermeasures to gain market share. Hospital administrators responsible for building relationships with physicians started reaching out to them, and the hospital enhanced its continuing medical-education programs for certain strategic service lines. In addition, a revamping of the Web site, direct-mail system, and advertisements of the hospital raised awareness of it both among referring doctors and prospective patients.

Well-prepared hospitals evaluate the growth potential not just of initial care episodes in a given clinical area but also of related services. To do so, they must understand how patients typically flow within and between service lines. Such an understanding requires hospitals to study disease pathways, likely treatment regimens, and relevant treatment technologies. For example, along with a local physician group, the hospital then invested in a heart failure clinic and began making more regular contact with patients. It turned out that many of congestive heart failure patients could benefit from device therapy (such as implanted defibrillators or ventricular resynchronization). The hospital's focus on its long-term relationship with heart failure patients was critical to its success. Just as retailers and financial-services companies use customer data to their advantage in building enduring relationships, providers increasingly recognize the value of advanced customer-relationship-management techniques. When and where changes are necessary Identifying the most competitive service lines is only half the battle; hospitals also need to change the way they operate these service lines. Rewards for success can be substantial. For example, one hospital have purchased many new medical equipment, if it increased its annual profits by about $15 million within two years of undertaking an ambitious service-line reorientation. I believe that its medical equipment can let many surgeon patients feel medical service satisfaction.

● Calculation of salary level by performance measurement

Changing people processes Implementing a service-line strategy requires changing how a hospital manages human resources. Hospitals may need to recruit more people for critical service lines and fewer for others. Not least important, the professionals and staff of each service line must understand the new strategy and accept the plan so that they will be willing to change the way they work. Incentives that encourage the staff, particularly physicians, to act like owners—including more formal joint-ownership structures, such as equity sharing, investment partnerships, or even full employment—are typically necessary to align the physicians' interests with those of the hospital.

When on hospital changed its personnel processes to support its advanced cardiovascular service line and its elective general-surgery program, which focused on breast cancer. The hospital filled talent gaps by recruiting new physicians (including, for instance, a radiologist with experience and interest in mammography) and increased training to ensure the clinical competency of the operating-room support staff. Before updating an existing joint business plan to improve the alignment between the new goals and the interests of the relevant specialists, the hospital conducted extensive conversations with them. Measuring progress When it comes to performance, most hospitals track only gross patient volumes, net revenue, and, sometimes, hospital-wide profit margins. But to ensure that a service-line strategy is working, they must also track patient-level performance.

For every patient admitted and diagnosed, a hospital might assign a score indicating the clinical outcome and monitor both the cost to treat the patient and the patient's total charges. These cost-accounting figures, plus yields from managed-care contracts, are vital to tracking a hospital's progress. Furthermore, because service-line strategies may take years to implement and show results, it is important to track process milestones (such as the recruitment of key physicians) and traditional measures such as profit margins or the total volume of cases. Like many hospitals, Springfield General found that quarterly performance scorecards helped it track both its financial and nonfinancial performance at a greater level of detail than had previously been possible.

Measuring performance with this degree of precision is challenging, so hospitals should consider taking interim steps. A hospital might use the ratio of costs to charges from each department to gauge a service line's performance. Knowing how every patient is admitted (through the emergency department, electively, or by referral from a specific physician group) can help the hospital to uncover patterns of unusually high or low profitability or possible sources of additional volume.

In addition, tracking how much a hospital actually collects for a service line (after writing off bad debt) can help to judge its true profitability and inform future contract negotiations with payers.An added benefit of detailed performance metrics is that their use often generates a virtuous cycle of improved clinical outcomes. Hospitals should track outcome-specific patient-level data (for example, the time from the arrival of a postsurgery coronary-bypass patient in the intensive-care unit to the point when the patient no longer needs the help of a ventilator to breathe) rather than more generic measures (such as whether discharge instructions were delivered). The more specific approach allows hospitals both to pinpoint areas of care that need improvement and to reward effective performance by the administrative, managerial, and clinical staff.

Managing service lines that aren't a priority In most cases, service lines that are not a strategic priority will continue operating at some level to help hospitals meet basic community needs and cover fixed costs. Hospitals should avoid investing large amounts of capital, their physicians' management time, or executive leadership in nonpriority service lines. But such clinical areas often employ dedicated nursing staff, support personnel, and physicians, most of whom have a vested interest in the status quo. Hospital leaders must develop an effective communication plan to lay out the rationale for change and to set the staff's expectations. The hospital should tell its employees that it will maintain high safety and quality standards but probably won't be an early adopter of expensive technologies in these service lines and won't respond to competitive forces.

For the emergency department, when the hospital choose to limit capital investments, marketing budgets, and efforts to reach previously unaffiliated physicians, as well as to reallocate a portion of the department's expanded space to a gastrointestinal diagnostics unit. The initial reaction of the emergency department's physicians was predictably negative, but by communicating the strategy effectively and sharing the data underlying the decision-making process, the administrative team eventually gained the confidence of the medical professionals, including those in the emergency department. It also used this transparent approach to reassure the broader community that the new strategy was in its best interest as well. Although the emergency department was scaled back, the community benefited from expanded colorectal-cancer-screening outreach programs and gastrointestinal-disease seminars for both the public and the primary-care community. So, emergency department medical equipment need is essential to any hospital service improvement if the hospital hopes to innovate its medical service to let any emergency service patients feel satisfactory.

● What 4 Factors Should Determine a Hospital's Service Line Strategy?
These include the hospital's mission, market growth, margin and the likelihood of the service line's success, as well as the following factors:
   • Hospital mission: Type of patient care (secondary, tertiary, quaternary); types of education; and types of research.
• Market growth: Growth by service line; payor mix by service line; ability to feed into other key profitable service lines; and the ability to partner with payors and/or employers and shift share.
• Margin: Payor mix by service line; impact of reimbursement changes; and ability to partner with physicians to control costs.
• Likelihood of success: Necessary investments, such as physician recruitment and capital expenditures; internal capabilities; and competitors' capabilities.
The rate at which these lines are expected to grow is not directly correlated with their profitability, however. For instance, out of those five specialties, orthopedics is generally third in terms of profits and General surgery is the most profitable. Hospitals will need to cross-examine each specialty's expected market growth and its profitability, as service lines across hospitals and geographies can present different clusters of performance. While this data can help hospitals prioritize their service lines, some qualitative factors also need consideration, such as competitors' capabilities. Do competitors offer any specific services within their service line? Do they provide key feeder services for your hospital? Also, what is physicians' perception of competitors? How aggressively do they market their service lines? These questions can help bring a greater understanding to how likely a hospital service line is to succeed.

# CHAPTER TEN